THE OTHER
DIALOGUE

THE OTHER DIALOGUE

Joseph Gremillion

1965

DOUBLEDAY & COMPANY, INC.
GARDEN CITY, NEW YORK

ACKNOWLEDGMENTS

Grateful acknowledgment is made for permission to include the following copyrighted material in this book:

Excerpt from *A History of the English-Speaking Peoples. Volume I: The Birth of Britain* by Winston Churchill, copyright © 1956 by The Right Honourable Sir Winston Churchill, K.G., O.M., C.H., M.P. Reprinted by permission of Dodd, Mead & Company, New York, and Cassell and Company Ltd., London.

Excerpt from "Aid, Trade and Economic Development: Issues Before the U.S." by Isaiah Frank, *Foreign Affairs* (January 1964), copyright © 1964 by Council on Foreign Relations, Inc., New York. Reprinted by permission of *Foreign Affairs*.

Excerpt from "United States Policy in the Western Hemisphere" by Hubert Humphrey, *Foreign Affairs* (July 1964), copyright © 1964 by Council on Foreign Relations, Inc., New York. Reprinted by permission of *Foreign Affairs*.

Excerpt from *Ideologies of the Developing Nations* by Paul Sigmund, Jr., copyright © 1963 by Frederick A. Praeger, Inc. Reprinted by permission of Frederick A. Praeger, Inc.

CONTENTS

Finally the council will build a bridge towards the contemporary world. . . . And as Peter on the day of Pentecost felt the impulse at once to raise his voice and to speak to the people, so you also have unexpectedly determined to treat no longer of your own limited affairs but rather those of the world, no longer to conduct a dialogue among yourselves but rather to open one with the world.

Opening Address of Pope Paul VI to the
Second Session of Vatican Council II

INTRODUCTION

In his early months on the throne of Peter, Pope Paul VI clearly showed that he would wholeheartedly embrace and build upon Pope John's great advances, but still move beyond them. Paul quickly took initiatives which could uniquely mark his entire reign with a grander and deeper development of John's adventurous probings. He has brought additional content and a new positive character into the Second Vatican Council—and into the next century, which the Council will affect.

This acceleration and broadening of John's *aggiornamento* began with Paul's coronation sermon. He asserts therein his intention to pursue "the dialogue that has begun . . . [with] those who, without belonging to the Catholic Church, are united with us by the powerful link of Faith and of the Lord Jesus and marked with the seal of the unique Baptism—'one Lord, one Faith, one Baptism,' . . . the heritage of our unforgettable predecessor Pope John XXIII."

Then, in this same French portion of his sermon, Pope Paul states further: "But beyond the frontiers of Christianity, there is another dialogue in which the Church is engaged today—the dialogue with the modern world."

We find here an important element which is not only part of the heritage of John, but reminiscent of Pius XII, and still personal to Pope Paul himself. For surely the Monsignor Montini of the decade after the War contributed much to the profound thought of Pius' famed allocutions to the scholars and scientists, statesmen and thinkers of the modern world —many of them nonbelievers—on their frequent visits to Rome.

In his first formal address as Pope, Paul explicitly commits the Church to continue, and to expand and deepen, this *other* dialogue with these "profound voices of the modern world . . . beyond the frontiers of Christianity . . ."

What is the content of this conversation? As Paul interprets these voices, the modern world "aspires to justice, to a progress not only technical but human, to a peace . . . which permits finally an openness and collaboration of men and peoples in an atmosphere of reciprocal confidence." Justice, human progress and peace, with openness and collaboration of men and peoples, are then the causes voiced by the modern world which Pope Paul hears and with which he wants expanded dialogue.

"In the service of these causes," Paul goes on, "it is possible to practice to an astonishing degree the virtues of strength and courage, the spirit of enterprise, of devotion, of sacrifice. We say it without hesitation, all that is ours." (In the original French: *"tout cela est le nôtre";* that is, to paraphrase Pope Paul: All these causes and positive virtues of the modern world, we embrace them as our own as well, without hesitation.) In proof of this rapport Pope Paul cites "the immense ovation which has been raised everywhere at the voice of a Pope recently calling all men to organize society in brotherhood and peace."

In his address opening the Second Session of the Council, September 1963, Pope Paul returns explicitly to this theme. He lists the already well-known objectives of the Council: 1) examination of the intimate nature of the Church, her awareness of herself; 2) the reform and renewal of the Church (he uses both words; it is not a mere *aggiornamento*); 3) "the bringing together of all Christians in unity."

Then Paul adds a fourth objective, not heretofore made explicit to the Council by Pope John, though approached boldly in his great encyclicals: "the dialogue of the Church with the contemporary world."

This other dialogue is par excellence the concern of the

final schema of the Council, number thirteen. Among the titles given to drafts of this schema have been "The Temporal Presence of the Church," "The Active Presence of the Church in Upbuilding the World," and "The Church in the Modern World." The subjects include the vocation of man to the affairs of this-world; the human person in society; the family, marriage and the population issue; the values of human culture; social justice and the economic order; peace and the international community; the lay apostolate and the spirit of the dialogue.

Following Pope Paul's emphasis—he devotes 878 words of his address opening the Second Session to this other dialogue, more time than he spends on the dialogue among Christians—the Council and the Church are opening to a wider range of issues "beyond the frontiers of Christianity" than was foreseen before Paul's advent.

It might be said that Pope John's *aggiornamento* was principally directed to concerns interior to the Christian Faith: it sought renewal of the Roman Catholic Church and dialogue within the family of Christians. These compose, at most, one third of the world's people. Pope Paul's expanded objective explicitly directs the Council and the Church to external issues: to the whole family of man and the gamut of world issues. And he lists among these (all direct quotes from Paul's opening address):

—fundamental rights of man . . . crushed by principles and methods of political, racial or antireligious intolerance;
—atheism . . . bringing in its wake the derangement of the intellectual, moral and social order;
—the light of the science of nature, [and] progress, [while man's] heart is declining toward emptiness, sadness and despair;
—the Church looks at the world with profound understanding, with sincere admiration and with the sincere intention . . . of serving, appreciating, strengthening and saving it;

– the poor, the needy, the afflicted, the hungry, the suffering and sorrowing;

– men of culture and learning, scientists, artists . . . [the Church has] a great desire to receive the fruit of their experiences, to strengthen their intellectual life, to defend their liberty;

– the workers, toward the legitimacy of their hopes, toward the need . . . of social improvement and of interior elevation;

– the mission [of the workers] . . . to create a new world, of free men and brothers;

– rulers of nations, today you can give to your peoples many good things necessary for their life, bread, education, work, order, the dignity of free and peaceful citizens;

– leaders of nations . . . working together in justice and love, you can create peace, that greatest good, . . . and you can make of humanity a single city. God be with you;

– those other religions which preserve the sense and notion of the one supreme, transcendent God, creator and sustainer, and which worship Him with acts of sincere piety and base their moral and social life on their belief and religious practices;

– new generations of youth desirous of living and expressing themselves;

– the new peoples now coming to self-awareness, independence and civil organization;

– the innumerable men and women who feel isolated in a troubled society that has no message for their spirit;

– and to all without exception she [the Church] proclaims the good news of salvation and hope.

Again in his first encyclical, *Ecclesiam Suam* (*His Church*), Pope Paul shows his fundamental preoccupation with the other dialogue. He employs the phrase "ecumenical dialogue" to denote relations with the circle "which is nearest to us, the circle of Christianity." He stresses that the good news of

Christ's coming is the Church's principal concern, and that the acceptance of this Gospel ultimately does not "depend upon any favorable temporal conditions, for faith is a gift of God and God alone defines in the world the times and limits of salvation."

But before speaking of the ecumenical dialogue among Christians, Paul deals at great length with the dialogue which "should be potentially universal, i.e. all-embracing and capable of including all," excepting only those who are insincere or totally impervious to communication. The Church, Paul assures us, "sees clearly enough the astounding newness of modern times," and with frank confidence she stands astride "the paths of history and says to men: 'I have that for which you search, that which you lack.'" The Church does not thereby promise earthly felicity, but rather light and grace which make human happiness in this-world more easily attainable.

Because, Paul explains, in speaking to men of their transcendent destiny, the Church "speaks to them of truth, justice, freedom, progress, concord, peace and civilization." These are words whose secret is known to the Church, for Christ has entrusted the secret to her keeping. The Church has in consequence "a message for every category of humanity: for children, for youth, for men of science and learning, for the world of labor and for every social class, for artists, for statesmen and for rulers. Most of all, the Church has words for the poor, the outcasts, the suffering and the dying, for all men."

Ecclesiam Suam then opens the arms of Christ's Church to reach out and to welcome dialogue with all these great circles and on all the concerns of the human family: "the councils of nations. . . . (the) many, very many unfortunately, who profess no religion. . . . many who profess themselves, in various ways, to be atheists. . . . some of these proclaim their godlessness openly and uphold it as a program of hu-

man education and political conduct. . . . the cause of peace
between men."

Paul then turns to "another circle around us. This, too,
is vast in its extent, yet it is not so far away from us. It
is made up of the men who above all adore the One, Supreme
God Whom we too adore." Perhaps for the first time in a
public document of such import a pope addresses himself directly and openly and fraternally to the great religions of the
world.

> We refer to the children, worthy of our affection and
> respect, of the Hebrew people, faithful to the religion
> which we call that of the Old Testament. Then to the
> adorers of God according to the conception of monotheism,
> the Moslem religion especially, deserving of our admira-
> tion for all that is true and good in their worship of God.
> And also to the followers of the great Afro-Asian reli-
> gions.

Pope Paul forthrightly states that, in all honesty, he must
declare his conviction that there is but one true religion, that
of Christ. But he does express his recognition and respect
for the moral and spiritual values of the non-Christian religions. He desires to join with them in promoting and defending common ideals of religious liberty and human brotherhood, for the advance of human culture, social welfare, and
civil order. "For our part, we are ready to enter into discussion on these common ideals, and will not fail to take the
initiative where our offer of discussion in genuine, mutual respect, would be well received."

In *Ecclesiam Suam*, Pope Paul acknowledges that the very
breadth of the concerns which he proclaims might appear out
of touch with reality in view of "the actual relations of mankind with the Catholic Church." This range of concern is indeed immense, so immense that "its limits stretch beyond our
sight and merge with the horizon. It is that of mankind as
such, the world. We gauge the distance that lies between us

and the world, yet we do not consider the world as a stranger." Paul makes his own what has become the dominant theme of schema thirteen of the Council on "The Church in the World of Our Time":

> All things human are our concern. We share with the whole of mankind a common nature, human life with all its gifts and problems. In this primary, universal reality we are ready to play our part, to acknowledge the deep-seated claims of its fundamental needs, to applaud the new, and sometimes sublime, expressions of its genius.

Since 1960, the intellectual energy of Catholics has been deeply absorbed in the Council and particularly in its themes of renewal and ecumenism. Most of the Church's outstanding scholars, and many other Christian thinkers, are understandably dominantly drawn into the vortex of currents revolving around the nature of the Church and Christian unity. Pope Paul now expressly determines that this dialogue among Christians should not absorb us to the detriment of the larger dialogue with the rest of the human family and the great issues of this-world. It would seem that the more we Christians approach at least a psychological solidarity (long before we reach the further remove of doctrinal and juridical unity), the more we should be concerned about talking with "the others," with "every creature," as Mark's Gospel puts it. The very fact that we Christians are once again talking to each other does make Christ's message more "hearable" to the rest of mankind. Indeed, the universal acclaim given to *Pacem in Terris* is probably due in large measure to Pope John's having sensitized the ears and hearts of the world by his dialogue with other Christians. So, the two dialogues today are closely related.

The sixteenth-century split among Christians sharply deflected the influence of Christ from the modern world and its successive primordial movements: the new science and nationalism, the Enlightenment and positivism, philosophical liberalism and Marxism. And just as this theological fury contributed to the sectarian division of Christianity, and this division alienated the secular world from the bearers of the Christian message, so today will theological love, even before theological unity, help to redress this sad relation of Christians with modern man.

Like John the Affirmative, Pope Paul is full of hope. In his coronation sermon, he admits that, "In a superficial examination, the man of today can appear to be more and more a stranger to all that is religious and spiritual. Aware of the progress of science and technology, intoxicated by spectacular successes in domains until now unexplored, he seems to have divined powers of his own and to want to do without God . . ." But behind this façade, Paul assures us, "it is easy to find the profound voices of the modern world, also affected by the Holy Spirit and by grace." It is at this point that he claims as his own these voices and causes which seek justice, human progress and peace, with openness and collaboration of men and peoples, in the spirit of enterprise, of devotion, of sacrifice. All these causes and positive goods of the modern world the Holy Father embraces as his own, "without hesitation."

This view of life and the apostolate is not new to Paul *as pope*. They were his as Monsignor Montini, at the side of Pius XII as he wrote his profound allocutions. They were his as Archbishop of Milan, leading his people to love the world as God had so loved it, sending His Own Son to partake of its matter and spirit, of its tears and joy, of its power and energy.

His Lenten pastoral of 1963 was on "The Christian and Temporal Well-being." He begins with the statement that "The Christian is *a priori* an optimist before the vision of the goods of this-world." He recalls "the marvelous and mysterious words which frequently reappear in the Bible: 'And God saw that it was good.' What a moving experience it would be to see the essence of things in some way with the eyes of God Himself." Far from absorption in angelism, the Christian should have the most complete and most noble vision of temporal values, approaching them with greatest realism, administering the things of this-world most effectively.

To lay leaders of his archdiocese, in 1961, he states that: "the fundamental attitude of Catholics who want to convert the world must be to love the world. Here is the genius of the apostolate: our technics, our art, our sports, our times, our civilization, our world." (The accent is on *our*.) He extols *Mater et Magistra* for lighting in human hearts a great hope and a great love: "love for our times, our country, for our society, which expect from Christ—and which expect in consequence from our own humble action—their regeneration, their solidarity and their peace."

Archbishop Montini sees in the dynamics of social progress, in the *élan* which motivates human research and advance, the movement of man toward truth and the Divine: "In your way, you seek God . . . Yes, I would say that every time you seek your own perfection . . . , both in leisure as in your work, from which you demand answer to the idea you possess of these, each time you are on the straight road of the truth." (To workers of Milan, 1957.)

Commenting on the 1958 paschal message of Pius XII, the Archbishop rejects the idea of Christianity as a static and socially conservative force: "Christianity holds no fear of renewal in any human order whatsoever. Christianity wills and aspires to renewal wherever higher justice is desirable and wherever a more perfect type of humanity can be realized . . . Constantly concerned with reforming itself as well as reforming the world, Christianity is always the optimist, never disillusioned . . . hunger and thirst for justice constitute one of her 'beatitudes.' "

He praises the instinctive dynamism of modern business, which now creates abundance sufficient to soften the hard insensibility of avarice, and which accords with Christian mentality in the measure that today's economic thought tends to regard temporal goods as means, and not as ends in themselves. "We must make our way in the profane universe with the religious sentiment that a Divine Presence, even a Divine expectancy, is there to be found, in part hidden, in part manifest, of dimension beyond reckoning." (Lenten pastoral, 1963.)

As pastor of a sprawling industrial metropolis, the Archbishop does not view the contemporary world as presenting only obstacles to pastoral work. Today's world also offers numerous advantages for evangelization: "A great number of aspects of modern life—want and desire and yearning for Christ—haunt so many souls still far from the Church . . . and these too can be interpreted as providential dispositions for the Gospel message: it suffices to read by intuition 'the signs of the times.'" (*Osservatore Romano,* 1958.) In July 1963, Pope Paul shows that, for him, such intuition is not enough. To find out "why the world of the worker is moving away from God," he directs that a study, "with an attention and care that requires true specialization," be made of the psychology of the worker. (New York *Times,* July 11, 1963.)

Pope Paul not only understands that the Church, and all Christianity, must talk with the modern world, he is also at home with the ideas and views at issue. He is a pastor who is also an intellectual, or rather an intellectual who became a pastor in his late fifties. Those oft-cited ninety boxes of books he brought from Rome to Milan and back again do not add up to conclusive proof, but *ninety* cases do provide weighty cumulative evidence of where his deeper interests lie. He has an affinity for French thinkers. Many of the above references remind one of Cardinal Suhard's pastorals. Quotes from Camus and Bernanos, Fathers de Lubac and Chenu interlace his writings. He translated into Italian several works of Maritain.

In the past year the dialogue among Christians has brought about an incipient psychological solidarity which is the palpable, public fruition of thoughtful communication among theologians, liturgists and scripture scholars over the past decade and more. Open manifestation of fraternal concern and fellowship must be nourished from these deeper wellsprings of truth. The promise of this dialogue is that thinkers who share faith in Christ have gathered about Him at Jacob's well—to see and to seek together, in quiet and profundity. Christ is the Logos, the Word, the Idea of God's Intellect, made Flesh, become Man. Since our mandate from Christ is that we incarnate Him, the Idea-made-Flesh, here in this-world, today and tomorrow, then ideas take on dominant import in the Christian dialogue—ideas and men who think.

Thinkers have an equal role in Pope Paul's *other* dialogue, perhaps a more telling role, among Catholics especially, because Catholic thinkers as a whole have been, until very recently, quarantined from the formative thinkers who have begotten and continue to shape the modern world. About a hundred years ago the pervasive influence of the new science, and particularly its key creed of all-embracing evolution, began contaminating the very roots of Catholic dogma, generating the corrosive heresy of Modernism condemned in 1907. But anathematizing Modernism, a basic error fraught with danger to all Christian doctrine, was accompanied by an atmosphere of malediction on much that modern man cherished outside the direct scope of dogma. Driven in greater part by the Church-State combat in Italy, Pius IX went so far as to condemn the proposition: "The Roman Pontiff can and should reconcile and harmonize himself with progress, with liberalism, and with recent civilization." (The final proposition, number 80, of the *Syllabus of Errors,* 1864.)

In the context of that day's concrete issues, the "why" of such a sweeping anathema *can* be understood. Pope Pius IX had in mind specific anticlerical programs of Cavour and his

Piedmontese nationalists, publicized under the slogan of "progress, liberalism and modern civilization." But much of this same defensive emotion and fortress mentality pervaded the guardians of doctrinal purity, so that for a century, into our own decade, it remained difficult for Catholic thinkers to communicate with the philosophers and scholars of "progress, liberalism and modern civilization." Besides facing obvious obstacles such as a ban preventing publication, the basic vehicle of any scholarly dialogue, Catholic thought was hidebound in its very language. It could not develop the modern idiom intelligible to our times. Maybe the guardians of doctrine had no other recourse. At any rate, this policy has until now frustrated meaningful intellectual interchange with the makers of the modern mind.

Pope Paul now accelerates and expands the changes of atmosphere he inherited from Pope John's policy of opening the windows. Equally concerned with dialogue number two, Paul and the Council Fathers are giving freer rein toward fresh and deepened views of the philosophy (and theology) of science and history, of authority and freedom, of power and socialization, of evolution and human progress. The other dialogue is under way.

Part One

THE MULTIPLICATION
OF HUMAN RELATIONSHIPS

Chapter One

MAN'S CREATIONS AND
THE CHURCH'S CONCERN

The subjects of the other dialogue are the stuff which make up the workaday world—the Monday morning concerns of factory and office, store and stock exchange, Congress and military camp, school and kitchen. The morning headlines and evening television reports bring these issues into every home every day.

Courts and Congress debate civil rights for all our citizens. Republicans and Democrats argue over remedies for poverty amidst our affluent society. Labor contracts are negotiated, automation is applied, featherbedding is eliminated, men are fired. An industry moves away, a depressed area results, fathers seek work. Their children now eat spaghetti without meatballs, and mother lets out the cuffs on Johnny's single Sunday suit. The babies of the Second World War's baby boom now have children of their own. More boys and girls, millions more, enter school and college. A drive for building funds, a new bond issue, is launched. New taxes are voted on; one carries, another fails. Tuition climbs higher. All schools, public and private, clamor for governmental assistance.

Does God the Father care about these concerns of his children? Has Christ, Who knew Monday morning toil and sweat in Nazareth, forgotten about the anxiety and fatigue of workmen in Pittsburgh and Smolensk, Nairobi, Calcutta and Rio? But the Holy Spirit, sent by Christ to teach all things—does the Spirit of Truth know all this? Does the Love of Father and Son, Divine Love personified, really care about the ups and downs of millions and millions of little men, weak and wanting?

Global issues arise beyond our national borders. Frustrating dilemmas face policy- and decision-makers, business, university and governmental leaders. These complex problems, affecting the fate of millions for war or peace, are often dismissed as "globaloney" by many citizens and officeholders. But a yearning for the good old days and simplest panaceas, like sending in the Marines, cannot deal with irrevocable social change and new world realities. Conferences and meetings must multiply while men, inept and able, patiently seek fresh creative solutions for mankind's new challenges and ailments.

Presidents and prime ministers shuttle back and forth among the national capitals. Cabinet secretaries and ministers at all echelons meet in all corners of the globe on all manner of human concerns. Business and technical experts exchange data and plans.

They confer over the annual $900 billion income of a few wealthy have nations in the "Christian" West, and the daily, gnawing need of a thousand million have-not humans. They puzzle over surplus food from Minnesota and the hunger of half the family of man. They fret and fuss over fertilizer factories and human fertility, finance deficits and development funds, malaria and mass education, commerce and cosmonauts. Men of many lands gather to track the destiny of microscopic mesons and macroscopic galaxies. They fix the fate of nations, forge the future of man for war or peace, and fly into the depths of space.

Does God pay any attention to all these debates and debacles day by day? Does tax reform, a treaty to unite Europe or East Africa, to ban the bomb or to run the Panama Canal; does a contract to work thirty-five or fifty hours a week, to buy copper from Chile, to sell machinery to Rumania or wheat to Russia; does a new steel plant in India or a new hybrid seed corn in Iowa, a laboratory finding on genetics, or a new literary masterpiece; does Telstar and baby's bottle —really mean anything to God?

Does God truly value these works of man, our human creations, great and small, technical and cultural?

We humans spend most of our time on such as these, the things of this-world—dreaming, discussing, and striving, building, advancing, perfecting. Our creative powers and workaday hours are lavished on these profane concerns as engineers and teachers, as lawyers and accountants, as men of business and the arts, communications and politics. Does God give a care? What difference to Him how it all turns out, provided we keep ourselves "clean and unspotted from the world"? Can we do so?

These questions touch and grip followers of Jesus Christ in a profound manner and degree. In Him we are baptized, cleansed and configured. With His Image and Inner Life we are marked and confirmed. His Eucharistic Body nourishes us. Christ *is* God, God joined to Man. In Him, Creator and creature unite in a manner and degree unique in all history, past and to come.

St. John tells us that through Christ is made all that is made: the whole of creation, all electrons and atoms, crystals and cells, plants and protozoa, doves and dinosaurs, horses and humans. In the great arch of time's upward thrust, all come forth from the mind of God the Father, from His own Idea: The Word, The Logos, His Son, who is Man-God, Christ. And from the Will of Father and Son, from their Love personified, who is the Holy Spirit.

God knows and loves every bit of stuff that we call being. He conceives it, wills that it exist, sees that it is good.

And, loving man, His crowning creation of all the earth, God gives this creation to man, God shares with man His dominion over every other creature. God wills that man know and love all being as He, God, knows and loves all that is. God bids man to name the rest of creation, to call all by name, to become aware of the nature and traits of each atom and cell, galaxy and social group. God wants man to research, investigate, and grasp the interrelations of creatures with each other and to man himself. Thus perceiving their being, man learns the better who he is, and who is God.

God directs man to dress creation, to bring creation into fuller perfection, unto higher states of existence. And in the process, to dress man, to bring man into fuller perfection, unto higher states of existence. Even unto the summit of becoming perfect as the Father is perfect, always with His help.

To perfect creation and to perfect himself, to become more like unto God in his knowing and loving, in his possessing of creatures, man also creates, as God creates. Man creates what the headlines proclaim, what the news commentators tell us about every evening on TV. Man creates law and treaty, congress and contract, steel plant and wheat farm, laboratory and literature, Telstar and baby's bottle. Each of these human creations enables man to dress the bare creation of God, to refine the raw materials from His hand, to bring God's creation unto fuller perfection. And each of these human creations enables man to advance God's crowning creature of the earth, man himself. And in this way to honor the Creator.

Or to degrade man. And in this way to insult the Creator.

So it is basic to Christian belief that God does value the works of man. He understands and cares much more deeply than we humans can care or understand. God cares so much that as the God-Man Christ He took to Himself not only our human nature, but also our human work, as the carpenter of Nazareth. Becoming our brother in the flesh, our comrade at work, Christ became indeed kinsman even to every clump of clay, living leaf and creature within and beyond our ken.

And the Church cares and understands—as Pope John so clearly tells, with the Piuses and Leo XIII before him, and now Pope Paul—because the Church continues Christ the

God-Man in time and space, today and tomorrow and to the end of the world, in New York, the Congo and Cuba and over the whole earth. We who are the Church are Christ. In and with and through us Christ expresses His care for the creation which He with the Father brings into existence unceasingly.

In the opening sentence of his encyclical *Christianity and Social Progress*—*Mater et Magistra* is the Latin title—Pope John tells us why the Church cares about the things of this world:

> The Catholic Church has been established by Jesus Christ as Mother and Teacher of nations, so that all who in the course of centuries come to her loving embrace, may find salvation as well as *the fullness of a more excellent life*.

Pope John then explains why the Church is concerned not only about salvation, but also about the fullness of a more excellent life for men:

> For the teaching of Christ joins, as it were, *earth with heaven*, in that it embraces the whole man, namely, his soul and body, intellect and will and bids him to lift his mind from the changing conditions of human existence to that heavenly country where he will one day enjoy unending happiness and peace.
>
> Hence, although Holy Church has the special task of sanctifying souls and of making them sharers of heavenly blessings, she is also *solicitous for the requirements of men in their daily lives,* not merely those relating to food and sustenance, but also to their *comfort and advancement* in various kinds of goods in varying circumstances of time. [Italics added.]

The Church is solicitous about the same human concerns which make up the front pages and evening news reports. The Church does care for the requirements of men in their daily lives: for work and food, health and peace, home and family; for comfort and advancement in various kinds of goods: for education, communication and cultural creation; in varying circumstances of time and place: postwar Europeans and post-empire Africans striving to unite, Marxism readapting itself, Latin America in social revolution, men and nations striving for equality and human progress.

True, the Church's special task is sanctifying souls. But the earthly affairs of man concern her as well, because man becomes Christ-like amidst the fleshy affairs of earth. And because the Church continues Christ, through whom man is sanctified and brought back to God, through whom all things are made as well, including man himself. In Christ man is sanctified, brought back to God, by sanctifying all creation, bringing all creation back to God with man himself. Creation and man must not be split apart, as the God-Man, Creator and Redeemer, must not be split apart.

Because the Church continues Christ in His full role, she is solicitous also about man's need and advancement at the natural level of creaturehood. One of the most kinetic elements in our century's dynamic history is the startling expansion of human needs, stirred by human advancement, especially by science and its technological application to economic production. Human advance begets human need, at least in our present state. Here is a paradox indeed: man's progress in affluence multiplies his needs. Yet human advance is today's great imperative.

There is no call to venture into the depths of philosophy, psychology or rhetoric. The niceties of ultimate causes, subconscious reflexes and symbolic logic we can leave aside for the present, for the norms of daily experience and common sense.

Most of us would agree that when Johnny and Jane learn to read and write, to add and subtract, Johnny and Jane make progress, which is good. Most of us would concur that when Mike and Mary and their children are vaccinated for polio and acquire a typhoid-free water supply, they advance as humans. Mike and his family will live longer, with less pain, capable of steady, more productive work. More productive work makes possible greater security and leisure, a more human existence, the basis for improved family and home, a more moral life.

Let us remain within this simple consensus, that schooling and improved health are good for man, that this is progress and desirable for the whole human family. Good and desirable not only for us of the West, of Europe and North America, but good and desirable too for the Mikes and Johnnys, Marys and Janes of Africa, Asia and Latin America —and for their little ones by the hundreds of millions.

Rid of malaria's chill and fever, no longer lethargic through weeks on end, Mike's body requires more food. He can perform more work, so Mike wants more acres to till, more sheep to shear, more opportunity to work.

If we put ourselves in his shoes, we might hear Mike reason along these lines:

"Neighbor Johnny has learned to read and write, so the plantation boss has made him foreman. We are the same age, reared together, but now Johnny is my boss. He tells me about places where land and food abound, where work is regular and paid for in cash. Wish I had ten dollars cash. It could buy a shiny new cooking pot, a radio, medicine for baby's worms.

"Here I hardly ever see cash. From the plantation commissary I am allowed each month a ration of corn, lard, beans, and brown sugar, matches and salt. For this I work four days a week on plantation lands. I get two scrawny acres, which I work for myself and on which I have built my adobe hut, one room, earthen floor, no windows, no chimney. I buy extras on credit at the commissary, and pay with potatoes from my two acres, and, until now, with piglets from my sow that ranged in the woods. But the sow died last week; 'cholera,' Johnny says. I should have given her shots, like the government nurse just gave us for smallpox. But that costs money, cash money.

"I ought to buy another sow. Even a young one costs ten dollars. The commissary manager said he would loan me ten dollars at 20 percent interest each month. I don't know how to figure out this interest business, but Johnny said that would be two dollars a month, without really paying for this sow. Now, a piggy is worth about two dollars, so it would take a new piggy every month to pay for this interest. But the sow would still not be mine. Besides, I never had a sow that had twelve piglets a year, not piglets that lived, anyway.

"This credit and loan and interest business is certainly complicated. Wish I could read and add and figure like Johnny can. Maybe he and the store manager are fooling me. I sure don't like being fooled. It makes me disgusted, mad. Are they making a fool of me? Now, if I went to school I could find out, and straighten things out my way. I have to get my son to school when he is old enough. But that takes money too.

"If only I had more land, my own land. If I complain about anything to the plantation boss, about those extra workdays—the weevils in the commissary corn, mold on the lard, or the plantation hogs eating my potatoes—I might get the gate. Maybe I should move to the capital, where there is plenty of work for cash, like Johnny reads about, like I heard about on his radio. Wish I had a radio."

Such are Mike's musings, musings which now thunder around the world. The one thousand million Mikes and Johnnys, Marys and Janes of Africa, Asia and Latin America are moving from this revolution of rising expectations to the revolution of rising demands.

To get schooling and medicine for their youngsters, land of their own and work for steady cash, a second room on the house, maybe even a stove and a ten-dollar radio, Mike and Johnny, by the millions, are risking daring deeds. They are breaking with the past, they are shedding the familiar ways and traditional customs of their fathers and grand-fathers. For centuries they have been bound by the chrysalis of custom: What is good for father is good for son. Working this land under this proprietor, under this chief, is my fate. He is the superior man, he has learning and power, he controls much land and rules many people. To the end of life this valley is home, or prison. Such has fate decreed, such is the custom of this my people, for centuries and millennia handed down.

As Mike and Johnny break out of this chrysalis of custom, they cut away roots of family and community which provided orientation and nourishment to the human personality through the whole of life. Sayings and values, taboos and rites, the village elders and the holy men offered a rule, norms to govern the orderly rhythm of work and rest, birth and death, sickness and health, love and hate. Now these accepted ways, this second nature which unrecorded time has grooved into their very souls, are questioned by Mike and Johnny, doubted and gradually rejected because they cannot provide the new needs they discover pulsating within, the bright attractions shining without.

To obtain work for cash, land, schooling, freedom from the old authority, that second room, gadgets, medicine—"the fullness of a more excellent life" promised by Pope John—Mike and Johnny break from the past, from the family-land-community relations of their fathers, and form new associations. As a rule this is not their decision alone, arrived at in the isolation of their own valley or ridge. Urgent instruments probe and pierce the chrysalis of custom from without, reaching out from national capital to provincial city, from provincial city to market town, and from market town to hamlet, until now secluded in the valley, forlorn on the ridge, entombed in the jungle.

No longer is any human habitation secluded, forlorn, entombed. The forces of national development, of human progress, private and public, seek them out: departments of

health and welfare and schools, commissions of agrarian reform and land tenure, rural extension services, bureaus of
cooperatives and credit, agencies of adult literacy and basic
education, institutes of self-help and community development, housing authorities, regional planning boards for resource survey and utilization, industry and banks, salesmen
and advertising, road and transport systems, communications
media, peasants' leagues and sharecroppers' unions, labor
movements, patriotic and cultural associations, civic and professional clubs—and other organs of the new social body
now aborning in some eighty of the world's nations.

These stimulate and reinforce the desire of Mike and
Johnny for the new, for change, for reform. Quite often these
private and public forces of social progress, for "the fullness
of a more excellent life," promise more than they can fulfill,
more than resources and training and time allow. As desires
wax into demands, frustrated demands, the move for reform
shifts gear to the drive for revolution, violent if necessary.

Mike and Johnny, Mary and Jane, feel the pressure and
attraction of these mighty currents reaching them from successive levels of market town, provincial city, and national
capital. Of course, the national capital is itself pressured and
attracted by currents from beyond the frontier, by forces rising out of the West and East, from Europe, Japan and North
America, from Moscow and Peking: technology, rationaliza-
tion of industry and commerce, ideas about man and God
and society, ideals concerning humanity and culture and
social progress, economic and social systems.

International industry and organized labor; the United
Nations and regional groups like the French Community and
the Organization of American States; the private foundations,
universities and numerous voluntary associations; technical
and financial assistance like the Alliance for Progress, the
Colombo Plan, the Peace Corps and development programs
of the Common Market countries and of Russia; political
and ideological movements like those of the Communists and

Socialists, of the Arab League and Christian Democrats; diplomatic relations among countries, bilateral and bloc; the communications media, public and private; and the churches and religions—are the principal carriers of these powerful currents out of the East and the West to the capitals and hamlets of eighty countries.

And a thousand million Mikes and Johnnys listen and begin to understand. They find an awakening response within— to the call to change, for the new, from without. They, too, want "the fullness of a more excellent life, . . . not merely in those things relating to food and sustenance, but also to comfort and advancement in various kinds of goods . . . ," which Pope John, and Christ as well, also wants for them.

Mike and Johnny now want things which the old system, and they individually, cannot satisfy. That new sow and better seed, the right to complain to the overseer and negotiate sharecropping terms with the landlord, can come about only by joining hands. So Mike and Johnny join with other fellows to form peasant leagues, labor unions and cooperatives. Obtaining those typhoid shots and schoolrooms is not only beyond the power of individual families, but outside the scope and ken of the individual village, market town and slum. Teachers and technicians, instruments and books from provincial city and national capital must be brought in. The local village and slum form school and health committees, which associate in the provincial education and health boards, which petition the respective national services of the capital right up the line. Or, more often, the whole process is introduced from the top by the national government or commercial firms, and meets the village mixture of apathy and interest somewhere along the way.

Teachers and technicians, instruments and books are naturally in short supply in view of the pyramiding demand. So national government and commerce go beyond the frontiers, seeking aid and trade with other countries.

One way or another, obtaining typhoid shots and schoolbooks; acquiring technical training and tools for farm and shop and factory, and the forging of a countervailing force to *ancien régime* property, production systems and profits; all this striving for human progress, and all this joining together of Mikes and Johnnys, their wives, children and neighbors for "the fullness of a more excellent life"—all of this brings about what Pope John calls "the multiplication of social relationships," or "socialization," on a world scale.

"The fullness of a more excellent life" requires this multiplication of social relationships because Mike and Johnny, and their wives, cannot attain their now dawning goals alone. The Church, as a solicitous mother, urges her children, all of them, to seek and obtain the human perfection of education and health, and the human dignity of freedom and security. Since these achievements can come about only through the multiplication of social relationships, through socialization, then Mother Church looks upon socialization affirmatively, as a good thing, as a perfection of human creativity itself, in conformity with God's will for His universal creation.

Chapter Two

SOCIALIZATION AND THE BIRTH OF CIVILIZATION

From the earliest days of his life on earth, man's quest for human progress has led inevitably to a "multiplication of social relationships." Man can satisfy very few of his needs alone. Most human goods can be obtained with greater abundance and speed, and with more constancy and security for the future, if men and social groupings pool their respective resources, talents and acquired skills, as well as the fruit of their combined enterprise. Man cannot survive infancy alone. He cannot acquire any significant knowledge alone. He cannot love alone. In short, alone, man cannot be truly human.

So from the beginning man formed the family; and the extended families, seeking security and identity, combined to form the clan and tribe. It was only about nine thousand years ago that the food-gathering and hunting tribes learned that wild weeds and roots planted in prepared soil with sufficient moisture would become wheat and rice, maize and potatoes, to yield year after year a hundredfold. Agriculture was born. The food gatherers halted their seasonal wanderings, planted their own roots and grain and put down roots themselves. The stable human habitation became possible; the primitive village arose.*

[1] William H. McNeill's *The Rise of the West* (University of Chicago Press, 1963) gives an excellent short account of the birth of the Middle Eastern civilizations, especially pages 3–109. The present writer is indebted to this work for valuable insights, which are viewed here in the context of socialization.

The hunter of this period might bring home a fawn, a pup, a calf, a chick, a pony—the offspring of his kill as a pet for the children, or maybe as a totem with religious overtones. These animals, once domesticated, provided food and fun, transport and draft power, to the struggling Neolithic villages which began to dot the earth. Transport and draft power from burro and bullock meant energy and physical capacity beyond man's own, a big step in human progress and toward socialization. Because he had more food, energy and physical capacity at his disposal, more than was required for mere survival, man's horizons broadened, his needs and wants multiplied—a paradoxical phenomenon noted in the previous chapter.

The culture of the pre-agricultural food collectors and hunters is called Paleolithic (Old Stone). Their hand axes, clubs, spears, scrapers and knives were chipped and rough, and were usually made of flint. They also made tools of bone, antlers, horns and tusks. From the earliest record of human artifacts, going back perhaps to 500,000 B.C., it seems that man's Paleolithic way of life underwent little change. Then came additions to the tool kit, at least in Western Europe, to begin the Mesolithic (Middle Stone) period, about 8000 to 4500 B.C., with the bow and arrow, fish nets and hooks, dugout canoes, sleds and skis, as well as domesticated dogs, probably as pets as well as trailers for the hunt. There is evidence that these vast improvements, man's first significant triumph over his natural environment in some half-million years, were introduced into Europe by newcomers from the East.

It is in the Middle East that the next great step, agriculture, is first recorded. By radio-carbon dating, archeologists place grain culture at about 6500 B.C. and the first settled villages some two to four hundred years thereafter. This began the Neolithic (New Stone) age, with the polished stone implements which characterized those community sites. The cutting edge of stones harder than flint was required to strip off bark to kill a tree, to cut through the trunk and to dig about the stump to clear land for agriculture. Stronger, sharper axes were needed to fashion hardwood branches into hoes and plow-like implements. Tools to make tools began to multiply; clay pottery in which to cook cereal porridge, and cloth made from flax, began to appear.

Most Neolithic families met their own needs with their own growing skills. But here and there among the twenty to forty families of the village, one man showed greater skill than all others as a stone polisher, a potter, a weaver: the specialist appeared and "the division of labor" began. The part-time specialist exchanged his product, surplus beyond his own need, for the extra grain, meat or firewood of another; or for assistance at his work in lifting a heavy load, or in finding and carrying stone and wood of peculiar hardness from far-off places, or clay of choice viscosity. Barter trade and exchange of goods-in-kind for work performed, commerce and wages of the most primitive type came upon the human scene.

Prior to their concentration in large valleys, river deltas and lake areas, begun only about 4000 B.C. in the Middle East, the Neolithic village was a lonely outpost in a forest clearing or mountain vale. Neighboring villages were a day or more away—twenty, fifty, a hundred miles in any direction. These were not regarded as neighbors at all, because there was no regular communication or joint concerns among these scattered centers of human life. The men saw each other by chance while on the chase or in a slugging match over a choice carcass; the women, when a wife was bought or stolen.

It must be emphasized further that Paleolithic men did not all move through the Mesolithic and Neolithic periods at the same time, and some indeed never did. That man began his polished stone, pottery, cloth-making and farming culture about 6500 B.C. by no means implies that all men of his region, much less of the world, did the same. In the miles of wilderness comprising the interstices between the Neolithic village sites, Paleolithic and Mesolithic man continued to gather food and hunt deer, eschewing agriculture.

When Columbus came to America, the Plains Indians of the Midwest were still at this collector-hunter stage, while the Mohawks and Iroquois of the Hudson and the St. Lawrence valleys may be considered advanced Neolithic, quite beyond the isolated village in their concept of authority and nation and organized war. The Aztecs and Incas to the far south were in full-fledged civilization, while the Navajo and cliff dwellers of Arizona and New Mexico were somewhere between Neolithic and the more complex relations of civilization.

As the Neolithic advances diffused from the original creative center, imitation of these developments was quite uneven. Not all men were equally attracted to the sedentary way which agriculture demands. The thrills of the chase, the satisfaction of the kill and the pleasure of wanderlust countered the growing security and monotony of the man with the hoe. When the grass was right, many groups hit a compromise by becoming nomadic stockherders, moving their sheep and goats, tents and leather utensils, and their kinsmen over several hundred miles of range and back again as the season required. Such was Abraham from Ur of the Chaldees, who set out for the north and west about 1900 B.C. Horseback riding did not become habitual until about 900 B.C. So pastoral nomadism remained arduous and relatively insecure, providing neither surplus of produce, nor stability of habitation and division of labor, nor the continuing common problems and bonds among several contiguous, interacting centers of human society—the socialization which true civilization requires.

Areas of exceptional fertility and optimum moisture, like flat, rockless river valleys and deltas, naturally attracted the first raw agricultural settlements in greater density. With population growth spurting upward, due to a stable food supply and better nutrition, especially for pregnant and nursing mothers and their infants, the villagers spread their holdings outward and the village units became increasingly contiguous. By about the year 4000 B.C., forty- and fifty-mile stretches along the lower Tigris and Euphrates, in modern-day Iraq, were almost solidly cultivated areas, one village's lands extending four or five miles downstream and up, meeting in each direction the neighboring village's area of concern and control. Along the Nile and Indus Rivers agglomerations of these human concentrations, never before experienced by man, gathered by about the year 3500 B.C.

The stage was now set for the true beginning of socialization and human civilization, for the two are intimately related, even reciprocal.

The isolated Neolithic community had been held together by bonds of blood and face-to-face relations. The fifty to a hundred inhabitants were kinsmen; they all knew each other, each spoke to each almost daily. Many owned and cultivated the land in common, without individual ownership. In some Neolithic villages, the inhabitants ate from a common pot or roasting spit, and slept under the same roof. They evolved their own religious ceremonials, rites of passage and totem practices in which all the village partook. The holy men shared in the authority of the headman and elders. Neolithic horizons and concerns hardly ever reached beyond this extended family of a few score persons. The villages were quite self-sufficient, except perhaps for occasional exchanges, warlike and peaceful, with other communities, especially for wives.

Then came the concentration of villages in the great river valleys and deltas. Intervillage contact and concern multiplied. Village chief and elders had to treat with heads of other villages. Harder stone, stronger wood and better clay became known and coveted from the second and fourth and tenth village up the river, fifty and eighty miles from home base. Log rafts were devised to float the cargo past the riverbank village sites. Boundary disputes must be settled. "The

multiplication of social relationships"—socialization, and civilization—began first in the lower Tigris-Euphrates Valley,
about 4000 B.C., and along the Nile and Indus valleys some
five to eight hundred years later.

Undoubtedly, a new technological development to improve
primitive agriculture played a major generative role in the
birth of the first civilization, the Sumerian, in the area of
modern-day Iraq. This technical advance was irrigation, the
controlled impounding and channeling of water for crops
and for animal and human use. Probably this development,
more than any other, broadened and multiplied social relationships, which became stabilized in complex new institutions to beget the first human civilization.

Seasonal floods in river flats lay down silt deposits which
built up the banks nearest the stream, so the land level over
the centuries slopes downward away from the river. The first
irrigation, the first human attempt at directing the water flow
to man's advantage, probably consisted in simply cutting
trenches of modest size, one or two feet deep, twenty to fifty
yards in length, through the riverside embankment to facili-
tate the temporary flooding of inland areas. As these ditches
grew in size to become canals and to increase the water's
volume and spread, the acres of neighboring villages were
radically affected. Too much water, or any water at the wrong
time, ruined the crops for miles around; and in dry years
water control became vital. Disputes and altercations ensued;
consultations were held and agreements entered into among
neighboring villages.

The time of planting of crops, location of canals, control
of water flow, allocation of water in dry years, and other issues of joint interest had to be agreed upon by the heads of
villages. They selected men especially skilled in water lore as
their managers, men who had an eye for land levels and
contours, who understood seepage and could devise primitive
gates and sluices, who could foretell the seasons from the
moon, stars, sun and migratory fowl. These "technicians" be-

gan keeping records of the river's seasonal rise and fall, with axed notches on trees along its edge, by notches on clay tablets kept year by year with increasing care. This process brought to power a priestly caste of "scientific" seers, who shared with selected initiates their precious lore for interpreting and controlling nature's forces, which in time were personalized into river gods and earth-fertility goddesses. This led in turn to centralized control of grain production, granaries for surplus storage, careful record-keeping, and numbers and writing systems. The cuneiform writing of the Sumerians resembles a series of notches or wedge marks. These were probably at first literal reminders (one unit per notch), which gradually became differentiated into patterns to express phonetic and numerical values.

As developers, trustees and transmitters of this powerful "science," the priestly college in due time obtained *de facto* managerial control of the grain from a score of villages, and with the passage of centuries they obtained *de jure* possession of land, water and produce in the name of the gods they represented—the gods who personified the earth and river, storm and flood from which plants and food, life itself, and death, came forth. Between 3500 and 3200 B.C. the village communities, with their local loyalty based on kinship, lost their inner cohesion and self-sufficiency to the stronger magnetism of the much larger temple city, an attraction concretized in the monumental temple itself, the many-tiered ziggurat. Twenty to forty villages became the satellites which revolved around the much richer and highly differentiated life of the urban nucleus, the prototype of the city-state of Greece and Renaissance Europe.

The city's god owned the land, so he had first claim to surplus produce beyond the family needs of the farmers. This surplus was stored in temple granaries. These accumulated "savings" above annual consumption became "currency" for exchange with neighboring cities and for paying distant hillmen for livestock, timber, stone, and, later, metal, especially tin for bronze. There was an increase in shipping going down the river, packtrains going upstream, and caravans penetrating the hills and deserts which border the river basin. Commerce on a large and regular scale began. Agents of the temple rulers became merchants.

Guards, who defended settlers from the marauding barbarians and the nomads who invaded the fringe farms, and who protected the caravans and mining expeditions, became full-time soldiers. Their leaders became military chiefs, and intercity warfare was frequent by 3000 B.C. The military chiefs became kings, who gradually assumed for themselves the juridical and economic prerogatives the priestly caste had until then exercised. This concept of kingship—sovereign authority residing in one man—may have arisen from the extraordinary powers which must be deputized to a military leader in time of war, and may have been brought into Mesopotamia by the pastoral nomads of the surrounding hills and desert who organized their tribes under the stern discipline of one chief.

Royal authority became sanctioned by arranging approval from the gods. Myth and ritual developed to sanctify it, leading to the crowning annual ceremony of ritual marriage between the king and the goddess of the city. By 2500 B.C. most of the temple cities had ceded jurisdiction to the local king.

The surplus grain from the temple tracts, "savings" above annual consumption accumulated in central granaries, not only became "currency" to sustain commerce, but were translated into "capital" which further improved and expanded the means of production. The grain, or its equivalent in other goods, provided wages for the extensive labor forces needed to reclaim new land, to build larger canals and levees, roads and bridges, dams and monuments. (The close parallel with the Russian Communist control of grain under Lenin and Stalin for capital formation and industrial growth, as an economic base for the "take-off" of economic development, must be noted.) This secure supply of food aplenty also freed men from steady toil and allowed for more experimentation. The wheeled vehicle, bronze fittings for chariots and weapons, and sailing vessels able to leave the river mouth and probe along coasts of the open sea, were introduced.

Other men had leisure, sufficient sustenance without usefully productive work, to spend their time adorning the temple and its furnishings, to weave colorful designs into cloth and decorative draperies, to design and paint graceful pottery, to form clay and stone into human and animal figures. Art on a grand scale was born. Men had the leisure to record oral myths, traditions and their own imaginings on clay tablets. History, poems and literature came into being, among them the famed *Epic of Gilgamesh*. The first civilization, the Sumerian, was in full flower. The civilizations of the Nile and Indus valleys followed in close parallel, with some variety in specifics and in chronology. The three civilizations knew of, and interacted on, each other.

With the improvement of technology and the expansion of transport and commerce, with the enlargement of the waterworks and road systems, and with the broadening of man's inner vision beyond his city-state to the wider universe of his physical, exterior reach, and his musings on what might be beyond those horizons, the temple city became too small as a social, economic and political unit. The multiplication of social relations extended ever outward. Cities grouped, by suasion and by force, into larger units. About 2375 B.C. Lugalzaggisi of Umma united most of the cities of Sumer under his dominion, the first ruler known to have done so. Sargon of Akkad put together a more enduring political empire a generation later, about 2340 B.C., covering an area some 400 miles long and 200 miles wide, a territory almost identical with modern Iraq.

After five centuries of war and peace, which saw the breakup and reassembly of the Tigris-Euphrates basin in many molds, Hammurabi of Babylon gave the region cohesion and unity about 1700 B.C. Socialization attained a broader scope and greater intensity, as leaders devised more effective methods for dealing with large groups of men in distant cities, now so different from the day-to-day, face-to-face, man-to-man relations which had obtained since Paleolithic times over the half-million years before. The contractual, legal, impersonal relations of a complex civilization replaced the social cement of kinsmen and primary groups. Among these new socializing techniques were five of the highest significance:

1. Administrative technique—i.e. the communication of orders from the top to lower echelons, and from the power center to far-off representatives, and the supervision and evaluation of executive performance—was vastly improved, especially through written messages, directives and reports.

2. Generalized policy and decisions of the sovereign authority were laid down in written and codified laws, the famed Hammurabian Code. Application of norms of right and wrong to human conduct became stable and predictable. Rule of law over rule of man made its first precarious appearance.

3. Trained administrators, a civil service and bureaucracy, and a professional army, came into being.

4. Political theory and loyalty developed, giving the "whys" and rationale for the new social institutions, providing a psychological substitute for traditional bonds of family and village.

5. Uniform regulations were applied to commerce, business contracts and taxes on goods, facilitating trade in an extensive common market. A powerful merchant and manufacturing class arose who were favored by the central government in its surveillance of local authorities. By standardizing weights, measures and customs duties, by controlling piracy, and by constructing roads and clearing river channels and dock areas, the central government enabled the commercial and artisan class to range hundreds of miles within and be-

yond the empire. This trade system bound the distant villages together by the interdependent ties of buying and selling. Nomadic tribes and primitive villages on the fringes of the empire were gradually introduced to a more complex, more civilized, way of life. In time, commerce linked together the three old civilizations of Sumer, Egypt and the Indus Delta.

From 7000 to 1700 B.C., some 5000 years, man, after some 500,000 years of stagnation, suddenly moved from Paleolithic hunter-food collector—to primitive Neolithic farming village, to the civilization of the self-sufficient city-state, and on to the greater social macrocosm of empire. These first three empires were rooted in the same basic elements upon which all subsequent civilizations have rested: law, administration, commerce, agriculture, manufacturing, training, army; artists and thinkers, rulers and priests; farmers, workers and technicians.

New technology played a key role in each human advance, enabling man to concentrate greater energy, physical and mental, and to unify larger, ever larger, numbers of his fellowmen, to bring about fulfillment of their needs, potentialities and desires, which showed an astonishing capacity for expansion. This multiplication of social relationships, this process of socialization, brought about civilization and a deeper, wider realization of "the fullness of a more excellent life." War and servitude, crime and injustice, and other potentialities for evil increased proportionately.

Chapter Three

POPE JOHN AND
MODERN SOCIALIZATION

Prime Minister Nehru of India was among the millions who perked up their ears when Pope John praised socialization in his encyclical *Christianity and Social Progress*. Like many others, the Indian leader appeared to have wrongly equated socialization with socialism, which is the collectivization of productive property under state ownership and management. Owing in part to this confusion of meanings, some English translators of the encyclical avoided the word "socialization" and used instead "multiplication of social relationships," an apt rendering of the official Latin text. However, the Vatican version in Italian in the *Osservatore Romano* used *socializzazione* from the first.

Amleto Cardinal Cicognani, Vatican Secretary of State, writing in English to the National Social Action Conference of Canada in 1963, uses the word "socialization" twelve times. He also quotes the word right out of *Christianity and Social Progress*. So the Holy See shows no timidity in asserting its own meaning for the English term, which to many sensitive Americans did at first sound dangerously evocative of socialism. To set all at rest, Cardinal Cicognani clarifies the point at the very start of his 1963 letter to the Canadians:

It is well to emphasize, in the first place, that socialization, as discussed in the encyclical letter *Mater et Magistra*, is in no way to be confused with socialism. Socialization,

when freely and prudently actuated, is entirely in conformity with the social nature of man, and is a source of true
human progress in every field, economic, social, moral and
cultural.

Pope John brings up socialization in his encyclical immediately after the section entitled "Private Initiative and State
Intervention in Economic Life." He affirms that "in economic
affairs first place is to be given to the private initiative of individual men who, either working by themselves, or with others in one fashion or another, pursue their common interests."
John then asserts that, for reasons pointed out by his prede-
cessors, "it is necessary that public authorities take active interest, the better to increase output of goods and to further
social progress for the benefit of all citizens." (Pars. 51, 52.)
In the very next sentence John defines this "active interest"
as the "intervention of public authorities." The use of the
word "intervention" should be noted. The choice of this concept implies entry by an outside agent into an ongoing affair,
an interference which, though necessary, is regrettable and
should be minimized. The negative nuance is then happily balanced by a positive affirmation: "This intervention of public
authorities that encourages, regulates, supplements, and complements is based on the *principle of subsidiarity* as set forth
by Pius XI in his encyclical *Quadragesimo Anno*." (John's
italics.)

The principle of subsidiarity is so basic to Christian social
teaching and is so constantly operative in the complex process
of socialization that, at this point in *Christianity and Social
Progress,* John quotes what Pius XI said back in 1931:

It is a fundamental principle of social philosophy, fixed
and unchangeable, that one should not withdraw from individuals and commit to the community what they can accomplish by their own enterprise and industry. So, too, it
is an injustice and at the same time a grave evil and a disturbance of right order, to transfer to the larger and higher

collectivity functions which can be performed and provided for by lesser and subordinate bodies. Inasmuch as every social activity should, by its very nature, prove a help to members of the body social, it should never destroy or absorb them. [Par. 53.]

Since Pope John discusses the principle of subsidiarity in clarification of public intervention in the economy and to introduce the wider subject of socialization, it must be stressed that subsidiary function should obtain as well within all social bodies, public and private, whether their purposes are economic, political, civic, recreational, religious (i.e. within the Church herself), or for some other human end. Subsidiary function means that in practice:

1. The individual person must seek to satisfy his needs and wants through his own efforts before he asks the collaboration of his family or other individuals;

2. The family group must strive to fulfill its own needs and wants before requesting a voluntary community effort;

3. Voluntary and private groups must expend their own resources and abilities before expecting the local, municipal or other public authority to address itself to the need felt by a significant number;

4. The local political body should refer a problem, or an opportunity for human progress, to the county, state, provincial or departmental government only when local efforts prove inadequate to the task;

5. The intermediate public or private authority or group should turn for assistance to the federal or national government only when its powers are exhausted;

6. The "sovereign" nation ought to go beyond its borders by treaty and by the sharing of its powers with international bodies only for goals which are outside the nation's own scope.

Furthermore, just as the lesser and subordinate bodies should not indiscriminately thrust their needs and demands upward onto the shoulders of the larger and higher bodies, these latter are not to impress their solutions of human wants and problems downward upon the less powerful groups without due cause. This applies equally to the economic community.

After the direct quote from Pius XI's statement on subsidiary function from *Quadragesimo Anno* (1931), Pope John immediately asserts strong reasons why it is, now "to a greater extent than heretofore," within the power of the state to intervene in economic affairs. Recent developments of science and technology provide these current additional reasons, giving public authorities the power to reduce economic imbalances of three types: "between various sectors of economic life, or between different regions of the same nation, or even between different peoples of the world as a whole." (Par. 54.)

These three phrases provide theoretical bases for state-promoted mutual help among members of a given nation and members of the human family. Such programs embody the fundamental principle of the interdependence of all human beings, with stress upon the concern which the strong must have for the weak. This cuts across social and economic strata—effecting, it is true, a sort of leveling whereby those with needs beyond their present powers benefit from the strength and sufficiency of others. This valid and fundamental principle echoes throughout the political and social philosophy of the American and French Revolutions, Jeffersonian and Jacksonian Democrats and Lincoln Republicans. It finds expression in the recent evolution of "One World" Willkie-ites into Eisenhower and Rockefeller world-viewers, and the New and Fair Dealers into New Frontiersmen.

State-promoted collaboration to reduce imbalances between various sectors of the economy, between different regions of the nation, and even between peoples of the world as a whole, rudely uproots the bases of exaggerated capitalism. Economic imbalances and consequent political and social stratification are not to be passively accepted as inevitable effects of the free market, the immutable natural law of supply and demand, "the invisible hand" of Adam Smith. Laissez-faire is out, not only among the factors of production, such as labor, capital, raw material, management and technicians, but also among sectors of the economy such as agriculture, industry, commerce and services. So public subsidies or other means of buoying a sector toward parity with others is definitely called for when the imbalance reaches crucial proportions. Later in the encyclical Pope John explicitly applies this to agriculture.

If public authorities are to reduce imbalances between the haves and have-nots of different regions of the same country, then a depressed-areas program—a Tennessee Valley Authority, a SUDENE for Brazil's Northeast, a *Casa Mezzogiorno* for southern Italy—might well be called for. If imbalances, "even between different people of the world as a whole," are to be mitigated by governments, then foreign aid—the Colombo Plan, the Alliance for Progress and Inter-American Development Bank, the United Nations Conference on Trade and Development, international commodity stabilization treaties, the World Bank and International Monetary Fund—assuredly have their role to play. The United Nations and the Organization of American States must not only be allowed to exist; they must be strengthened. Pope John makes this abundantly clear in his second great encyclical, *Pacem in Terris*.

National economic planning, at least for some sectors and commodities, inter-nation regional coordination leading to free trade areas and common markets, and world planning for production and pricing of commodities chronically in surplus, like coffee, sugar and rubber, quickly follow from Pope John's thesis toward economic parity among production sectors, geographic areas and have and have-not nations. He does not stop there.

These same recent developments of science and technology, John goes on, make it possible to keep fluctuations in the economy within bounds, and to provide effective measures for avoiding mass unemployment. Since public authorities are responsible for the common good, this Johannine doctrine of economic collaboration concludes, it is again and again requested "that they [public authorities] intervene in a wide variety of economic affairs, and that, in a more extensive and organized way than heretofore, they adapt institutions, tasks, means, and procedures to this end." (Par. 54.)

Pope John is anxious that these precautionary activities of public authorities in the economic life should avoid restricting the freedom and fundamental rights of the individual person. Rather, this public intervention, to his mind, should increase freedom and rights, especially "the right and duty of each individual normally to provide the necessities of life for himself and his dependents." If private initiative is lacking, political tyranny prevails and "much stagnation occurs in various sectors of the economy, and hence all sorts of consumer goods and services, closely connected with needs of the body and more especially of the spirit, are in short supply." (Pars. 55, 57.) Surely this is applicable to Communist countries in general.

On the other hand, John warns that where "appropriate activity of the state is lacking or defective, commonwealths are apt to experience incurable disorders, and there occurs exploitation of the weak by the unscrupulously strong, who flourish, unfortunately, like cockle among the wheat, in all times and places." (Par. 58.) Surely this is applicable to many Latin American countries. It is at this point in *Christianity and Social Progress* that the term and concept of socialization are introduced under the heading "Complexity of Social Structure." (Pars. 59–67.)

Pope John states that the multiplication of social relationships, or socialization, is a principal characteristic of our time. This daily more complex interdependence of citizens introduces into our lives numerous varied forms of association, many of which are recognized by law. Among the factors bringing about this phenomenon are technical and scientific progress, increased productive efficiency and a rising standard of living. Human motives definitely contribute to this growing social complexity. Man has a natural inclination, scarcely resistible, which impels him to enter voluntarily into association in order to attain objectives which exceed the capacity of single individuals.

These developments in human society are both a cause and a symptom of the growing intervention of public authorities in matters of serious moment. This intervention involves some danger because it reaches into the more intimate aspects of personal life, like education of youth, care of the sick and the choice of one's vocation. In recent years socialization has given rise to national and international organizations with economic and social goals, and dealing with cultural, professional and political affairs.

In the judgment of Pope John this advance in social relationships undoubtedly brings numerous services and advantages. "It makes possible, in fact, the satisfaction of many personal rights, especially those of economic and social life." These personal rights relate to the necessities of life, to health services and training, to labor and housing, and to suitable leisure and recreation. Furthermore, individuals can now participate in human events on a world scale, due to the ever more perfect organization of media for the diffusion of thought by press, radio, television and the movies.

But all the results of socialization are not good. Rules and laws which control and determine the relationships of citizens are multiplied. The opportunity for free action by individuals is restricted. Often an atmosphere is created in which one finds it difficult to make decisions without undue external influences, or to undertake anything on one's own initiative. The proper fulfillment of rights and duties and the full development of one's personality are easily impeded.

Pope John asks the question directly: "Will men perhaps then become automatons, and cease to be personally responsible, as these social relationships multiply more and more?"

And he immediately responds: "It is a question which must be answered negatively."

This increased complexity of life is by no means the result of a blind drive of natural forces beyond the control of man, John explains. Quite the opposite: this is the deliberate creation of free men, responsible for their acts. These free men must, however, take into account the laws of human progress and of the development of economic life. They must recognize, too, that men are not altogether free of their environment. Men are the creators of this new environment, but they remain creatures also.

In order that advances in social organization may yield maximum advantages to citizens, while disadvantages are either averted or minimized, the common good must be correctly understood by public authorities. The common good, Pope John makes plain, "embraces the sum total of those conditions of social living, whereby men are enabled more fully and more readily to achieve their own perfection."

This calls for varied intermediate bodies and numerous social groupings at all levels, through which men give expression to the expanding social structure. These intermediate bodies—some private, some public, and some of mixed character—must be autonomous, ruled by their own laws. But they must seek sincere concord among themselves, in keeping with the common good. More important still, these intermediate associations must take on the nature of a true community, in which individual members are treated as human beings, and in which each person is encouraged to participate in the affairs of the group.

As relationships multiply between men, binding them more closely together, two key factors must be kept in balance to obtain appropriate order in each commonwealth. Citizens as individuals and as groups must remain free to act autonomously, while cooperating with each other; and this must be balanced by state activity to regulate suitably, and to foster, the initiatives of private persons and groups.

Pope John concludes on a very positive note:

Now if social systems are organized in accordance with the above norms and moral laws, their extension does not necessarily mean that individual citizens will be gravely discriminated against or excessively burdened. Rather, we can hope that this will enable man not only to develop and perfect his natural talents, but also will lead to an appropriate structuring of the human community. Such a structure, as our predecessor of happy memory, Pius XI, warned in his Encyclical Letter, *Quadragesimo Anno,* is absolutely necessary for the adequate fulfillment of the rights and duties of social life. [Par. 67.]

Today's socialization, which Pope John defines with such insight and evaluates so favorably, is a logical continuation of the process which began when our Paleolithic hunting ancestors first took up nomadic stockraising and Neolithic farming, then coalesced their villages into the temple city-states from which arose the Sumerian, Egyptian and Indus "water control" civilizations. These brought forth the great society which was the Middle East from 1500 to 500 B.C., to which all civilized humans have been indebted. This interacting social macrocosm in due time provided many of the fertilizants for today's world socialization, begetting for the first time a civilization which promises to be truly universal, embracing all the family of man. And this process of travail brings also birth pangs and danger, revolutions within and outside of man, peaceful and violent, creative and traumatic, liberating and oppressive. The new wine bursts the old skins; new containers for these fermenting forces take shape.

Pope John discerns two key motors, or factors—in the root sense of "makers" and "doers"—operative throughout this millennial process: "that human and natural inclination, scarcely resistible, whereby men are impelled voluntarily to enter into association in order to obtain objectives which each one desires, but which exceed the capacity of single individuals"; and "technical and scientific progress, greater productive efficiency."

Both these factors or motors are highly accelerated in our day, speeding up the multiplication of human associations and extending these to most areas of human concern, to weave a social fabric of astonishing complexity. This social fabric has become in reality *the new human environment*. Man in his struggle to know, to control and to direct his natural environment—earth, water and air; cold, heat and energy; plants and animals; distance and time—has created, step by step, a new social environment: hunting bands, nomadic tribes, farming villages, city-states, nations, empires, alliances and international treaties; commercial partnerships, legal contracts, trade agreements, cooperatives and industrial corporations; artisan guilds, labor unions, peasant leagues and professional associations; centers for training, research and education; groupings for cultural and civic, recreational and humanitarian, secular and religious purposes, in unimaginable variety.

The head of the household no longer wrestles heroically with water and darkness, cold and heat; he treats rather with the utility company, which negotiates in turn with the labor unions and city planning board, with the conservation department and the Federal Power Commission. To get meat and milk, potatoes and transport, the family no longer trails deer and digs the earth, corrals goats and lassoes horses; they call up the supermarket and airline, which in turn bargain with General Foods and General Motors, the Farm Bureau, and the Federal Aviation Authority, Congressional committees and Madison Avenue.

Other associations form to study, to direct, and to coordinate this new social environment at local, state, national and international levels: federations of labor, farmer and industrial organizations; of technical and professional societies; of private and public agencies. Still other organizations are formed to analyze, synthesize and animate the whole complex creation: public opinion polls and public relations agencies; White House conferences on youth and old age, education, race and "National Goals for Americans"; world assemblies on technology and development—and thousands and thousands more.

Man's enemies are no longer beast and bacteria; and, for half the human family, food and shelter seem sufficient for our generation. Human fears now arise from the new social environment: "Will men perhaps then become automatons, and cease to be personally responsible, as these social relationships multiply more and more?" Pope John asks. Will organization man lose all initiative, become the passive ploy of big government, big labor and big business? A grain of sand in the totalitarian concrete mixer? Will man abandon his identity, his "I-ness," his personality, to become a nameless, numbered nomad in the lonely crowd—in the words of Paul VI, "isolated in a troubled society that has no message for their spirit"? Will this driving technology and world socialization pollute the very air man once breathed in Paleolithic plenty and purity with smog and radioactive fallout, that noxious debris of socialization that pierces man's very innards—lungs, blood and nerves—with physical symptoms of spiritual malaise?

Socialization has transformed the atmosphere in which man lives into a "sociosphere," to adopt a neologism attributed to Teilhard de Chardin. It is this new human reality which imparts high significance to the dialogue with the contemporary world which Paul VI inherited from his predecessor, and which he now places in the main current of the Church's concern.

Part Two

THE REVOLUTIONS OF THE WEST

Chapter Four

CONFLICT AND RENEWAL
IN THE WEST

Socialization creates a new atmosphere, a new habitat, in which man lives and loves, hopes and fears, plays and works. Man and his environment continue to undergo elemental changes, changes of revolutionary dimension on a global scale.

These societal revolutions are many, complex and closely intertwined. However, four primordial transformations can be discerned, more basic and causal than the rest. These four primordial revolutions are: science applied to economic and social processes, progress through this-world betterment, equality among men and nations, and spiraling population growth.[1] The order given is not necessarily chronological nor in priority of importance.

The *first* revolution is the ever accelerating advance of *science,* and the rational application of technology to the *economic and social processes,* to accumulate massive savings over consumption, to build up investment and capital formation for plant, equipment and training, and to nourish further research. This makes material betterment in this world tech-

---

[1] Barbara Ward introduces comparable basic concepts in her excellent book *The Rich Nations and the Poor Nations* (New York: Norton, 1962). The present writer is indebted to her for stimulating initially much of his own thought on the four revolutions. However, another order of development is followed herein, and distinctive applications are made to the central theme of this volume, the Church and world socialization.

nically possible for the many, because now necessities and niceties can be multiplied beyond man's historic dreams. Further, the scientific method (exact measurement, repeatable and predictable behavior, mass generalization) is applied to man and society as a whole through "social engineering," group psychology, and direction of learning and motive processes.

The *second* revolution is the idea and ideal of *human and social progress,* spread by the new communications media and concretized by material betterment in this world, the here-and-now, as distinct from spiritual joys, bodily asceticism and rewards in the next world. This rising expectation and demand for progress through material betterment requires drastic restructuring of the social, political and economic institutions of national and world society. Such temporal reform for this-world progress is morally justified by Pope John:

> Such an advance in social relationships definitely brings numerous services and advantages. It makes possible, in fact, the satisfaction of many personal rights, especially those of economic and social life; these relate, for example, to the minimum necessities of life, to health services, to the broadening and deepening of elementary education, to a more fitting training in skills, to housing, to labor, to suitable leisure and recreation. [Par. 61, *Christianity and Social Progress.*]

And, adds Pope John with obvious approval, "through the more perfect organization of modern means for the diffusion of thought—press, cinema, radio, television—individuals are enabled to take part in human events on a worldwide scale." To John this is human and social progress, for which he rejoices. Other moral and religious leaders mitigate formerly harsh ascetic ideals, opening the door to widespread human yearning for this-world improvement.

The *third* revolution is the idea and ideal of *human and social equality,* a growing inner awareness and conviction of the value and dignity of every human being, of the equality among men and social classes within each nation, and of the equality of nations and races among themselves. This personal consciousness is transferred to collective consciousness of the value, dignity and equality of social groupings, and re-enforces the demand for exterior reform of societal structures to promote the material betterment of all classes, in all nations and races, as well as the private and public acknowledgment of human equality. Concepts of social justice and the common good are extended beyond tribes and nations to the whole human family.

The *fourth* revolution is the sudden recent acceleration of the rate at which *human population multiplies itself,* in particular regions and over the earth as a whole, due to the three revolutions already named, especially to scientific advances in public health and preventive medicine. The new social bodies which have been organized nationally and internationally to apply this technical progress to all men with growing equality, without regard for race, nation, religion or social class, spread the population spiral to every corner of the earth.

These four revolutions all began in the North Atlantic region, in Western Europe and North America. In the century between 1775 and 1875 these four primordial revolutions transformed this region from agricultural, dominantly authoritarian, class-structured societies, into increasingly industrial, democratic and egalitarian nations, with built-in drives for further economic and social reform leading to the technological, welfare, consumer society common to all the North Atlantic nations today. These deep transformations gave the Atlantic community political, economic and social qualities which set it radically apart from the rest of the world, and imparted powers which brought the continents of Africa, Asia and, to some degree, Latin America under Atlantic control for about a century and a half, from about 1800 to World War II.

In our present decade the four primordial revolutions are sweeping through the rest of mankind. Two thousand million people, almost two thirds of the human family, now feel the impact of driving scientific change, of progress through this-world betterment, of equality among men and nations, of spiraling population growth. Each of these revolutions provides prime fuel for socialization; operating together, they accelerate the multiplication of social relationships unprecedented in scope and pace. This process of world socialization is sometimes called Europeanization or Westernization, emphasizing its origins.

The Church and Christianity as a whole, excepting the Orthodox Churches, have had their home base in the North Atlantic community, in the West. Western religious history of the past two centuries has been deeply influenced, first, by the rapport of the Church with the modern world within Atlantica during this process of socialization brought about by the primordial revolutions, from 1775 to the present; and, secondly, by the interplay of the Church's own movement for world expansion with the universalist drive of the secular revolutions from the West.

The rapport of the Church with secular Europe and North America, as they became the modern West, must be quickly characterized as antagonistic. Church and secular society were often in open conflict. At their onset Church leaders felt uneasy before the revolution of egalitarian democracy, social progress and the new science. Time after time, in their concrete personifications, the makers of the modern world were regarded with mistrust, and even as downright enemies of the Church and of the best interests of man. The men of the Enlightenment and of the French Revolution, the followers of Marx and of Comte, of Descartes, Kant, and Darwin, reciprocated this distrust and enmity with malevolent largesse.

The Church of the 1800s had inherited privileges and encumbrances from Constantine, Charlemagne and ten centuries of agricultural, feudal society. With these conservative structures she was identified, so the "enlightened" revolutionists against the secular *ancien régime* saw the Church also as their enemy, often enough with good reason. The glorification of human reason and individual freedom into philosophical absolutes provided doctrinal cause for further division between Church and secular reformers, at those inner depths of idea and spirit where enduring revolutions are born and nourished. Anticlericalism flourished and became institutionalized; atheism spread.

So for the century of democracy's ascent which began about 1775, the Church as an institution could not come to satisfactory terms with liberty, equality and fraternity. At last Leo XIII began the definitive reconciliation. Michael Fogarty states:

> The General Election in 1876 [France] represented the final and, as quickly appeared, irrevocable victory of liberal democracy. The dream of a restored monarchy could still flutter aristocratic Catholic hearts. But henceforward it was in a democracy that they must live, and a few years later Leo XIII told them squarely to face the fact and adapt themselves to the new republican ways; which from the Church's point of view were as legitimate as any others. [*Christian Democracy in Western Europe* (University of Notre Dame Press, 1957), p. 170.]

But reconciliation with the new political realities did not follow immediately. Nationalism as manifested by Bismarck's *Kulturkampf* and anticlericalism as institutionalized in the French and Italian governments provided constant struggle until World War I. "Separation of Church and State" forced the closing of Catholic schools and exiled teaching societies from France, and led in Italy to the "non-expedit" of Pius IX, which forbade Catholics from participating in political affairs from 1867 to 1919. Similar strain and struggle occurred in Belgium, Holland, Switzerland, Austria, Spain, Portugal and Latin America between the Church and the modern world as it came into being.

The application of the new technology to industrial production, leading to a massive influx of rural dwellers into bursting cities, and the hardening of social strata into have-not workers and have-all capitalists, created additional crucial problems for the already embattled Church. Just when her leaders were at last transferring temporal allegiance from the landed aristocracy to the politically liberal bourgeoisie, socialists and syndicalists were forging new forces against the bourgeois entrepreneurs. The proletariat of the West became conscious of its power, and from 1850 to 1950 in the name of social justice the class struggle raged, with the Church again identified by and large with the propertied conservatives. The exceptions to this phenomenon—e.g., much of North America, some scattered areas of North Italy and France, the Rhineland and Flanders—were very exceptional indeed, so exceptional that Pius XI must needs lament that the scandal of the nineteenth century was the Church's loss of the working class.

This succession of struggles between the City of God and the ever evolving City of Man gives one pause. Is there something within the Church so extremely "not of this world" that each new formative force that begets the next era of man's world automatically regards the Church as an enemy, and vice versa? Is there some element natural to human society so extremely "not of the Spirit" that the Body which is "souled" by the Holy Spirit cannot at first assimilate new creations of the social body?

Are these successive struggles explainable by merely human reasons—the ignorance and misjudgment of the Church's leaders and the vindictive and excessive zeal of social innovators? Or are they the perennial battle of good and evil, in a diffused sense of creaturely inadequacy or in stark personification of the enduring struggle between Christ and

Satan? Or does this interplay suggest a creative dialectic of
societal thesis and ecclesial antithesis (and, at times, the
converse), spiraling ever upward to new levels of combined
human achievement? Has the scandal of Christian disunity
contributed to this exile of Christian influence from contemporary affairs?

Suffice it, for the moment, that the questions are posed.
The fact is that the Church could not, or did not, cope adequately with the makers of the modern world for the past two
centuries. Just when the Church had begun a *modus vivendi*
with such practical consequences of the Enlightenment as
public education, political democracy, and civil rights (at least
for property owners); just when the daughters and grandsons of eighteenth-century revolutionists had begun attending
Ursuline academies and Jesuit colleges—then the nineteenth-
century proletarian revolution burst forth and the Church
was again "on the losing side."

Divine providence is surely at work in these seeming disasters, for God writes straight with crooked lines. Only divine
wisdom can read the full script. Human knowledge tries to
decipher a phrase or two in imitation of the Idea in whose
image man is made. The Good Lord probably smiles with
fatherly pride and delight at our boyish efforts to know, "to
do what Daddy does." And so we strive to understand.

Striving to understand brings up the Church's third and
greatest failure in the modern era. For it is, above all, in the
realm of science and philosophy, cultural and intellectual
achievement, that the Church has suffered near total eclipse
in the past two centuries. This twilight of the Catholic mind
appears all the more disconcerting in view of the Church's
commitment to, and creative role in, scholarship and the arts
for the first fifteen hundred years of her life. From apostolic
times, despite their minority, persecuted status, Christian
thinkers sought to communicate with and to nourish secular
scholarship and culture and to assimilate these great human
creations into the living Christian body.

Justin, Origen and the Alexandrine school in the second and third centuries follow quickly the lead of John the Apostle, whose Gospel prologue (the Last Gospel of the Mass) points to strong familiarity with and appreciation for the Neoplatonism prevalent in his day. Athanasius, Basil and the Gregorys in the first ecumenical councils were so at home with the philosophical concepts of their time that they incorporated them into the first key doctrinal formulas to elucidate the "whoness and whatness" of Christ. Such "pagan" concepts as person and nature, substance and essence, became bedrocks in the upbuilding of Christian theology.

Along came Augustine of Hippo in Africa to introduce to all human thinkers the first true philosophy of history, a "first" of such significance that over a thousand years later, Hegel and Marx, Spengler and Toynbee must needs tread in many of his footsteps. Then followed the Irish monks, Bede, Boniface, and Alcuin, the monastery libraries and cathedral schools, which gave birth to the university.

In the intellectually dynamic atmosphere of the West's— and the world's—first universities, Albert Magnus and Thomas Aquinas conversed with wonder and delight across the centuries with pagan Aristotle, and across the frontiers of Christendom with the Moslem philosopher-scientists Avicenna and Averroës. From this "progressive" give and take, a dialogue severely condemned by many isolationists of that day, came those brilliant syntheses of reason and faith, the *Summa Theologica* and the *Summa contra Gentiles*. In fact, the very brilliance of this last dialogue with contemporary and non-Christian thinkers appears in retrospect to have mesmerized Catholic thought ever since. The assumption has come down through seven centuries, to our own generation, that Thomas has already said everything, in the only form and manner that truth can be expressed. Catholic thought came to mean mere memory tasks in most seminaries and Catholic universities of the present generation—until Vatican Council II.

Returning to the centuries immediately following St.

Thomas, Dante and Chaucer were assuredly in open dialogue with their cultures and awakening nations. Roger Bacon and the master builders who designed and engineered Chartres and Rheims fully grasped the physics, mechanics and mathematics of their time, and did not hesitate to experiment further. And speaking of experimenters, Michelangelo and da Vinci dared break all manner of artistic, engineering and scientific conventions to "throw the Pantheon into the sky" and, in blueprint, a flying machine into the air. The Polish priest, Copernicus, searched for knowledge to the very stars. He found that the earth revolved around the sun and published that truth. With him and Galileo, the great eclipse began; or, rather, the intellectual obscurity became increasingly visible. The twilight of Catholic intellectual life must have begun some generations before. Anyway, for three centuries after Galileo, no Catholic thinker appeared who approached the caliber of the makers of the modern mind—no one, for instance, comparable to Descartes and Rousseau, Kant and Hegel, Marx and Darwin, Einstein and Bergson.

Pascal might have been a candidate, but he got bogged down in otherworldly Jansenism and fratricidal debate with the Jesuits, which prevented effective dialogue with this-world. Besides, Pascal's startling intuitive gifts seem to have affrighted, rather than attracted, followers; he developed no intellectual system, no school of thought, as did the other giants. And, too, he died so young.

Newman also comes to mind. Certainly he sought to speak to his contemporaries, and to create an atmosphere and institutions for enduring dialogue—although his opacity before the social questions of his own Birmingham and Manchester are hard to excuse. However, he was an Oxford man. The First Vatican Council's handling of the Church's relationship to science and democracy, freedom and progress appalled him and his fellow progressives. But they were too few and too early for their own day. However, they came not too soon in the one long day in which the Church truly lives, for Newman heralded both of today's dialogues. He is spiritual father to much of the kindly openness and pastoral concern, non-legalism and theological perspicacity, of Vatican II. All this he began a century ago; not too early at all, for by now the Church recognizes her need for his spirit, and the world vaguely senses its thirst for the Spirit of Christ.

Why did the Church, as a social institution and apart from its supernatural claims, after fulfilling such a major role for over fifteen hundred years in begetting Western civilization, experience this notable inadequacy as the modern world dawned? Were her successive inabilities to assimilate, let alone create, political democracy and civic equality, social justice and science, derived from prior intellectual bankruptcy as a body directed by humans (keeping aside in these considerations prerogatives given and preserved by Christ)?

Again, as a social institution ruled also by the will of men, did institutional pride, triumphalism, collective hubris, take hold of the Church in her human and visible expression? Can the body in and through which the meek and humble Christ lives on be guilty of pride? And suffer in consequence humiliation and persecution in penance and reparation?

And can the Church as a social body, created and directed in part by mere men, recover her creative role in time, without injury to her central role for eternity?

It would appear that the Church might, in these very decades, have begun to recover her creative role in and with the world of time, or at least to feel more at home with today. These signs of recovery in the West, where the Church has until now had the greatest visible presence, can be only superficially indicated here. In the next chapter some comment will be made about the other continents, which are only now experiencing pervasive socialization through the same four primordial revolutions which shaped today's community of the West, Atlantica.

Some indications that the Church is currently beginning

"to find herself" amidst the West's continuing socialization now appear.

The Church is at last at home with political democracy; in certain ways she has become indeed its champion. An unforeseen reversal of roles has occurred in fifty years and less. One need but compare the Church's pre-World War I struggles with Clemenceau and Cavour, Ferry and Mazzini, Juarez and Freemasonry, with her post-World War II accord, even cooperation, with Adenauer, Schuman and De Gasperi.

Due in some degree to the influence of Christian thinkers and leaders, the nineteenth-century political democracy of the European liberal bourgeoisie has grown beyond its property base toward equal civil status for all, including property-less workers, who share also in the evolving economic democracy of mixed-economy, collective bargaining, welfare society.

This has stimulated clearly identified social and political movements which are called expressly "Christian democracy" in some countries, such as Germany, Italy, Holland, Belgium and Austria, and notably in Chile and Venezuela in Latin America. In other countries, like France, Britain, Canada, Australia, Eire and the United States, this recent Christian contribution to a maturer, expanded democracy is less recognizable, but it is still considerable despite anonymity.

Christian democracy in both these manifestations extends far beyond the merely political arena. It can be defined as that society-wide movement led by modern Christian leaders who, as lay citizens, are engaged on their own responsibility in the conception, upbuilding, and operation of a humanly just and viable political, economic and social order; they operate under the general inspiration of principles of the natural law and public philosophy and of Judaeo-Christian-Hellenic ideals, and conclude from these principles, and from historical and practical experience, that government in the economic organization, social grouping, local community, and at intermediate, national, and international levels, should be of, for, and by the whole people.

Another sign of recovery is in relation to socialism, originally Marxist-inspired. Due in great part to the contributions cited above, the Church has done much through clergy and lay leaders to mute the class-struggle thesis, dictatorship-of-the-proletariat means, and this-world paradisiac ends of Marxist socialism. In most Western countries socialist pluralities among workers and intellectuals now approach doctrinal and platform positions concerning the human person, family, property, work, wages, profit, government and international peace and justice which closely correspond to the position of Christian democracy. And hopeful interaction increases, as dramatized in the political arena by Italy's "opening to the left" by Christian Democrats to join hands with Nenni Socialists' "opening to the right."

The expectation of the United States and Britain after World War II was that socialism would inspire and direct the political and economic structures in the chaos of Europe's reconstruction. Stalin felt certain that this would lay the ground for takeover by Communists within each country. To the surprise of almost everyone, a social democracy of a more mature, all-embracing species sprang up, held its own in the first decade of postwar struggle, obtained dominant power by the mid-fifties, and now gives a uniting Europe promise of full partnership with her ally across the Atlantic and of world leadership of a new scale and kind. This astonishing postwar democracy owes much to Christianity, and the free world owes much to this victor over Marxist socialism.

In Western Europe this same Christian inspiration did much to exorcise the demoniac forces of excessive nationalism which have wracked and wrecked the continent with chronic convulsions for over a thousand years. The Coal and Steel Community and the Common Market offer long, sure steps toward psychological and ultimate political unity. The names again of these great Christian leaders tell half the tale: Schuman, Adenauer and De Gasperi.

In Eastern Europe, the Church—Protestant, Orthodox and Catholic—survives as the one institution still able to bear witness to the dignity and inviolability of man. Hers is the principal voice still heard upholding family identity and true national rights. Her bishops, clergy and lay leaders are to-day's champions of justice and democracy, heroes of freedom in a way Voltaire, Rousseau and the Jacobins could have never imagined.

Catholic thinkers begin to command some attention: Bloy, Peguy and Bernanos, Maritain, Marcel, Suhard and Guardini, Newman, de Lubac and Congar, Bea, Kung and Rahner, Weigel, Murray and Teilhard de Chardin.

A succession of great popes have turned the world's de-rision of Pius IX during Vatican I into respect and distant admiration, confidence and, with John, simple, unabashed love and devotion. John becomes the foremost champion of progress, liberalism and modern civilization (condemned by the *Syllabus of Errors,* 1864) for all the people of all the world.

And now Pope Paul not only invites all his brothers in Christ to continue the dialogue among themselves. Paul VI expressly dedicates himself, the Council and the Church to the other dialogue with the contemporary world beyond the frontiers of Christianity.

It would be a grave error to consider these latter-day signs that the Church has recovered this-world relevancy as a Catholic experience alone. Protestants have also developed their "social Gospel" during the recent decades, as evidenced in North America and especially in Britain's labor movement. Some churches pioneered in the drive for civil liberties and minority rights. Orthodoxy, as already noted, plays an indis-pensable function in preserving and stimulating national identity and human dignity behind the Iron Curtain, and a democratizing, liberating role outside as well.

Rapprochement of Protestants and Catholics on temporal issues made Christian democracy possible in Germany and Holland after the Second World War, after four centuries of intramural Christian hostility, politically and socially manifested, to the profit of atheistic materialism. Indifference to the crassest racial inequality by white Christians and Jews of the United States is now tardily softened by beginnings of Protestant, Catholic and Jewish collaboration in the Conference on Religion and Race.

The ecumenical movement of the World Council of Churches and Vatican II opens fresh prospects for joint dialogues with the contemporary world in revolution, as the family dialogue progresses among Christians of the West, East and everywhere.

Chapter Five

THE INTERPLAY OF CHRISTIAN UNIVERSALISM WITH WORLD WESTERNIZATION

From 1775 through our day, the status of the Church and the spiritual life of five hundred million Christians have been deeply affected by the revolutions of advanced socialization which have remade the North Atlantic community. After some two hundred years of chronic institutional conflict between the Church and the secular society of the West, some hopeful indications of fruitful dialogue have begun to appear in our generation, especially after World War II.

Since World War II these same social forces which transformed the West have been sweeping through the rest of the world at greatly accelerated speed. Two thousand million persons, the remaining two thirds of the human family, now feel the revolutionary impact of driving scientific change, of human progress through this-world betterment, of equality among men and nations, of spiraling population growth. In Africa, Asia and Latin America each of these four revolutions provides the same prime fuel for generating socialization as they have provided for two centuries in Europe and North America. Operating together, they are crushing and sweeping away the millennial bonds of traditional social organisms like family and village, land tenure and feudal systems, to leave way for the multiplication of new social relationships of unprecedented scope, and at a pace much more accelerated than that experienced by the West in the two previous centuries.

Since World War II most of the eighty economically un-derdeveloped nations have undertaken changes and reforms broadly comparable to those identified in the West with the American and French Revolutions; with the Industrial Revo-lution, the rise of the proletariat, class consciousness and class struggle, workers' and farmers' movements; with the New Deal and Europe's welfare societies, the American Civil War and today's struggle for racial justice.

All these achievements and changes of two hundred years of gradual Western development, all this "fullness of a more excellent life," the peoples of Africa, Asia and Latin America now want to attain "in a decade of development," at most in a generation. Their leaders—the sincere ones as well as the demagogues—under pressure of the massive daily squalor, usually promise more work and wages, schools and houses, water and medical care than time, resources, and training will allow. The orderly economic and social advance of the de-veloping continents is further complicated by the rapid in-crease of their rates of population growth, again especially noteworthy since the Second World War, due principally to inoculations and public health measures such as malaria control programs and water purification techniques.

The rate of population growth in the developing nations is two to three times higher today than was the rate of popula-tion increase in Western Europe and North America at a comparable stage of Western industrial and social advance four generations ago. In the decade 1841–50 the annual net increase in population (live births over deaths) per one thou-sand inhabitants was only 7.1 persons in the very heartland of Europe; that is, an annual net population increase of .71 percent, or about seven-tenths of 1 percent. These data cover France (4.1 annual live births over deaths per thousand pop-ulation), Germany (9.4), Great Britain (10.2), Belgium (6.1), and Holland (6.8). Current rates of population in-crease in Africa, Asia and Latin America are respectively 21, 20 and 27 persons per year per thousand inhabitants, or about 2.1 percent on the average (giving due weight to the dominance of Asia's numbers). The rates anticipated for 1975 are 17, 23, and 28, respectively, or an average annual increase of about 2.3 percent for the three continents.

This expanding rate of population increase among the have-not nations is almost twice as high as that experienced at anytime in the West during its two centuries of modern socialization. Annual rates of net growth are currently 8 and 18 live births over deaths per thousand population in Western Europe and North America, respectively, for an average of 1.2 percent for the industrial West as a whole. Never before in history has the human family experienced population expansion at the rate now seen in Africa, Asia and, especially, Latin America. Their present rates of increase (2.1, 2.0 and 2.7 percent respectively) are all the more notable when compared with their relatively static demographic situation prior to our generation.

The population of Asia, for instance, increased only by 19 percent during the quarter-century from 1900 to 1925. But in the next twenty-five years this rate doubled to 35 percent, and has risen to 60 percent in our present quarter-century (1950–1975). So, Asia's rate of population increase has trebled in the forty years since 1925. In the same period the growth rate of Europe, including Russia, has risen only from 19 to 31 percent, while that of North America has fallen from 56 to 43 percent per quarter-century. Currently Latin America's population is increasing at the rate of 90 percent each twenty-five years.

On the scale of human history the recent population spiral is even more striking. It took mankind over 500,000 years to reach, in the year 1900 A.D., a population of 1500 million. This total, which required 500 millennia to attain, suddenly doubled in the next 60 years to 3000 million in 1960. Now, barring world catastrophe, the earth's population will be doubled again, to 6000 million, by the year 2000 A.D., quadrupling the number of living human beings within the twentieth century. If this rate of increase continues, and the world's population quadruples again in the next century, the population in 2100 A.D. will be 24 billion humans.

Of the four primordial revolutions which the West has introduced into the rest of the world, the revolution of spiraling birth rates is one of the most elemental in any evaluation of socialization—for the simple reason that the greater the number of people who live within restricted borders, the more multiplied are their social contacts and relationships likely to be. This is all the more verified if their horizontal movement and communication are facilitated by technology, if their vertical mobility from one social stratum to the other is exteriorly promoted by social and economic opportunity and equality, and if they are inwardly motivated by newly felt desires for progress and position in the world.

All these generators of socialization have become operative in the eighty have-not nations of the world at a greatly accelerated pace and with society-wide impact. Western expansionism began during the sixteenth century; gradually, it has increased in intensity and evolved in quality during the last hundred years. It was accompanied by the Church's determined effort to teach all nations. This global process and the interplay of the Church's universalist role may be divided into three periods stretching over five centuries.

I. First Period: 1450–1800

The European powers establish trading posts and forts in coastal ports of Africa and Asia, and on strategic islands in all the seas. The Americas are colonized: in the north, the aborigines are all but destroyed; south of the Rio Grande, the authoritarian, feudal civilizations of the Aztecs and Incas are taken over by the conquistadores. Russian colonizing traders expand through the 4000-mile land mass of Siberia, and cross the Pacific into Alaska and California.

Christian missionaries accompany, and sometimes precede, secular armies and commerce, and are in general identified with Western secular authority. British and Dutch Protestant colonies settle the Atlantic coast of North America; French Catholics sparsely settle the St. Lawrence and Mississippi valleys and Great Lakes area. Spanish and Portuguese Catholics, even fewer in number in proportion to territory, settle selected coastal areas in Latin America, India and the Philippines. Orthodox Christianity is introduced to northern Asia by the Russians. Most other Orthodox peoples fall under the Moslem influence of the Ottoman Empire with the fall of Constantinople in 1453.

This European expansion is possible because of technological advances. Principal among these are navigational instruments and sailing methods; better use of horse power and wheeled vehicles; the invention of gunpowder and printing; and improved organizational techniques in government, the military and business (e.g., the stock company, insurance and banking). Europeans leave home to encircle the globe, spurred by awakened human needs, "for their comfort and advancement in various kinds of goods": silk, dyes, spices, precious metals, tobacco, sugar, fruit—and cheap labor, slaves. They are also motivated by curiosity, the yearning to know, plus a strong dose of individual and national self-glorification, and to some extent because of the Good News of Christ.

II. Second Period: 1800 to World War II

During these four generations Western ideas and institutions make a deep impact upon the whole world. European powers take over military control and political administration of 95 percent of Africa, all of the Indian subcontinent, South Asia, and Oceania. The United States takes the Philippines from Spain and, in concert with the northern European powers, opens the closed civilization of Japan to Western influence and takes over *de facto* control of most of China. Russia—czarist, then Communist—consolidates in Siberia and penetrates into western China and the Middle East. During the

Great Depression, between the World Wars, Russia adapts Communism to its dream of world conquest. Through a hard core of trained leaders and popular-front tactics, directed by the Comintern apparatus, it exploits human misery and just aspirations for social justice and national freedom, to gain for international Communism increasing political and ideological influence around the world. The Moslem Ottoman Empire collapses during World War I, and the Western powers take over the Middle East, vying with expansionist Russia for control of that area. Russia takes over Eastern Europe during World War II, and its brand of Marxism notably infects China.

Western Europe and North America are transformed from traditional agricultural, authoritarian nations into the highly industrialized, democratized Atlantic community, with close commercial and cultural bonds. The Atlantic nations introduce plantation agriculture, increasingly industrialized, and extractive mining operations into Africa, Asia and Latin America. By and large, these three colony-continents provide raw materials for processing in the "mother country," and industry does not develop outside the West, except in Japan and, by force, in Russia. The Great Depression deepens criticism of laissez-faire, private-property capitalism, strengthens the countervailing force of worker movements, and leads to social and economic experimentation toward the mixed economy—e.g., in Britain, France and North America, and to statist economic socialism in Germany and Italy with fierce nationalistic and emotional drives.

Christian missionaries, Catholic and Protestant, spread over Africa and Asia in a new wave of zealous universalism. They are usually very closely linked with Western military, political and economic powers, often depending upon these for protection, transport and material support. Besides their message of spiritual salvation, the Christian missionaries bring beginnings of this-world blessings. They introduce "the fullness of a more excellent life." Through schools and hospitals they launch the war against want, often subsidized by the secular powers. With education and humanitarianism the Church introduces the great truths of human dignity and the basic equality of all men, nations and races.

But, on the whole, the spiritual apostolate of the Church is not successful in Asia and North Africa, as measured in numbers, public acceptance, and influence within social institutions. In the Moslem world—extending from the Atlantic through the Sahara and its borders, on through the Middle East and Pakistan to Indonesia, eight thousand miles to the east—the Christian apostolate is notably without visible fruit. Less than 1 percent of the population are Christians, and most of these have been transplanted from without. Among the 400 million Hindus and the 800 million living in the Buddhist cultural sphere, there are perhaps 25 million Christians, about 2 percent of the whole, many of whom are partly European in ethnic origin. Almost all Christians in the Moslem, Hindu and Buddhist cultural spheres are identified openly or subconsciously as collaborators with Western secular powers and with Western cultural imperialism.

The spiritual mission of the Church enjoys, during this second period of Western expansion, much greater acceptance in Africa, south of the Sahara, among the Negroid peoples, and in the islands of the Pacific. Their evangelization begins in earnest only in the late 1800s. The Church encounters here no highly developed civilization, nor the millennial culture systems of Asia, but rather hunting and pastoral nomads and agricultural villages with strong tribal bonds. The Church plays an important role, especially through its schools, health and social services, often in close concert with Western secular authorities, in recasting the fragmented, isolated centers of nomadic and tribal life into increasingly integrated units of the broader society and into modern administrative departments. This process of socialization begins to break down tribal identity and local parochialism and to direct loyalties toward the new multitribe unit of society—the colonial territory. Within this chrysalis the ferment of the new nationalism begins, preparing for the post-World War II outburst of thirty new nations.

In Latin America, from 1800 on, the breakup of the Spanish and Portuguese empires begins, leaving a score of new nations, geographically isolated from each other, with anticlerical governments of the French Enlightenment, Grand Orient Freemasonry, and positivist orientation. Many Church leaders, for the most part closely identified with Hispanic secular hegemony, are expelled by the new nations and, worse yet, lose the loyalty of the "lower clergy," the intellectuals and the small but influential bourgeois business class. The de-Christianization of one third of the Catholic world begins.

About two thirds of Orthodoxy, some 60 million Roman Catholics, and the millions of staunch Protestants of Central Europe, fall under Russian Communist rule. The other third of Orthodoxy, after liberation from four centuries of the Moslem Ottoman yoke, are presided over by Western "protectors" and annoyed by self-confident Latinizing Catholics after World War I.

In North America the Protestant ethic of individual initiative, hard work, and messianic drive, subdues a continent— mountains, plains and deserts, Indians and Catholic settlements in the St. Lawrence and Mississippi valleys and the Southwest—by 1850. With the coming of rationalizing science, Biblical criticism and industrial urbanization, the Protestant ethic declines. Waves of proletarian Catholic and Jewish immigrants pour in from Ireland and South and Central Europe, and by World War II the United States is a three-faith nation. French Catholics in Canada, after more than a century of eclipse, regain cultural identity and political influence. Culturally and spiritually, North America remains at one with Western Europe, the motherland; they form together the Atlantic West, and in concert they Westernize the rest of the world.

Western expansionism during this period is impelled by

two motives more basic than others: technology, applied to economic production and management; and the twin psychological drives of nationalism and material betterment in this-world.

Scientific advances made from 1800 on are well-known: the steam engine, mining and metallurgy, farming methods, locomotive, steamship, automobile, chemistry and electricity. Less obvious, but of equal importance, are the creative social inventions by which the energy and speed supplied by technology become mighty tools in the hands of larger, ever larger, concentrations of workers through the business corporation, bonds and mortgages, the stock market and clearinghouse, labor unions and technical schools.

Until World War I most of the world-embracing economic drive made feasible by technology is nationally oriented—i.e., it remains a closed affair between mother country and the colonies held by that nation. Indeed, nationalistic competition among Western nations heightens the compulsion to take over Africa and Asia and to get concessions in Latin America. British, French, German, Dutch, Belgian, Spanish, Portuguese, American and, finally, under Mussolini, Italian citizens are incited to heroic feats for national glory in far-away lands and are rewarded by domestic material betterment made possible by colonial resources.

In the name of national destiny, fratricidal wars break out in the heartland of the West during the closing decades of this period. Recurrent economic crises are further exacerbated by trade quotas and tariffs, raising even higher the barriers dividing the Western nations among themselves. In the words of Carlton Hayes, "nationalism becomes a religion." And forced drafts of all men form nationalist armies to bring the good news of pride in blood and soil and collective ego "to every creature" and to offer their bodies as holocausts at home and everywhere.

This nationalist fanaticism reaches its apogee in Nazism and Fascism. Communism wins many disaffected intellectuals and labor leaders by countering exaggerated nationalism in general and Hitler and Mussolini in particular, and by stressing its universalist embrace—"Workers of the world, unite!"—against nationalist-oriented capitalism.

This nationalist-colonialist capitalism divides each nation into two warring camps—the working class and the bourgeois entrepreneurs—each with their camp followers, intellectuals, artists, reformers, do-gooders. And it divides the globe into the have imperialists of the West and the have-not colonial subjects, usually non-Caucasian, of the rest of the world. This rather simplist formulation is propagated especially by Marx, and later put to work by Lenin and Stalin.

It is rooted in truth sufficient to nourish another religion, Communism, an atheistic materialism, which takes over Russia during World War I and starts a holy war-to-the-death against nationalist-colonialist capitalism: first, within the Western nations themselves, and in a second phase, in the Western empires around the world. Atheism becomes institutionalized, with state-financed centers of research and doctrinal development, paid staffs of writers and lecturers, organizers and popularizers. The Christian religion is the choice target. Its leaders are imprisoned and humiliated, exiled and executed. Jews also suffer. The other transcendental religions —Islam, Hinduism and Buddhism—increasingly feel the attack of atheistic materialism as it moves into their cultural spheres.

III. Third Period: After World War II

The political and power structures of the world are unbelievably transformed within two decades. The Western empires are liquidated with a wondrous minimum of violence. Some fifty new nations gain independence in Africa and Asia over a period of fifteen years. The United Nations, formed by the wartime allies, offers these young nations "rites of passage" by which they are initiated into the councils of the world as peers of their Western elders.

The Cold War begins. The Iron Curtain countries, now including China and totaling one third the human family, vie with the free world by wiles and violence for the allegiance of Africans, Asians and Latin Americans. World-embracing military and political alliances give, at first, a two-bloc structure to the Cold War. The free nations are led by the United States, which inherits the burden of keeping the peace in the power vacuum resulting from the sudden dismantling of the Western empires.

Western Europe moves toward unity, moved by economic group self-interest, disgust with nationalism, fear of Communism and prodding of the Americans. Russia holds restive Eastern Europe by force of arms, but cracks in the Communist monolith appear. Yugoslavia and Rumania adapt Marxism to their own national needs, Russia and China show mutual disaffection, Communist parties around the world take sides. Simultaneously, the continental European nations, pushed by General de Gaulle, tend toward looser ties with the Anglo-Saxons, Britain, and the United States. The latter experiences traumatic shock at the rise of a Communist threat in Latin America, dramatized by Castro's Cuba. Khrushchev's rockets in the Cuban power play of 1962 bring the world five minutes from the brink of nuclear catastrophe.

Fear of fallout and the search for world peace become the indispensables of the sane. Armed coexistence, uneasy and vigilant, tiptoes warily onto the world political stage. The nuclear test ban offers a first toddling step toward disarmament.

In the economic sphere the drive for industrialization grips the whole world. Material this-world betterment is demanded by all citizens, spurring have-not nations to five- and ten-year plans of development, herculean and too often utopian, and introducing further advances of the welfare state in the affluent West and Russia. The latter's international power moves are sharply affected by citizen demand for consumer goods and the good life, free of war, and contribute much to the ideological break with China.

Africa, Asia and Latin America, which previously provided raw materials for Western factories, now strain to industrialize. Lacking capital and technical know-how, they turn to the West, Japan and Russia. Programs of development aid, loans and investment are set up, but are insufficient by far to the immensity of the task. The pioneering Marshall Plan enables Western Europe, with her skills and hard work, to recover from the economic death rattle of the 1940s, from the mortal inner virus of class-struggle Marxism, and from the naked threat of Red armored divisions. The Common Market, successful beyond imagining, raises Europe's standard of living to unexpected new levels.

The Communists and the African, Asian and Latin American countries also move toward economic integration. The very brilliance of the Marshall Plan obscures the more checkered achievement of American aid via Point Four, the Alliance for Progress, and multilateral programs. American voters, publicists and Congressmen, disenchanted with foreign aid results and problems, reduce appropriations year by year. Russia, China and Europe launch technical-assistance and development programs on the selective basis of spheres of interest.

International trade increases rapidly and world-girdling business enterprises multiply, often with management and capital drawn from several nations. Private foundations, universities and voluntary agencies undertake broad programs of technical and organizational training for social and economic development, often in concert with industry and government. These are complementary to the far-reaching aims of the specialized agencies of the United Nations, like the Food and Agriculture Organization (FAO), the World Health Organization (WHO), the United Nations Educational, Scientific and Cultural Organization (UNESCO), the International

Labor Organization (ILO), and a dozen other multinational bodies.

The Church continues and intensifies her universal apostolate, characterized by fresh qualities of critical self-evaluation, social emphasis and ecumenical openness.

The Church's relatively improved stance in Western society —by her affirmative position on democracy and social issues and the belated appearance of some intellectual vigor—is further strengthened by her adamant stand against raw Communism. The heroism of Church leaders behind the Iron Curtain and Christian-inspired programs for social justice, especially in Europe and Latin America, help to erase the image of a self-serving, antiliberal, social anachronism which the Church had assumed to many minds throughout the modern era. These Christian positions also mitigate the charges of rationalized acquiescence in the face of Nazi and Fascist atrocities by Catholics and Protestants alike.

However, the brutality of World War II and its aftermath of living hell, the fact that Nazi Dachaus, Allied saturation bombing and Hiroshima *could* happen in the *Christian* West, the sweep of atheism into Europe's heartland by force of arms and into millions of Western hearts by dint of intellectual and social attraction—all of these at last shake ecclesiastical complacency and traditionalism. Reassessment of inherited religious and ritual formulas and renewed investigation of the Word of God and His truth, revealed and natural, produce live theologians and able Scripture scholars, even a few contemplatives, saints and thinkers. And a goodly number of martyrs manifest heroic faith, hope, love and courage. Their light suddenly bursts upon the official Church through Pope John's open window, the Second Vatican Council, like the star of another Nativity. The Holy Spirit bestirs the minds and wills of Christians.

The Fathers of the Council, sincere and seeking, humbly recognize and rejoice that Christ is again reborn, in His Church and in themselves. Brother Christians share their joy.

In growing fraternal confidence and human friendship, all Christians ponder together how to beget the birth of Christ every day and everywhere, in the heart of every man and in this new world which man daily creates from the raw material and boundless energy the Creator provides. Pope Paul adds this challenge of the temporal as a distinct Council objective.

Western nationalism gravely distorted Christian individual psychology, group identity and social allegiance throughout the five hundred years of the modern era: fifteenth-century Europe through the century-long religious wars (1530–1648, Treaty of Augsburg) and the divine right of kings, the Napoleonic Leviathan and industrial nationalism of the 1800s, to the god-status absolute the nation assumed under Hitler and Mussolini. In the Atlantic West, World War II signaled the twilight and death of the nation-gods, at least for people in the next few decades who remember. This *Götterdämmerung* affects all the nations of the West, not only Germany. The way is cleared for a truer and more universal incarnation of Christ in today's society. Protestants are the first to discern this Christian release from the bonds of nationalism and parochialism. It begins to take shape with surprising speed in the World Council of Churches.

For centuries some Catholic leaders had been decrying the excesses of modern nationalism. Pius XII and Pope John strongly endorse the remaking of Europe after the Second World War and the new search for world solidarity through the United Nations. In the encyclical *Pacem in Terris,* the universal common good and international social justice replace national self-interest as the motivating consensus and moral ground on which to build the future.

This twilight of nationalism occurs in the West just as national self-awareness dawns and reawakens in the rest of the world. The ethos of most of the fifty new nations is inspired in great part by religio-cultural values long belittled in the West, derived from the Moslem, Hindu, Buddhist and animist religions. The last-named gradually wanes; the three others wax anew in this current cross-fertilization with Western-style nationalism. The rise of the Zionist ethnic theocracy, Israel, a reaction against Nazi excesses, serves to exacerbate Western and Christian relations with the revived nationalism of the Moslem Arabs.

This postwar outburst of the four primordial revolutions—driving scientific change, human progress through this-world betterment, equality among men and nations, and spiraling population growth—generates the multiplication of social relationships at dizzying rates of acceleration. The concomitant and causal technological wonders of jet travel, rockets, orbiting satellites, computers, and nuclear explosion provide fitting "hardware" symbols of the concomitant and co-causal wonders of world socialization—the drawing together of man in a depth and scope of human convergence never before envisioned.

The Church is herself a society. Her members create and live in society. She is Christ here and now, knowing and loving, serving and suffering for, and redeeming the whole human family—man-in-society, in the this-world of today and tomorrow—the chrysalis in which is begun and begotten the City of God for all eternity.

The challenges, problems and opportunities of this-world profoundly affect the Body of Christ. These great issues, which accompany and contribute to world socialization, are of increasing concern to the Church. They are the daily subject matter of the other dialogue.

Part Three

THE GREAT ISSUES

Chapter Six

RACE

When Bishop Robert Tracy of Baton Rouge, Louisiana, spoke for racial justice in the Vatican Council, the bishops of the world broke the rules: they applauded him. The New York *Times* put his picture on the front page. The story read in part:

> The Americans sought to amend a Council document so that it would be absolutely clear that racial inequality . . . was contrary to the Church's fundamental beliefs.
>
> It was taken by many observers as particularly dramatic that the spokesman [for the Americans], Bishop Robert E. Tracy, was from a southern state that has had more than its share of trouble over racial segregation.
>
> It was also recalled that the racial problem in Louisiana had involved the Church itself in difficulties with some segregationist Catholics. [October 25, 1963]

The present writer, Louisiana-born and -reared, for ten years worked closely with Bishop Tracy to promote racial justice in all its implications. I know first hand that a basic barrier to acceptance of the Church's teaching on race equality and civil rights for all is the history of *de facto* acquiescence in segregation by Christian leaders for the past two centuries.

Why, ask segregationists, this sudden sensitiveness by Negroes to our traditional way of the South? Why this new repudiation by the Church of our society's values and long-accepted structures? Why is the Church now leaving the sanctuary to meddle in political and economic affairs like voter registration, housing and job opportunities? If segregation was accepted a hundred years age, ten years ago, why is it suddenly wrong? Why can't I choose whom I eat with, whom my children may play and go to school with, whom I employ? We have done so for generations without condemnation from the Church, without a word of criticism from the pulpit. Why has the Church "changed her mind"? Can the Church change her teaching on these things?

These are the segregationists' questions. They have puzzled many a bishop and pastor, lay leader and priest—myself among them. To the degree that early satisfactory response is given, the more rapid and peaceably will civil rights be acknowledged, the more sincerely and deeply will human and interior solidarity take root, to ripen into understanding and friendship among whites and Negroes, North and South. And this happy cure of cancerous hatred and disdain within the leader nation of the West will have telling side effects on the rest of the world, especially on non-Caucasian countries.

Though often repeated, it is too often forgotten by the haves of the West that the have-nots of Africa, Asia and Latin America—the hungry, diseased, illiterate *les misérables* of our day—possess physical traits different from the Caucasoid. In their physical sameness, in being different from Westerners, they find self-identification, solidarity, and strength in their struggle for "the fullness of a more excellent life." If the West—the heartland of Christianity for a thousand years, the home of Christian missionaries to other races and cultures—does not accord human respect and rights to the Negro, who has dwelt as a Christian neighbor for two hundred years, then the African, the Oriental and the Andean Indian can well conclude that our Lord's promise of God-given dignity and brotherhood is not worth the paper the

Bible is printed on. Nor are Pope John's ringing encyclicals; nor the joint Christian social statements, present and future. They too can ask questions similar to those of the segregationist: Why after centuries of silent acquiesence does the Church at last speak out? Is it principally to allay our alarm, now that we know, via press and radio, film and TV, of the shameful treatment accorded our blood brothers by you who would teach us of Christ? Do Cold War motives enter in as well?

Does the Church change her social teaching chameleonlike to suit the social environment? Or does her teaching change society itself, bringing it closer to Christ's image?

The Church never taught that segregation provided an ideal social relationship, but the resigned sufferings of Christ have been invoked from the time of Paul to induce patient acceptance of a lowly role in this-world: Servants be subject to your masters, as to the Lord. Political and societal structures based upon leadership by the very few, and passive obedience by the very many, have dominated the seven thousand years of human civilization. The select leader class have been the stronger, the propertied, the educated. Their *de facto* power was often given *de jure* legitimacy by the subjects' consensus, perpetuated by blood descent to their progeny, and justified by the desire for internal peace and protection from foreign foes.

Thus in the West were created the orders of aristocracy, nobility and royal prerogative, usually upheld by divine-right sanctions. Most primitive tribes of all races adhered to a similar chieftain system, and indeed the principle of kingship was often introduced into higher civilizations by tribal chiefs through military might—for instance, in Sumeria, India and Europe. That society should be based upon superiors and subjects became embedded in tradition beyond human memory, became germane to the human psyche: That's the way things have been, are and should be.

This authoritarian order among people of one nation and

one race, universally accepted, prepared the way for the subjection of one race by another either in faraway colonies or
at home. The stronger, better educated, more organized class
of one tribe or race made subject to themselves the weaker,
less technically advanced, more poorly organized. In the same
way, servitude of one race to another has also, alas, long
obtained. The Church did not always supinely accept this
racial presumption of "manifest destiny." The defense of
the Latin American Indian in the sixteenth century, led by
Father Barthélemy de Las Casas, and Christian campaigns
against slavery in Africa and America in the nineteenth century are beacons in the otherwise unrelieved darkness.

Space does not permit a negative apologia based on the
declining influence of the Church in the temporal order of
the past two centuries. Nor is a positive apologia, based on
Christianity's educational and cultural contribution to the
progress of subject and segregated races at home and abroad,
appropriate here. Apologias tend to obscure the root reality,
the fact that a new species of society has evolved in the West
and now involves the world. This results from socialization,
caused by the four primordial revolutions.

Christ in his Church now speaks to a different world: to
human minds changed because they know more now than
formerly, to human wills expanded by fresh wants and vision,
to human hearts newly awakened to feelings and aspirations
for advance and oneness, slumbering until our day. Science
applied to economic and social processes, progress through
this-world betterment, equality among men and nations now
re-create the world our Lord must save, a world of ever multiplying social relationships, generating a new atmosphere in
which man works and plays, strives and dreams, thinks and
plays.

As human society develops from seeds ever present in the
hidden greatness of man, Christian social teaching also develops from roots ever nourished by the Vine, roots awaiting

always that new soil and air, rain and sun—the new social climate, the sociosphere—needful stimuli for sprouting forth. Sometimes, gradually, the Vine remakes the social atmosphere; sometimes not. Either way, social teaching must be current, in close touch with the actual situation of society at a particular stage of history. For this reason Pope John writes *Christianity and Social Progress (Mater et Magistra)* in *our* day. It would have made no sense a thousand years ago, except as a prophecy of things to come à la H. G. Wells and Aldous Huxley.

So, in answer to the segregationists' question, Christian social teaching does not change by contradicting former positions, silent or vocal. It develops, moves forward and upward with human advance and social progress, at least in our generation. (We will not enter here into the profound question of human and social retrogression and the problem of evil applied to society and history as a whole. This volume, whatever its pretensions, does not claim to be a philosophy or theology of history.)

There can be valid criticism of the rhythm and rate at which social teaching develops and becomes concretely applied. By and large, conservatives hold that it moves too far too rapidly, and progressives contend that too often it lags behind current events and fails to anticipate and promote necessary social change. The present writer is a declared progressive. Remarks critical of the Church's slowness in understanding the West's new natural creations—political democracy, the industrial revolution and modern science—have already been voiced.

Such criticism must also apply to the field of race relations in the West, especially in the United States and in the "colony continents" now attaining freedom. These observations are made with the advantage of hindsight and without bearing the hard responsibility of day-to-day administration, which superiors, clergy and citizens alike must shoulder.

II. A CHRISTIAN VIEW ON RACE

In race relations, as in all social issues, the first responsibility of the Church is to teach.

At the end of the Second World War a number of Catholic leaders in the southern United States began to teach the truth about racial justice and love. They began to apply Christian truths to the daily gnawing reality. Among these men were Archbishop Joseph F. Rummel of New Orleans, Bishop Vincent Waters of North Carolina, Fathers Vincent O'Connell and Joseph Fichter of New Orleans, and Father Maurice Shean of South Carolina, as well as laymen, like Paul Williams of Richmond. The Benedictine monks of Belmont Abbey must also be singled out. These men formed the nucleus of the Catholic Committee of the South, whose aim was the application of Christian social teaching to Southern problems like segregation and the sharecropping system.

These Catholic social pioneers found ready cooperation from the National Association for the Advancement of Colored People (NAACP), the Urban League, and from the liberal leaders of the Southern Regional Conference, among them the Conference's executive director, George Mitchell, and Ralph McGill of the *Atlanta Constitution*. These last two were among a score of outstanding collaborators who were not Catholics. Through conversations on the race issue, the Church of the South began both dialogues in the 1940s— among Christians, and with the contemporary world.

Catholic protagonists in the early struggle had received enlightenment on racial justice principally from Father John LaFarge. His books and articles reached us as college students, seminarians and young priests. His persuasive understanding, gentle manner and persistent courage gradually opened our minds and hearts, and our sleeping eyes, to the full meaning of the Faith. An objective critique of segregation and a new Christian concern began to question our boyhood inheritance as beneficiaries of the sharecropping system and as grandsons of slaveholders and Confederate soldiers. We began to ask ourselves, our parishioners and neighbors, whether our Lord wanted us to change, and whether He wanted us to change our Old South society. The usual response, from ourselves within and from others without, was negative, and frequently combatively so: "Why change a social system that has worked satisfactorily for so many generations? Why let Northern agitators and a few 'nigger' soreheads returning from the war stir up so much trouble? Fight back hard, and don't give in!"

We soon learned that arguments advanced from reason or the American Constitution alone lacked compelling force. These had to be seasoned with arguments from Faith which could penetrate and uplift the soul, which could overcome selfishness and pride, which could fire justice and love. So we advanced the reasons of Christ, the cause of the Church of Christ, and of all who are and can be sons of God. These reasons of Christ have been formulated in different ways. Reviewing our Catholic statements of the past two decades, Christian concern arose from four principal motives, which are still basically valid.

First, we must receive the Negro, on a status fully equal and without reserve, into our Church, schools and society in order to advance the worldwide mission of Christ. He has given the command: Go and teach all nations. Most of us—priests and people, sisters and students, parishioners and citizens—will not go abroad as missionaries. We will spend all our days within our country and Southland, perhaps even within our home state and diocese.

But, strange as it seems, the fabric of history and the network of world communications are so interlaced that we Christians can teach the whole of mankind from our southern towns and homes. Because what happens in the South deeply affects the racial policy of all our nation, and because the United States stands in the world's spotlight as the leader of the West, the heartland of Christianity—what happens here profoundly influences the judgments of those two billion human beings who are not Caucasian. So the South, we argued then, and now, which prides itself for being the most church-going sector of the nation, has an impact of grave significance upon the real-life reputation of Christianity itself. From the South we must teach the lesson of justice and fraternal love and expose the heresy of racism and hatred to the whole human family.

Secondly, we must receive the Negro, on a status fully equal and without reserve, into our Church, schools and society, because to deny him such status is to be guilty in practice of the heresy of racism. In the 1940s the Catholic document most frequently cited in discussing racial justice was the first encyclical of Pope Pius XII, in which he offers:

> . . . a marvelous vision, which makes us see the human race in the unity of one common origin in God, "One God and Father of all, Who is above all, and through all, and in us all" [Ephesians 4:6]; in the unity of nature, which in every man is composed of material body and spiritual, immortal soul; in the unity of the immediate end and mission [of man] in the world; in the unity of dwelling place, the earth, of whose resources all men can, by natural right, avail themselves to sustain and develop life; in the unity of the supernatural end, God Himself, to Whom all should tend; in the unity of means to secure that end. [*The Unity of Human Society* (Latin title: *Summi Pontificatus*), October 20, 1939.]

From these principles we argued two decades ago, and still do, that the heresy of racism manifested itself concretely in the "Southern way of life."

For, assuredly, to believe that the Negro people are cursed by God is heresy. To believe that the Negro people are predestined by God, and by a nature created by God, to inferior status as hewers of wood and drawers of water, as janitors, field hands and cooks, is heresy.

To believe that we Caucasians are possessed of a unique superiority—endowed with special qualities of intellect and will, faculties of spirit and gifts of genius—that substantially differentiate us from other peoples and form a height of excellence unattainable by the majority of the human family, who are qualitatively inferior—all this is erroneous doctrine.

To judge a person's rights and to choose one's neighbors, in our society, primarily and habitually on the basis of thickness of lip, straightness of hair and shade of pigmentation, and to relegate sons of God to a position of inferiority precisely because the Father made them in a particular form and appearance—all this is immoral and sinful.

To acquiesce supinely in a social system derived from slavery, a system of human bondage in which our grandfathers bought and sold human flesh as chattel—all this is to acquiesce in a social system built upon heresy. Considering their disabilities, the American Negroes have made greater cultural, educational and social progress than any of the racial or ethnic groups that came to our shores in quest of freedom and a more excellent life. We white men never can appreciate adequately the debilitating effects of the slavery from which the Negro had to recover.

It is helpful to read the Black Code, the slave law promulgated in 1728 by Bienville de Lemoyne, the first governor of Louisiana. It is instructive to recall that these decrees came forth from Louis XV, King of France, the most enlightened nation of the West and the eldest daughter of the Church. Further, they were produced by the generation which was the immediate beneficiary of the grand sermons of Bossuet on the will of God in the philosophy of history and of his Christian social teaching on the divine right of kings. And Bienville's Black Code was the product, too, of the policies elaborated by Richelieu, Cardinal of the Catholic Church. Here are a few excerpts from the Louisiana law under which our ancestors settled the Mississippi Delta, strove and prospered.

We declare that slaves can have no right to any kind of property, and that all that they acquire either by their own industry, or by the liberality of others, or by any other means or title whatsoever, shall be the full property of their masters. [Art. 22.]

Slaves shall be held in law as movables . . . , they shall be equally divided among the co-heirs. [Art. 40.]

The original French term was *meubles,* meaning movables in the sense of chattel or furniture. I, the present writer, have examined the will of my great-grandfather, Jean Baptiste Rabalais, to find that his slaves were bequeathed to his children in the same listing as wagons and plows, four-poster beds and marble-top dressers, mules, hogs and cattle. Other articles of our Louisiana law, given to us by our mother country, so very enlightened and Catholic:

We forbid slaves belonging to different masters to gather in crowds either by day or night, under the pretext of a wedding, or any other cause . . . under the penalty of corporal punishment, which shall not be less than the whip . . . and should there be aggravating circumstances, capital punishment may be applied. [Art. 13.]

Thefts of importance, including the stealing of horses . . . or cows, when done by slaves . . . , shall make the offender liable to corporal, even to capital, punishment, according to the circumstances of the case. [Art. 29.]

Such was the depth of inhumanity from which the Southern Negro has risen in the past century, through some eighty years of the semiserfdom of the sharecropping system. We know by faith that there is no master race destined to rule and no inferior race cursed by God to subjection. By faith this heresy is condemned *a priori.* The Negroes of the South have proven racism erroneous in practice *a posteriori,* by the very progress they have made toward full equality.

The third argument we Catholics have advanced is that we must receive Negro Catholics into the full life of the Church and society because they are members of the Mystical Body of Christ. This position is based on the purely supernatural belief that the baptized and believing Christian is the temple of the Holy Spirit. God dwells within him. Segregation advances the strange doctrine that the white Christian is to refuse association with him in whom God dwells—because his body is brown, his hair is kinky, his nose is flat, and because, principally, *his* grandfather was bought and sold like furniture by *my* grandfather.

In his 1942 encyclical, Pius XII teaches us that the Third Person of the Blessed Trinity is the Soul of Christ's Mystical Body, the Church. This means that we are unified and joined together by the Holy Spirit, the Personified Love of God Himself. This means that, as the parts and organs of my own human body are inspirited, given life and oneness by my own personal soul, we members of Christ's Body are souled, given life and oneness by the Holy Spirit. My left hand is joined to my right hand by my immortal soul as the principle and source of natural life. In like manner, human beings are joined together by the Holy Spirit, God Himself, into the unity of Christ's visible Body here on earth, and with eternal continuity in heaven.

Discrimination against the Negro is discrimination against the very Body of Christ. Racial discrimination forms a blood clot, an occlusion in the flow of grace and love within Christ's Body. This obex, this obstacle to grace for the full flowering of Christ, must be removed.

The fourth and final argument is that we must receive the Negro into the full life of the Church and society because this is the way of Christian perfection. Conviction in this matter among citizens *as Christians* does not depend upon Congressional laws and court decisions on civil rights. Real as these are, they are secondary reasons for interracial justice among convinced Christians, who by baptism and confirmation set out on the way toward Christian perfection, nourished by Christ Himself in the Eucharist.

"Be you perfect as your heavenly Father is perfect," is the height toward which we strive. "Thou shalt love thy neighbor as thyself" must be the Christian goal, a goal set for us not by a supreme court or an NAACP, but by Christ Himself.

III. THE HUMAN VICTORY

While I still adhere to these convictions evolved in the South in the 1940s, I discern in them today a thread of pastoral paternalism which was beyond my grasp before the combative demonstrations of more recent years and the admirable nonviolence of Rev. Martin Luther King. Changes in the racial struggle have given rise to changes in my own paternalistically tinted outlook.

The key word in each of the four propositions which I have discussed is the verb *receive*. My thesis, four times repeated, is: "We must receive the Negro, on a status fully equal and without reserve . . ."—as though such a transformation of the social structure hinged solely on the white man's benevolence; as though the Negro were the passive object of the decisions of white men, Christian or otherwise; as though the Negro were not capable of forging deliberately his own social advance through the twin instruments of countervailing force and well-earned admiration.

Dignity cannot be *given* by one racial group to another. The Negro cannot *receive* equality from the white man. Dignity and equality must be acquired by the Negro himself by his own endeavor. These attributes must be demonstrated, shown forth. Only then can there be true acceptance—"receiving"—by the white majority. This is now coming to pass, in a way unforeseen a decade ago—in Mississippi, in Chicago, in the Andes, in the slums of Brazil, in the young nations of Africa and in the old cultures of Asia.

As the grandson of a Confederate soldier, born on a sharecropper plantation in the deepest South, my boyhood concept of the Negro people *as a group* was typical of my time and class. We learned as children that the "nigger" is inferior because he is:

1. Violent, given to passionate outbursts, and controllable only by force;

2. Disorganized, without leadership, unreliable, lacking the constancy and disciplined cohesion which modern social progress demands;

3. Cowardly, obsequious, ready to betray his own kindred if it will serve his individual, passing desires;

4. Ignorant, unable to learn, without either ability or desire for education, without a role in our literate, technological society.

The drama of the past decade is this, that the Negro has taught the white man, by living example daily headlined, the great human virtues which reverse the Uncle Tom caricature.

The Negro has shown himself capable of marvelous self-restraint under the most bitter provocation. Martin Luther King's nonviolence becomes an epochal demonstration that man's interior strength can and does vanquish exterior force, that spirit can and does hold sway over matter, ideals over might. The sight of town bullies splashing mustard and catchup over the serene heads of college students at a lunch counter; of specially trained police, protected by helmets, dogs, guns and the imposing accoutrements of modern war, manhandling women and children, who rejoice at becoming victims—to assure the continuance of injustice clearly condemned by law, civic conscience and Christian command—all these astonishing displays of self-control and sacrifice fully reverse the caricature of Negro violence.

No white man could be proud of the performance of his "superior" race. Every human should rejoice that, through the Negro's conduct, all mankind rises to new heights of superiority over the evil within us all. The victory of the Negro over himself becomes my victory too. And I am grateful to him.

The Negro in our decade has shown qualities of leadership, ability for organized constancy and social discipline seldom equaled in the human record. The rapid rise of this new cohesiveness and its prairie-fire spread over the nation bring an aura of awe and authenticity to the racial movement. We Americans sense of a sudden that we are witnessing and participating in a social revolution unique in our national history. As several white participants in the Freedom March on Washington (August 1963) observed to me: they wanted a role in the making of history. In the proud story of America's minorities striving to "arrive," yes; but also, many desired to enrich their own personal and family heritage. I believe that is why so many fathers and mothers with young children joined the march. They want their grandsons to be able to stand up in fifth-grade history class, and say: "My mother and dad helped out the 'good guys.'" They want their little ones to say a half century hence: "I was there."

Only the exceptional leadership and organized discipline of the Negroes make possible this admiration and desire for self-identification with a cause. To insiders, the greatest wonder of all is that the leaders themselves have stuck together, that men of such diverse background and motive—Martin Luther King, Roy Wilkins, Whitney Young, James Farmer, John Lewis, Philip Randolph—could agree on a program of action, and adhere to it in the face of insults and scourgings, prison and death.

Personal cowardice draws particular scorn among Americans. Our authentic heroes of the American Revolution and of subsequent wars, and the folk heroes of pioneer and cowboy vintage, win ready admiration. The Negro arrived here in the early 1600s. Immigrants of every other race and nationality have found niches in state historical museums and pedestals in public parks. But where are the monuments to

Negroes? Where is the Negro Nathan Hale or Daniel Boone or Davy Crockett?

I have seen but one community-erected statue to a Negro in all the United States. It is a tribute to the Negro *as a race* by the citizens of Natchitoches, Louisiana. On the main street of this cotton and cattle town of fifteen thousand population, the oldest town in the Louisiana Purchase, founded in 1714, is the white man's image of the Negro, set in bronze. An Uncle Tom bows his head, stoops his shoulders, raises his crumpled hat from his woolly head. He does not lift his eyes to greet the white "marster" face to face. Beholding his boots suffices to stir Uncle Tom's sycophant smile. Engraved in the stone pedestal are these sentiments of the noble white man: "Erected by the City of Natchitoches in grateful recognition of the arduous and faithful service of the Good Darkies of Louisiana."

Minstrels, Amos 'n' Andy and Uncle Remus stories have given this spineless, scraping caricature popular currency and literary respectability over the years. All had some foundation in fact, the fact of a race in chains. Chains of iron until Lincoln freed the slaves. Chains of fraud, forced ignorance, poverty and endemic disease through the more subtle oppression of sharecropper servitude. The cowering, beholden-to-you attitude became the defensive reflex necessary for keeping alive.

Now, of a sudden, these "cowards" brave police dogs and bullies, bombs and telescopic rifles. Not for immediate gratification, not for personal gain, but for a cause, for their race. To redeem Uncle Tom. But to redeem also the soul of our nation and modern world.

Threats of assassination often reach Reverend King. He knows that sudden death hangs over him daily. Responding to a *Time* reporter's query, he says:

> I just don't worry about things like this. If I did, I just couldn't get anything done. One time I did have a gun.

. . . As a leader of a nonviolent movement, I had no right to have a gun, so I got rid of it.

The quality, not the longevity, of one's life is what is important. If you are cut down in a movement that is designed to save the soul of a nation, then no other death could be more redemptive. [January 3, 1964]

In the face of such valor the self-proclaimed superior race is bound to reassess its clichés. The millions who watch TV know who are the cowards today. And so does a resounding majority of our lawmakers.

In the sharecropper South I knew as a boy, the Negro was seldom called "ignorant." That was insufficient abuse. Usually the epithet was "dirty ignorant." The two went together. And their foulness, to us planters' sons, was interior as well as outer. Squalor of clothing and cabin were exterior signs of inner baseness. The Negro lacks, we learned from family conversation, the ability to learn. He has no ambition anyway. If he can sign his name, add and subtract well enough to weigh cotton and count cattle, that suffices for his actual and potential needs.

As boys we played together as equals. I recall especially Cornelius Johnson and Jonail Turner. They were my acknowledged superiors in many boyhood pursuits—hunting, fishing, riding, swimming, baseball. Throughout the summer vacation I often followed their leadership at play. They were alert, imaginative, creative. But when school opened in the fall we went our separate ways. The school bus picked me up at our front gate and took me to the brick, steam-heated, consolidated public school four miles away. Cornelius and Jonail walked a mile and a half to a leaky shack where eight grades gathered in one room. The one teacher did not have a high school diploma.

My personal investigation in later years of the school's daily records of the 1920s and '30s showed that the teacher did not know how to spell correctly the names of my boyhood friends; that attendance averaged less than fifty days a year during the five-month term of one hundred school days; that many children remained in the same grade four years in a row; that the first graders' ages ranged from six to twelve years old. And recent conversations with one of the teachers of my boyhood friends, now principal of the new county seat high school, have brought me some understanding of the cold and hunger, squalor and chaos of that environment for learning. It must be added that thirty years ago our whole county had no high school for Cornelius and Jonail to attend, should they ever "graduate" from our local institution. The closest was forty miles distant, the Peabody High School in Alexandria, named for the national foundation which built it.

Knowing that similar and worse conditions existed throughout the sharecropper South, we can but marvel that so many Negroes overcame these awesome odds and became educated men. The most heroic ones in this struggle over ignorance, socially imposed, have been the mothers. How often a few questions will uncover that this cook, this laundress, this clean-up woman, this field hand, saved and scraped and sacrificed to see a son through college, a daughter through nursing school, a grandchild through a doctoral degree. Here is a characteristic of "Mammy" that we whites have overlooked, a quality all the more remarkable when we recall that "Mammy" herself was usually illiterate. Without personal experience of education, she knew intuitively and by observing its results, that her child must have this advantage, whatever the struggle and sacrifice.

A hundred years ago America as a people made the same judgment made by the Negro of the last generation: We must acquire knowledge. It is in the great American tradition. This is the principal reason for today's successful racial revolution. And now the same determination echoes around the world, in Africa, Asia and Latin America, among the entire human family.

When a people, supposedly violent, exercise noble self-restraint, when a people purportedly addicted to social chaos produce great leaders and organization, when erstwhile "cowards" show bravery and redemptive self-sacrifice, when the "innately ignorant" struggle up the ladder of learning—then all mankind shares in their progress, rejoices in their "fullness of a more excellent life." And God is pleased that his creation moves toward the fuller being of greater perfection, becoming more like Himself.

From the Negro we learn that his greatness was within him all the while, obscured and stunted by our white blindness and greed. The American Negro is teaching us to open our minds and hearts to all peoples in order that man can grow great together—for it has not yet entered into the heart of man what things God has prepared for us, even in this-world. And the justice and love of this-world nourish the root beginnings of the next.

IV. THE COUNCIL

The Second Vatican Council has already had telling influence on the role of the Catholic Church of the United States in the movement for racial justice and friendship. While basic teaching was quite clear, action *as a body* in cooperation with other churches was spotty and negligible until Pope John opened the windows. The Catholic interracial apostolate, spearheaded by Father John LaFarge, was outside the mainstream of official Church life in most dioceses. Local groups were permitted to exist, but they seldom enjoyed full chancery backing. Pushing the Negro cause was, above all, no way to climb the ecclesiastical ladder. Any cleric who messed around in that explosive field must certainly lack prudence. Such laymen seldom became Knights of St. Gregory.

They showed this imprudence by getting the Church mixed up in social agitation, by stirring up demagoguery, by harassing the business leaders and plantation owners, the respectable city fathers and old families whom we must always keep as our friends. Especially in the Bible-Belt South, the Church had first to exist before it could actively join the racial struggle. A degree of prudence was surely required. But most Catholic progressives believe it was inordinate, before and after the fact.

The first session of the Vatican Council brought about a deep change, just in time for the Church to enter the arena during the watershed year of 1963. In January 1963 I attended the assembly in Chicago which brought into being the National Conference on Religion and Race. This country-wide organization, with affiliated local chapters, is comprised of Jews, Protestants and Catholics. It appeared just in time to bring united church and synagogue participation in the crucial contests of 1963. While seldom at the forefront of the Negro revolution, as are CORE, SNCC, the NAACP, the Urban League and the Southern Christian Leadership Association, this coalition of religious bodies gives significant moral support to these activist groups and makes telling moral impact upon the nation's conscience. These effects have value beyond adequate reckoning.

This came through very clearly during the historic March on Washington for Freedom and Jobs in 1963. The signs proclaiming "Jews, Protestants and Catholics unite for racial justice," the many church groups marching under their banners, the hundreds of Roman collars, the presence and prayers of bishops and archbishops—all crowned the stately, almost prayerful, mood of the demonstration with a religious aura and sanction. This was not lost upon the press, TV and radio commentators, nor upon the millions around the nation—and the world—who must each make his decision to love or to hate, to smile or to scowl. Nor was it lost upon the police chiefs of many southern cities, who came to observe. Nor upon the men who make and administer our laws.

The point here is that Catholic participation in the Conference on Religion and Race, and in the March on Washington, would have been much less wholehearted were it not for Vatican II. Catholic teaching on the one human family is not now in question; it is rather the issue of collaborating with non-Catholics in witnessing *as a Church* to this truth. Persons highly knowledgeable of the decision-making process in the Catholic Church of the United States state categorically that episcopal and chancery-office support for this interfaith cooperation would have been much weaker were it not for "the ecumenical spirit" which Vatican II has aroused. Let me admit that my own presence in the March on Washington was partially motivated by this openness for fraternization and solidarity growing out of Pope John's dialogue among Christians, extended in this instance to include Jews on behalf of our Negro brothers, an experimental beginning of the other dialogue.

The Council's major doctrinal discussion on the collegiality of all bishops has also affected the world racial issue. The successors of the Apostles now grasp more clearly, and feel more intensely, that each is not only responsible for his own circumscribed diocese. Pope-and-bishops, together and in unison, are conjointly responsible for the cause of Christ throughout the world. A bishop of the South, of Harlem or South Chicago, of Brazil or Peru, of South Africa, Rhodesia or India now realizes more fully that he cannot act, or stand aside, at home without concern for the effect of his act, or silence, in every other diocese of the world.

The Council has helped the bishops to understand, in a way John's great encyclical alone never could, that "One of the principal characteristics of our time is the multiplication of social relationships, that is, a daily more complex interdependence of citizens, introducing into their lives and activities many and varied forms of association. . . ." World socialization for "the fullness of a more excellent life" makes its decisive impact on the local struggles for human equality— local struggles so numerous and, through modern communications, so shared by all, that these thousands of brush fires have become a gigantic flaming wave encircling the globe.

Chapter Seven

NATIONALISM AND THE WORLD COMMUNITY

The flaming wave of human equality affects nations as well as individuals and races. While racial groups in the United States and other countries seek domestic equality within their own frontiers, the new nations of the world seek international equality in relation to their erstwhile tutor nations of the Atlantic West. The worldwide "revolution of color" finds expression and structure through the birth of the African and Asian nations. This universal tide of nationalism provides a rallying ground for the multiple organization of human endeavor which modern education, health, and industrial development—"the fullness of a more excellent life"—require. Nationalism, in Eastern Europe and in all the continents, offers a rallying cry against the new imperialism of Moscow and Peking.

Western Europe brought the modern nation onto the human stage. Currently, in the Atlantic arena, nationalism plays out its final act after the climactic *Götterdämmerung* of the Second World War.

I. THE CHURCH AND THE RISE OF NATIONALISM

Nationalism took shape between the fifth and tenth centuries among the barbarian tribes newly arrived in Western Europe, during the very years when the Christian Faith was being assimilated by these migrant nations. The Church played a mighty role in the genesis of these first new nations and in elaborating a continental fabric within which they developed themselves and their interrelationships as nations. The baptism of Clovis, King of the Franks, in 493, and the crowning of Charlemagne as Emperor of the West, in 800, at Rome, by Pope Leo III, and of William the Conqueror, King of England, at Westminster on Christmas Day, 1066, by Archbishop Aldred of York, mark the high points of this 500-year process through which Christian sanction, even the Church's blessing and consecration, entered into the warp and woof of Europe's new nationalism, within the larger web of Christendom.

Winston Churchill describes the early contribution of Christianity to the birth of England in the chaos which followed the Saxon invasions of the sixth century:

> Barbarism reigned in its rags, without even the stern military principles which had animated and preserved the Germanic tribes. The confusion and conflict of petty ruffians sometimes called kings racked the land. There was nothing worthy of the name of nationhood, or even of tribalism. . . . Nor did the seeds of recovery spring from the savage hordes who had wrecked the Roman culture. They would certainly have continued to welter indefinitely in squalor, but for the fact that a new force was stirring beyond the seas which, moving slowly, fitfully, painfully, among the ruins of civilisation, reached at length by various paths the unhappy Island. . . .[1]

Churchill describes the work of St. Patrick in Ireland, the coming of the Irish monks to Britain, and the sending of St. Augustine from Rome by Pope Gregory the Great in 596:

> The King of Kent [Ethelbert] had married Bertha, a daughter of the Frankish king, the descendant of Clovis, now enthroned in Paris. Although her husband still wor-

[1] This and the two following quotes are from Churchill's *History of the English-Speaking Peoples* (Vol. I, *The Birth of Britain*) (New York: Bantam Books, 1963), pp. 52–55.

shipped Thor and Woden, Queen Bertha had already begun to spread the truth through courtly circles. Her chaplain, an earnest and energetic Frank, was given full rein, and thus a powerful impulse came to the people of Kent, who were already in a receptive mood toward the dominant creed of Western Europe. St. Augustine, when he landed in Kent, was therefore aware that much had been prepared beforehand. His arrival infused a mood of action. With the aid of the Frankish princess [Bertha, descendant of Clovis] he converted King Ethelbert, who had for reasons of policy long meditated this step.

Churchill, after commenting on the refounding of Christian life at Canterbury, "destined to become the centre and summit of religious England," shows how Church interests and royal policy went hand in hand toward uniting the multiple fractions of dukedoms and kinglets into one nation:

Ethelbert, as overlord of England, exercised an effective authority over the kingdoms of the South and West. His policy was at once skilful and ambitious; his conversion to Christianity, however sincere, was also in consonance with his secular aims. He was himself, as the only English Christian ruler, in a position where he might hold out the hand to the British princes, and, using *the Christian faith as a bond of union,* establish his supremacy over the whole country. This, no doubt, was also in accordance with the ideas which Augustine had carried from Rome. Thus at the opening of the seventh century *Ethelbert and Augustine* summoned a conference of the British Christian bishops. [Italics added.]

This dynamic cross-fertilization of the Christian faith and national spirit continued through more than a thousand years in all the nations of Europe, Russia included. These twin themes dominate Western history until the French Revolution, with national identity sometimes ceding to dynasty and empire, and tensions frequently arising on religious policy within national frontiers vis-à-vis the supranational Catholic Church. These latter tensions contributed greatly to the breakup of Christianity in the 1500s and to the Protestant alliance, on the whole, with nation and king against Catholic Church and emperor. The religious wars, which ensued for a century, helped to sanctify the divine right of kings and to consecrate nationalism. Church authority and even Christian conscience were ceded to secular rulers in many nations under the principle *cuius regio, eius religio,* the principle that subjects must accept the religion of the nation's ruler.

This ultimate in pragmatism produced corrosive cynicism toward the Christian Faith; and in due order, nationalism, with the French Revolution and Napoleon, became an independent religion, often engaged in its own war against the Church.

Carlton J. H. Hayes devotes a book to this theme: *Nationalism: A Religion* (New York: Macmillan, 1960). He recounts how the French Revolution transmuted the Christian Faith into a new religion of *la patrie.* The Declaration of the Rights of Man and Citizen became the national bible, and the Constitution of 1791 prescribed the profession of faith. The flag was substituted for the cross. The National Assembly, replacing synod and ecumenical council, decreed in 1792 that "in all communes an altar to the fatherland shall be raised and on it shall be written the Declaration of Rights, with the inscription: 'The citizen is born, lives, and dies for the nation.'" In 1790 a priest, a minister and a rabbi introduced a rite of civic baptism, to be followed by civic marriages and funerals. Anyone refusing to swear loyalty to the nation-god was excommunicated, cut off from civil rights and ostracized into the limbo misery of "a man without a country." On the other hand, he who shed his blood in the wars of national glory was acclaimed a martyr in eternal memory; his monument and relics were inscribed: "Dead for the fatherland!"

Napoleon evangelized the whole of Europe with this same

national faith, and thus unwittingly brought about his own demise by arousing German, English, Italian, Spanish and Russian nationalists against him. The new religion spread to the Americas. It energized the United States with a new vision of national manifest destiny and gave impetus for breaking out of the Atlantic coastal plain to take over the continent and spread across the seas. Nationalism shattered the Spanish and Portuguese empires, gave birth to fifteen new nations by 1830, and set off a struggle between secularistic nationalism and the supranational Church, a struggle fulsomely religious in its totality and fanaticism.

By 1900 the new religion of the collective ethnic ego had taken over most of the millennial prerogatives of the ancient Faith—in education, family, welfare, property, and over-all social influence. This ethnically inspired secularism was most acutely expressed again in France and the Latin countries, with less thoroughness in the Anglo-Saxon and Germanic lands. A volatile mixture of national imperialism, competing for control of the African and Asian continents, and "national self-determination," involving the small, suppressed nationalities of Europe, exploded into World War I, and prepared the way for Stalin, Mussolini and Hitler.

Nationalism animated the individual combatants of the First World War to a degree new to history, despite the massive, impersonal nature of the fighting. Selfless devotion to national solidarity and glory was enflamed to new heights by the new media of mass communication. The present writer recalls a conversation with a dear old French priest who had lost an arm in battle. A good and holy man, he was at the same time strongly nationalistic. As a resident of the United States, he could have avoided the military draft to which his French birth and citizenship made him liable despite his years in the ministry. He gladly, proudly served as a soldier for *la belle France*. By this willing service and the sacrifice of his blood, he explained to me, he had helped to overcome the prejudices of his countrymen against the Faith; he had in some way "redeemed the Church" by his sacrifice to the nation.

Nazism, of course, was the absolute apogee of nationalism as religion, religion of the most intolerant, persecuting, jealous breed. Hitler decreed the extermination of religions that opposed him. In the name of Aryan ethnic purity, he killed six million Jews in an attempt to exterminate the Hebrew people. In the name of national ideological purity, he killed Christians by the tens of thousands—855 Polish priests, for instance, at Dachau alone.

European expansion into Africa and Asia introduced to those continents the new gospel of the nation-god together with the Gospel of Christ. After the Second World War, fifty new nations were born; and today, a whole new array of tensions between nation and Church, together with creative opportunities for joint action, present themselves in lively and pregnant ferment. The African and Asian scenes are somewhat mindful of the England of Churchill's description, when St. Augustine and King Ethelbert joined hands in the dawn of Europe. But this verisimilitude is much distorted by powerful new factors: the other transcendental religions; the Moslem, the Hindu and the Buddhist faiths; and the mightiest secular religion of all, pretending to be universal rather than national, atheistic Communism. Negroid and Mongoloid reaction against centuries of Caucasian political, economic and military control also adds a strong racial complexion to the current revolution toward equality among nations. And the overarching phenomenon of world socialization introduces psychological forces undreamed of by Augustine and Ethelbert, Napoleon and Bismarck. For, accompanying the centrifugal impulse which nationalism engenders by setting peoples apart as self-centered units, now universalized beyond Atlantica into Africa and Asia, is another unifying force which, like gravity, draws the individual nation-planets toward the ordered macrocosm of one world.

II. THE NEW "WE" OF ONE WORLD

Every front-page and television news report gives testimony to this multiplication of national relationships to form a world society. Presidents, prime ministers, even popes, crisscross national boundaries. Cabinet secretaries and intergovernmental specialists at all echelons meet in all corners of the globe on all manner of human concerns. Together they seek "the fullness of a more excellent life" for all the human family, not only for those who share their own language, physical features and national citizenship.

The most bitter national enemies of Western Europe, that womb of worldwide nationalism, have now proceeded, past the point-of-no-return, toward federation. The nation, even if newly born, is no longer a whole, but a part: part of the Atlantic West; of the hemispheric Organization of American States; of the Communist system, the Arab League, the African or Asian blocs; of the United Nations, and therefore the Food and Agriculture Organization, International Labor Office, World Health Organization, United Nations Educational, Scientific and Cultural Organization; and other organizations. National units of nongovernmental bodies—professional, commercial, labor, farm, humanitarian, recreational —coalesce into world associations.

Interiorly, peoples become increasingly conscious of their global interdependence, a *prise de conscience* of human solidarity kept fresh up to the second by transistor and Telstar.

The Church, whose very mark is *katholike*, universal, all-embracing; whose founder is Lord of all that is, but brother still to every other human, and fleshy kinsman even to every lump of clay, living leaf, and crawling creature within our ken; that Church which is the very Body of Christ continued in our time and place, projected forward into every era and all space; this living Body of Christ which exists to draw together all creation, embrace and return it to the Creator God:

this Church watches over the drawing together of the nations with understanding, self-fulfillment and hope.

Indeed, world socialization moves the Church to become herself more wholly one.

Pope John called the Council to bring the Church abreast of these events and devoted his two encyclicals to this new epoch in history. The ecumenical movement is deeply influenced by this natural phenomenon. Pope Paul expressly addresses the Council, the Church and himself to the "leaders of nations. . . . Working together in justice and love, . . . you can make of humanity a single city."

Pope Pius XII gave especial emphasis and content to this universal concern of the Church, this striving by Christ in His Mystical Body to reincorporate Himself constantly into today's world in all its dimensions, tensions and achievements. Pius XII attracted and awed all men by his unwearied determination to reach out and speak to everyone of every land on every subject imaginable. How cordially he welcomed secular associations of all categories as they gathered in Rome for their world congresses, and always he addressed to these bankers, builders, and bakers, teachers, physicists, and treaty makers, a few truths which bound up their international temporal affairs with the business of the One Eternal Father. It was Pius, too, who established official relations with the several agencies of the United Nations and began the custom of token contributions to their annual budgets.

While important Catholic leaders, clergy and lay, voiced, with patriotic isolationist fervor, open suspicion of the United Nations and all its works, and even rejoiced in its weakness and trials of infancy, Pius XII repeated his own thumping affirmative to the movement toward world community. His address to Catholic lawyers (December 6, 1953) sets forth his advanced thinking on the subject. This same allocution also contains the famous position statement on the Church and civil freedom.

Pius XII develops five points as reasons for promoting world community.

The first of these is the imperative of peace. Pius says:

The conflicts of the past have too often been motivated by a desire to subjugate other nations and to extend the range of one's power, or by the necessity of defending one's liberty and one's own independent existence. This time, on the contrary, it is precisely the will to prevent threatening conflicts that urges men toward a supranational juridical community.

Secondly, there exist what Pius terms "utilitarian considerations." Economic supply and demand govern here. One nation needs another's oil and ores in exchange for machinery and food. Business, financial and technical enterprises assume global dimensions; national welfare comes to depend upon world interchange; international bodies must supervise. Communications and transport must be regulated, monetary and fiscal policy systematized, world markets correlated, national production subordinated to global consumption. So international movements of labor, industry, and agriculture interact in coordination with intergovernmental programs. The economic progress or misery of a fraction of the world affects the welfare of all, especially since this "fraction" of the poor is greater than one half, and the number of the hungry and undernourished exceeds one billion.

Thirdly, Pius XII states that "technological progress" provides the physical means of communication and transport conducive toward inter-nation coalescing, and simultaneously fortifies the necessity for peace, because science renders war unutterably horrible. The planet, physically and psychologically, becomes a neighborhood.

This psychological sense of oneness calls for emphasis. We live in the era of the Peace Corps and Food for Peace, of the Alliance for Progress and Freedom from Hunger campaigns, of the United Nations Technical Assistance Board and of far-ranging private endeavors by foundations, universities and professional, business, labor and voluntary agencies for world social progress.

These organizations strive for social and economic development through technical, financial and human contributions which crisscross national boundaries. Only since the Second World War has any nation taken serious note of the gnawing needs of other nations. Surely the world has always been in want. Hunger, disease, infant death, family misery are the age-old scourges of the Apocalypse. But only in the midst of the Second World War did national statesmen acknowledge responsibility to the entire human family. Prime Minister Churchill and President Roosevelt proclaimed "Freedom from Want" as one of the four freedoms of the Atlantic Charter.

Pope Pius points out that technological progress is the cause of this epochal advance beyond narrow nationalism. Technically we can now do something about world misery; we can produce in superabundance and we can transport this product of the affluent society. Mentally we are conscious— as individuals and nations, via press, radio, television, cinema and travel—of human needs. We know that the hungry, illiterate, and ill are now themselves conscious that their lot is not decreed by God or fate, that this-world betterment is desirable and possible. Further, they, the have-nots, know that we are aware of their predicament, that we have the wherewithal, and the moral imperative, to lend a hand. And we and they both know that the widening gap between their near-nothing and our all must be bridged if we truly want peace to prevail.

We witness, in short, the birth of a new "we," a plural ego beyond the nation, the "we" which is the world. All humans can now say: You and you and you and I are one and we.

As a psychological unity binds together the attentive audience of theater or lecture room, so that they share the same thoughts, exude the same feelings, nod in consensus or object in unison, so a similar psychological oneness now binds together all men. Hundreds of millions on each continent simultaneously hear the same words, advert to the same events, weigh the import of the same acts—knowing that, come the horror of war or the calm of peace, we will all share the same fate.

Fourthly, Pius XII makes his most telling point. Peace, economics and techniques loom, after all, as very obvious causes of "this mutual drawing together" of the nations. Pius sees in operation, underlying these exterior binding forces, "the more profound action of an intrinsic law of development." He means that the seed of unity rests within man, in his powers of perfection and sociability. The world community *in fieri,* in the making, is not merely the accidental, pragmatic product of external forces and pressures. Something within man and essential to him tends toward a society which embraces all other men. Man develops, strives to perfect and to realize his latent powers. By reaching out to embrace all men, by becoming the worldwide "we," man becomes more fully and truly man. We are witnessing today the flowering of man through the flowering of this potency for world social unity, a potency dormant since the dawn of history and unrealized since the Tower of Babel, perhaps since Cain and Abel.

Finally, Pius XII believes that today's science and techniques have stimulated this intrinsic law of development, which has been dormant within man until now: "and finally, perhaps, it is precisely this mingling of men of different nations because of technological progress that has awakened the faith, implanted in the hearts and souls of individuals, in a higher community of men, willed by the Creator and rooted in the unity of their common origin, nature and final destiny." (The relation of these ideas to those of Teilhard de Chardin on the "Law of Convergence" should be noted.)

The continuity of development of papal teaching is strikingly demonstrated by Pope John's elaboration of these themes set forth by Pius. In *Pacem in Terris* John states:

> Recent progress of science and technology has profoundly affected human beings and influenced men to work together and live as one family. There has been a great increase in the circulation of goods, of ideas and of persons from one country to another, so that relations have become closer. . . . The interdependence of national economics has grown deeper . . . so that they become, as it were, integral parts of the one world economy. Likewise the social progress, order, security and peace of each country are necessarily connected with the social progress, order, security and peace of all other countries.

Pope John then asserts categorically that no nation is able to pursue its own interests and develop itself in isolation, because the degree of prosperity and development of one nation reflects and depends upon the prosperity and development of all other nations. Further, John, true to his image as a warm grandfather, patriarch of an extended family, insists on the unity of the human family and the need to promote "the universal common good, that is, the common good of the entire human family."

It seems strange, even bizarre, to the present writer that Catholics professing loyalty to, faith in and love for the Holy Fathers, and who demonstrate these convictions by devout acts of homage, are still able to ignore and set aside the pleas of the Holy Fathers for incarnating Christian social teaching, especially regarding the world community. How often the most pious among the faithful and the clergy, from the best-administered parishes and schools, in the "most Catholic" areas of the country, are precisely the most antagonistic to foreign aid, the United Nations and other international bodies, as concepts and institutions—bodies which are expressly supported by the Holy Father as the best available instruments for peace and "the fullness of a more excellent life" for all men. These "very Catholic" critics—inveighing against the very aims and institutional concepts of the world bodies, not merely critical of passing policies or programs—do not seem to grasp the fact that the Pope and the Church have a moral responsibility for the peace and social progress of the whole human family.

A father must provide bread and milk, schooling and security to *all* his children; he cannot favor a select few, nor the fairest. Our Holy Father must do his utmost to support the *institutions and world system* which will provide bread and milk, schooling and security to all men; he cannot favor the few have nations, nor the whitest. The Popes call upon Catholics, Christians and all men of good will to upbuild these institutions and world systems for the peace and benefit of all men. Strangely—perversely, even—"men of good will," on the whole, have given our Holy Fathers greater heed than have Catholics. The partisans for destroying the United Nations are the anarchists of our day, home wreckers of the human family.

Pope John does not ask for some utopian world government. However, he does want all to recognize "that at this historical moment the present system of organization [within the human community] and the way its principle of authority operates on a world basis no longer correspond to the objective requirements of the universal common good." John wants all to recognize today's reality, so as not to prolong yesterday's romantic dream of national grandeur. Things have changed:

> Today the universal common good poses problems of worldwide dimensions, which cannot be adequately tackled or solved except by the efforts of public authorities endowed with a wideness of powers, structure and means of the same proportions: that is, of public authorities which are in a position to operate in an effective manner on a worldwide basis. The moral order itself, therefore, demands that such a form of public authority be established.

Pope John then makes clear: that this worldwide public authority must be set up by common consent, not imposed by force; that its fundamental objective must be the recognition, respect, safeguarding and promotion of the rights of the human person; and that it must observe the principle of subsidiarity function in relation to the individual nations, other bodies and citizens. The purpose of the public authority of the world community "is to create, on a world basis, an environment in which the public authorities of each political community [each nation], its citizens and intermediate associations, can carry out their tasks, fulfill their duties and exercise their rights with greater security."

Immediately following this statement, *Pacem in Terris* reviews the history and purposes of the United Nations and its specialized agencies. Pope John praises the Universal Declaration of Human Rights, despite objections raised on certain points, as "an important step on the path toward the juridical-political organization of the world community." John the Affirmative then very directly expresses not only support for the United Nations, but the desire that it be strengthened and expanded.

In May 1963, when Cardinal Suenens of Brussels was sent by Pope John to New York to deliver formally a copy of the encyclical and a personal message to the world body, the Cardinal was asked whether the United Nations was the supranational organization envisaged by the Holy Father. He replied, "No, but it is a first step towards it." John's exact words are:

It is Our earnest wish that the United Nations Organization—in its structure and in its means—may become ever more equal to the magnitude and nobility of its tasks.

May the day soon come when every human being will find therein an effective safeguard for the rights which derive directly from his dignity as a person, and which are therefore universal, inviolate and inalienable rights.

This is all the more to be hoped for since all human beings, as they take an ever more active part in the public life of their own political communities, are showing an increasing interest in the affairs of all peoples, and are becoming more consciously aware that they are living members of a universal family of mankind.

Nationalism and nationhood still retain their significant role in the social affairs of men. National identity and ethnic self-awareness must still be cultivated and legitimately invoked to awaken the individual to truth, value and life beyond the ego of self, beyond the larger ego of family, locality or other narrow association of men. The nation remains a dominant focus and fulcrum for the organization of production and finance, for education and cultural expression. The struggle for "the fullness of a more excellent life" will continue, with the individual nation as principal protagonist and arbiter, for years to come on most continents.

But collaboration and gradual fusion among nations are increasing, with Western Europe, the progenitor of religious nationalism, showing the way. Before General de Gaulle came to power in 1958, it was possible to hope that Europe's fever of ethnic egoism might at last become a burned-out case. This new flare-up is not surprising for *la belle France*. The *grande dame* has suffered for many centuries from periodic seizures of self-grandeur of the most virulent type, hers being a cerebral affliction for the good reason that her brain is much, perhaps excessively, used. Possibly this recurrence of the mania was artfully induced by General de Gaulle for the sound purpose of reviving self-pride and unity sufficient to prevent the political chaos of post-empire trauma. Few people can endure utter humiliation without neurosis. The individual requires a modicum of self-respect and dignity; so does the nation. Under General de Gaulle, France recovered from the shattering defeats of the Second World War and the world revolutions which frustrated her national will and rent her soul. Hers is an especially delicate soul, cultivated by intellect and sensibilities beyond the reach of her neighbor nations of Atlantica. The lesser nations of the West should rejoice at the recovery of their ancient tutor and endure her whims for the sake of family solidarity.

Leaving irony aside, all the West should thank Charles de Gaulle for his contribution to the over-all health of Europe by his masterful ministrations to his ailing land. France is recovering her self-identity, and as confidence returns, delusions of grandeur will diminish. For the French are certainly *that* intelligent. A sounder France will help beget a sounder Europe, a Europe no longer at the fraternal mercy of the United States, a Europe which can become a full and equal partner of the Atlantic family. Americans should also thank de Gaulle for thus redressing the United States' aggressive self-confidence, nourished by her postwar sallies as sole champion of the free world when all allies and competitors lay supine, mortally wounded. Some American arrogance should be excused, because it was the young nation's debut as a star with top billing in the arena of the world. And, indeed, the United States did not handle the challenge too badly.

It must be noted that today's ecumenical movement enables the Christian spirit to enliven and deepen the European movement toward unity to a degree impossible since Martin Luther. For four centuries profound religious conviction aided and abetted devisive nationalism unto the spilling of blood in torrents. In a reversal of history which parallels the postwar coming together of Christian thinkers and theologians, it was Christian thinkers and national leaders like Adenauer of Germany, Schuman of France and De Gasperi of Italy who came together to unite Europe after the Second World War. These were all founders of Christian democracy. Probably history will also place General de Gaulle and Premier Erhard among this company of giants, along with men of good will like Monnet of France and Spaak of Belgium.

Joining Popes Pius and John, Pope Paul VI also wants to give to Europe "a deeper, firmer and more organic unity."

Paul also emphasizes the developmental process animating this forward movement. He appeals to "the spontaneous evolution of life which makes of this continent a community," manifest in the reality of being joined by a technical and economic network. This exterior unity, Pope Paul asserts, needs to be infused with a common spirit and to be recognized as the fruit of long, irreversible and beneficent work.

We see again that Pope Paul looks favorably upon international socialization, that the growing interdependence of man does not affright him. He indicates that reaching out of man for convergence beyond the individual person, family, grouping and nation, toward the larger whole, is a positive development upward and forward, innate to and in keeping with man's social nature: "The spontaneous evolution of life makes of this continent a community. . . . Hence the need to give to the facts the seal of the most appropriate legal formulae."[2]

III. OUTSIDE THE ATLANTIC WEST

In Eastern Europe, state-imposed atheism has threatened to smother the cause of Christ, represented there principally by the Orthodox Churches. For centuries these ancient bastions against Moslem and other invaders have been structured along ethnic lines into the Greek, Russian, Rumanian, and other Orthodox Churches. Much of the family struggle between these venerable bodies and the Roman Catholic Church has been rooted in Western determination to latinize oriental Orthodoxy, to the detriment of their national values and self-awareness. Happily, this penchant toward cultural imperialism inherited from ancient Rome has now abated. Identification of the universal Church with a cultural Roman "me" gives way to a truly catholic "we." After five centuries of not being on speaking terms, His Holiness, Pope Paul,

[2] References are to Pope Paul's talk to the International Council for the European Movement, November 1963.

and His Beatitude, Patriarch Athenagoras, have met with Christ in His own Holy Land. The dialogue has begun.

Patriarch Athenagoras, in his first message to Pope Paul, which prepared for the meeting in Jerusalem (January 1964), asked for a joining of hands in the struggle for human freedom against atheism and tyranny. Since two thirds of Orthodoxy is in Communist East Europe, the Patriarch pointed up his chief daily anxiety, which is shared by all Orthodox leaders and all other Christians, and by many other men of good will. National self-determination has become a principal instrument for cracking the Communist monolith. The Orthodox Churches of each nation may well fulfill an historic role in this breakdown of Russian imperialism, as well as in the liberalization of totalitarian control within the satellites and in Russia as well.

It appears that the Orthodox Church, as she begins with Catholics the dialogue already begun in the past decade with Protestants, is ready to enter wholeheartedly into what Pope Paul calls "another dialogue . . . beyond the frontiers of Christianity . . . the dialogue of the Church with the contemporary world." Orthodoxy, historically and geographically, seems well placed to join renascent nationalism in the struggle for human freedom in the very heartland of world Communism. This alliance of nation and national church against external tyranny could have telling impact not only on the respective nations, but on religion as well. It could re-energize, expand and deepen Christian life, bringing about something similar to Pope John's *aggiornamento,* but with an "updating" altogether in keeping with national culture and Orthodox tradition.

Drawing from experiences familiar to Westerners, the interplay of Irish and Polish nationalism and religion is instructive. In Ireland, priests and people joined hands, hearts and blood in the long struggle against British control. Beyond a doubt, this century-long making of common cause by nation and faith, and of legitimate temporal and spiritual aspirations, did much to beget the deep, sure "thing" the Church is to Irish people everywhere. The Polish case is not quite so clear, because, besides Lutheran Prussia and Orthodox Russia, Catholic Austria also preyed upon and subdued Poland for two centuries. Nevertheless, Polish priests and people made common cause in the repeated bloody national struggles for freedom. This recurred under Nazism, and continues today. The fact that the Church in Poland can stand up to Communism at all is witness to her inherited prestige as the champion of national freedom for centuries before.

This Irish and Polish evidence could be adduced in support of a thesis which can be stated tentatively as follows: To the degree that a religion makes common cause with the legitimate national aspirations of a people, to that degree is the religious loyalty of the people strengthened. (Possibly "legitimate national aspirations" could be broadened to "legitimate natural and human aspirations," but this would take us beyond our present subject and far beyond our evidence, already stretched rather thin. The present writer wishes to state clearly that he is concerned here with nonsupernatural and nonrevelationary influences on the religious allegiance and practice of a people as a whole. The grace of God, His light and His strength, do not enter into this discussion.)

The Italian and Latin American experiences might reinforce this train of thought. It can be asserted that Church opposition to the union of Italy, in defense of the Papal States against the national *risorgimento* of the nineteenth century, even long after Italian unity was a *fait accompli,* contributed heavily to disaffection from and hatred of the Church. The Papacy bore the brunt of this resentment. The very funeral of Pius IX had to be quiet and guarded to prevent his body from being thrown into the Tiber.

When the Latin American nations revolted against Spain in the early 1800s, the higher clergy—bishops, major superiors, university and seminary rectors—were mostly Spanish citizens, loyal to king and the old homeland. These Church leaders usually became enemies to the revolutionaries. They were exiled, assaulted and occasionally killed. Most importantly, the lower clergy, most of whom were born and reared in their American homelands, often joined the national leaders in overthrowing Spanish power, their own bishops and superiors included. Church discipline and administration collapsed in many places for many years. The new governments which took over were strongly nationalistic, usually anti-Church, even anti-Christian, and especially suspicious of hierarchy and Rome. The Church in Latin America never fully recovered from this conflict with national aspirations. Many of her present difficulties can be traced to this shattering of the national spirit, this struggle, rather than concord, between secular and Christian leaders over the soul of their people.

Today, however, the Latin Church dramatically redresses her error. She takes on new national prestige and arouses the allegiance of the popular masses by championing their legitimate natural aspirations for "the fullness of a more excellent life," spurred on by Italian popes who have embraced the results of their land's anticlerical *risorgimento,* and have been embraced in turn by their Italian flock.

The new flaming nationalism of Africa and Asia, and the revived fires of Latin America, are obviously much different from the old *élan* of Mother Europe. In all three continents it is strengthened and distorted by the world race issue, by reaction against colonialism, by the widening gap between rich and poor nations, by the exhilaration of independence, by the population spiral, by political inexperience, and by demagogic appeal by some to cover up local oligarchy and, by others, to stir up revolution against the existing power structure. And of course, there are the added fuels of Communist expansionism and religious intolerance.

Among the Africans, nationalism offers the gravitational pull needed to draw allegiance beyond the tribe and locality into the much larger collective ego. Ancient tribal antagonisms must be overcome. Only the nation can encompass the sufficiently extensive and diversified economic production and markets required for the this-world betterment which all citizens suddenly espy and demand. Indeed, most nations of Africa, as well as Latin America, seem much too small for industrial development of modern scope. Movements toward common markets and free trade zones will intensify, nationalists permitting. Regretfully, after a wondrous minimum of bloodshed in the revolutions against the empires of the West, to the credit of both sides, wars of national expansion might come in due course, although the need of *lebensraum* does not press immediately, except perhaps in Egypt and Rwanda. "Living space," however, already exerts great pressure among the nearly saturated nations of Asia. Inevitably, nearby open areas will be occupied by the multiplying have-nots, gradually, peacefully or violently. Southeast Asia and Oceania will probably suffer wars of national expansion for some time in the indefinite future.

In Asia and North Africa the Moslem, Buddhist and Hindu religions supply inspiration and consensus to the new nationalism, a role which has served to stimulate the old religions themselves. Unfortunately, however, in too many cases religion has helped to inflame nationalism to heights of bitterness which are only too reminiscent of the European Wars of Religion of the 1500s and 1600s. The enmity between Moslem Pakistan and Hindu India, even under the threat of atheist China, is an obvious example. Also, the great transcendental religions sometimes become rallying ground for national political maneuvering in a manner heretofore unknown, as experienced in Vietnam in 1963. Regrettably, but understandably in view of Western colonial history and Christian missionary methods, the ancient religions of Asia and Saharan Africa utilize their influence within the new nations to exclude or inhibit the spread of Christ and His Good News for all men.

It is most fortunate for the Catholic Church that the Vatican Council was held just at this juncture, for cogent reasons well advanced by many commentators. One by-product, closely tied to the great issue of nationalism and the new world "we," would alone have justified the Council: the Council brought together the bishops of old Atlantica and the bishops of the new nations under circumstances in which they could come to know, respect, love and minister unto each other. During several months "at school" together they learned much from the Holy Spirit and from each other. It is supremely fitting that the collegiality of bishops was the Council's principal concern, that the pastors became convinced theologically of what they learned from the group experience: that there is really but one flock, and Christ charges all bishops to feed His lambs and to shoulder His sheep, all of His flock, all of the human family. Many affluent Western bishops for the first time met and had serious converse with bishops of other races and cultures, bishops much more like the have-not Apostles Christ first sent forth. Friendships are ripening among the have and have-not apostles sent today to unite the world in Christ.

The movement, through and beyond the nation, toward world community provides the natural substratum for the Mystical Body of Christ. Christ calls Himself *Omega*—the end of all that is, the ultimate self-realization toward which every creature strives to converge. The apostles of Christ, their worldwide flock, and indeed all men of good will begin to hear and understand Him: You and you and you and I are One and We, through Me.

Chapter Eight

THE ECONOMY, PROPERTY AND WORK

The scandal of the nineteenth century is that the Church lost the working class.

This honest admission by Pope Pius XI explains why he gave so much attention to the things of this-world (property, labor, the economy) during his reign—the cruel, crucial years of the Great Depression. Building upon the foundations laid by Leo XIII in the 1890s, Pius sought between the Great Wars to make up for the scandal of the previous century. He began in earnest the dialogue with the modern world, in the field of economics and social justice. That the world is at all alive to the Church today, and sufficiently attentive to carry on the current dialogue on this-world issues, witnesses to the modest success of Pius XI's repentance for the scandal and his amends in the Church's name.

In his encyclical of 1931, *Reconstructing the Social Order* (*Quadragesimo Anno*), Pius singles out the central social consequence of the Industrial Revolution, the class struggle. The application of science to economic production divided human society into two classes:

> The first, small in numbers, enjoyed practically all the comforts so plentifully supplied by modern invention. The second class, comprising the immense multitude of workingmen, was made up of those who, oppressed by dire poverty, struggled in vain to escape from the straits which encompassed them. [Par. 3.]

Pius comments that this national division of men into two classes, the haves and the have-nots, was quite acceptable to the wealthy, "who looked upon it as the consequence of inevitable and natural economic laws." The rich abandoned to charity alone the full care of relieving the oppressed, "as though it were the task of charity to make amends for the open violation of justice, a violation not merely tolerated, but sanctioned at times by legislators." Pius XI thus begins laying the ground for launching the Christian revolution, the basic reconstruction of a society's structures, by peaceful means, through application of social justice, directives of justice which do not depend upon the legislator, but which, on the contrary, the legislator must obey. These laws of human and societal justice exist above and prior to national constitutions and congresses. Indeed, constitutions and congresses are themselves unjust unless they conform to these higher principles of social justice, which derive from the human person, his very nature and dignity, origin and destiny.

The propertied class, of course, adhered to a different version of "the natural law." They clasped "the invisible hand" of the free market, sanctified into laissez-faire capitalism by Adam Smith. Personal and corporate property assumed near absolute sovereignty. The few who owned land, plant and equipment—capital—exercised authority almost supreme over the working masses, the proletariat, who had only hands and muscle.

On the other hand, Pius points out, the working classes, victims of these harsh conditions, submitted to them with extreme reluctance, and became more and more unwilling to bear the galling yoke. Some, carried away by the heat of evil counsels, went so far as to seek the disruption of the whole social fabric. Others, whom a more solid Christian training restrained from such misguided excesses, convinced themselves nevertheless that there was much in all this that needed a radical and speedy reform. (Par. 4.)

Pius XI fully supported workers' organizations which offered the fundamental countervailing force "for helping each member to better his condition to the utmost in body, soul and property [quoted by Pius from Leo XIII] . . . to defend their temporal rights and interests energetically and efficiently." Many, perhaps even most, workers of the industrial West did "seek the disruption of the whole social fabric," skillfully advanced by Marxist socialism through suasion and force. Due to her tardy and incomplete grasp of the meaning of the Industrial Revolution and the class struggle it caused, and due also to her delay in recognizing and championing the just natural aspirations of the great majority of her flock, the Church lost to socialism—and especially to Communism, its most zealous and intolerant expression—the allegiance of millions.

The Church opposed Marxist socialism because of its atheist ideology, class-struggle means, and wholly this-world goals. Also, the ownership and management of all productive property by the government, which it advocates, concentrates such absolute power in the hands of the very few that not only the worker, but all society, is enslaved. Simultaneously, the Church equally opposed the laissez-faire capitalism of the Manchester School, under which, as Pius XI puts it:

> Capital was long able to appropriate to itself excessive advantages; it claimed all the products and profits and left to the laborer the barest minimum necessary to repair his strength and to ensure the continuation of his class. For by an inexorable economic law, it was held, all accumulation of riches must fall to the share of the wealthy, while the workingman must remain perpetually in indigence or reduced to the minimum needed for existence. [Par. 54.]

In the West the Church's social teaching and action programs have sought to bridge the chasms between absolute property and proletarian workers, between the excesses of capitalism and the tyrannies of Marxism. Christian-inspired movements of management and labor, professionals and thinkers, have collaborated with moderate socialists and capitalists and with men of good will to help evolve the highly successful mixed economy of today's industrial West. Recalling the sweatshops of Leo's day and the paralyzing unemployment of the Depression Pius XI lived through, and the bitterness engendered against the "bourgeois" Church and all its works, the current marvel of the Common Market and the new respect, even affection, shown the Pope, by the sons of hate-filled workers, appear miraculous indeed. In these coalescing affluent societies of Free Europe and North America the internal threat of Marxist takeover has about passed away after a full century of mounting strength which crested in the chaotic aftermath of the Second World War.

The prodigies of production and distribution which undergird Western affluence result from a pragmatic fusing of selected capitalist and socialist economic theories, with kaleidoscopic variation from Swedish centralization to German free enterprise, from Italian state corporations to French national planning, British welfarism and American corporative giants. While not fully realized, and much nuanced in time and place, the basic rationale running through the Atlantic West is that the economy must support the common good and supply material means to all people "for the fullness of a more excellent life."

This striking change from the exaggerated capitalism indicted by Leo and Pius has resulted from radical redress of the capital-worker relationship by asserting human rights over property rights. The absolute sovereignty of property rights has been gradually withdrawn from owners and shared with workers, government and professional managers. Labor unions and collective bargaining have played by far the principal roles in this historic process. Leo XIII receives highest praise today for affirming in 1891 the right of workers to organize. This pronouncement brought the Church back into the picture. Had the popes denied or ignored the right to organize, the workers would have doubly damned the "bour-

geois" Church; Marxism would have enjoyed added tri-
umphs; class-struggle socialism might well have taken over
all of Europe. It was a close victory.

Leo was under heavy pressure from Catholic paternalists
to deny workers the right to organize, or at least to compromise by saying nothing about labor unions, which were, in
1891, new, unproven, violent disrupters of the old order. In
many nations they were outlawed, or under such legal encumbrances that most rights that are accepted today were
then opposed by police and soldiery. Not only did autonomous workers' unions run completely counter to the economic
theory of private property's absolute sovereignty expressed in
the free market, but they also ran wholly contrary to the dominant political doctrine of centralized national government as
advanced by Hobbes, Rousseau and Hegel, and concretized
by both Napoleons, Bismarck and their lesser colleagues.

Under this theory of the state, widely accepted in the nineteenth century, the individual citizen has only two choices:
either he remains outside civil life altogether as a lone wolf,
preying upon his neighbor and fearful of attack; or he gives
himself over to the *general will* of all the people, personified
in the central government of the nation. In this *social contract,* Rousseau asserts, "by total making-over of each associate, with all his rights, to the entire community, . . . [the
citizen] unites with all others, yet obeys only himself, and remains as free as before. . . . Each of us puts in common his
person and all his faculties under the supreme direction of the
general will [i.e., the national government]."

In the last half of the nineteenth century, the religion of
nationalism won ardent loyalty from Europeans under
forms of government derived from these propositions. The
very concept of autonomous organizations of workers, outside
the apparatus of government control, was anathema. Rousseau's social contract drained the individual citizen of any
remnant of rights transferable to a worker organization for
collective bargaining and union contract: "Further, this

making-over [of the person and all his faculties to the body politic] having taken place without reserve, the union [of the nation] is as perfect as it can be and no associate [citizen] has anything more to demand." In short, the organization of workers was not only illegal; it was treason, it was political heresy. Hobbes expressly repudiated even the traditional rights of craftsmen's guilds. To him, all these nongovernmental bodies became nuclei of dissidence, "worms in the body politic." So independent labor unions were forbidden both by the economic "natural law" of private property and free market, and by the political "natural law" of social contract and the general will.

These twin theories of society are the "natural law" criticized by Justice Oliver W. Holmes, doctrines quite different from the natural law of today's Catholic social teaching. But in the 1890s all this was unclear, undeveloped, untried. Progressives saw that oppressed workers needed and had a right to form a countervailing organization to defend themselves. Catholic conservatives, statists, and proprietors, as a whole, would only allow softening of the iron law of wages to the point of paternalism. In the nineteenth century the Catholic capitalist who considered the worker not as a commodity, but as a child who must be looked after in Christian charity, was considered progressive.

The model of these progressive paternalists was Léon Harmel, head of a textile firm at Val des Bois in northern France, who introduced old-age pensions, family subsidies, credit unions, night courses and recreation clubs. Harmel (appropriately known to his workers as *Bon Père*), over a period of four decades, evolved a series of regular consultations with his workers which culminated by 1909 in the factory council to provide "real cooperation by the workers in the industrial and disciplinary management of the factory." Representatives elected by the workers met each fortnight with the management as "spokesmen of their comrades in demands to be made of the employer . . . to give their counsel on all wage changes, on disciplinary measures to be taken, on questions of safety, hygiene, apprenticeship and work." Leo XIII came to know Harmel personally and followed his developing paternalism with approval. In 1879 Leo invited "all employers and all workers in large factories to strive to follow the example of Val des Bois."[1]

During the ensuing decade Harmel initiated workers' pilgrimages from France, so that employers and workers together in solidarity could pay their respects and receive counsel from the Holy Father. These biannual affairs brought up to ten and twelve thousand workers with three or four hundred employers to Rome. During the pilgrimage of 1887 Leo said, "It is necessary that Harmels be multiplied. Harmels must be multiplied." In 1889 Harmel wrote an *Employer's Catechism* which was widely praised. The noted Catholic moralist, Father A. Lehmkuhl, called it "a perfect book," although some reservation was voiced because Harmel based wage determination on "social interest and Christian charity" rather than on justice. The worker remained a ward of the employer, a child of the *Bon Père*.

It was in this climate that Leo XIII wrote his Magna Charta on *The Condition of Labor (Rerum Novarum)*. To most clergy and employers, however avant-garde their paternalism, autonomous labor unions, independent of employers and government, appeared outrageous, out of the question. The pioneering paternalists and theologians wanted only a revival of the craftsmen's guilds of the Middle Ages. Leo in his 1884 encyclical, *The Human Race (Humanum Genus)*, asked that these medieval workers' corporations be re-established and adapted to modern times. He praised current effort in that direction, with Harmel's model paternalism in mind. But these mixed organizations, composed of workers *and* em-

[1] These citations and much material for this section are taken from the doctoral thesis of the present author, *The Catholic Movement of Employers and Managers,* a study of UNIAPAC (Rome: Gregorian University Press, 1961), especially pp. 24–37.

ployers, were a far cry from the combative, purely workers' unions which ultimately received Leo's approval seven years later in *Rerum Novarum*.

Father Georges Jarlot, S.J., a foremost historian of the development of Catholic social teaching, and recent rector of the Institute of Social Sciences, Gregorian University, Rome, points out that, prior to *Rerum Novarum*, Catholic leaders, apparently including Pope Leo himself, did not understand the right to organize as a right in justice independent of Christian brotherhood.[2] In the mixed union, the updated corporation or guild, Jarlot explains, "the moral and religious association precedes the economic association: the corporation is a sort of confraternity. . . . The employer presides, the employee has a consultative voice." In the first draft of *Rerum Novarum* such mixed associations or guild-like corporations of workers and employers together are proposed for dissolving the class struggle. The second draft of the encyclical defines the rights of workers more precisely, but labor organization retains its mixed character to include employers.

Only the very last text of *Rerum Novarum* teaches definitively that workers alone can form their own separate unions, and this comes within the context of praise for the medieval guilds:

> History attests what excellent results were effected by the artisans' guilds of a former day. They were the means not only of many advantages to the workmen, but in no small degree of the advancement of art, as numerous monuments remain to prove. Such associations should be adapted to the requirements of the age in which we live—an age of greater instruction, of different customs, and of more numerous requirements in daily life. It is gratifying to know that there are actually in existence not a few societies of this nature, *consisting either of workmen alone, or of*

[2] From Father Jarlot's study of the history of *Rerum Novarum* in *Nouvelle Revue Théologique*, January 1959, pp. 60–77.

workmen and employers together; but it were greatly to be desired that they should multiply and become more effective. [Par. 36. Italics added.]

Pope Leo and his collaborators, principally Father Liberatore and Cardinal Zigliara, hesitated until the end on the right of workers alone to organize. The phrase italicized above, admitting that right, was inserted in the text between the second draft of April 21, 1891, and the final version of May 15th. This historic insertion was made by Leo himself, an act attributed by Jarlot in great part to the influence of Cardinal Gibbons of the United States, who, four years before, had come to Rome personally to defend, successfully, the right of Catholics to become members and leaders of the Knights of Labor. This early American labor movement was not only composed of workers alone; it was also neutral and nonconfessional. This latter point is significant, because in the half-century after *Rerum Novarum* intramural debate among Catholics often centered on that issue: Granted that workers alone could organize, should Catholic workers form their own Christian trade unions? Or could they join up with men of good will in nonconfessional organizations? In the 1960s this issue bobs up still, especially in Latin America.

We see, in this short case history of the elaboration of the Church's position on the right of workers to organize, that Christian social teaching does develop step-by-step. It does not exist ready-made behind the scenes awaiting curtain call to step out full-bodied onto the stage of this-world. The social doctrine of the future does not now stand in the wings, script well memorized, watching for the papal cue. Far from such a *deus ex machina,* the social teaching of tomorrow exists as a seed in today, as it existed in all that has gone before, in the solid ground of man's perduring essence and dignity, origin and destiny, in the perennial light and warmth of revelation. From these implicit powers the teaching evolves organically, preserving continuity with the past and the future: a more excellent life for man here and hereafter. And we see that the development of this teaching is much conditioned by the objective and independent development of man and society itself, which cannot be foreseen beyond certain basic guidelines, and that clear statement of particular points depends upon pastoral prudence, which is often influenced by subjective human and personal judgment.

We see, further, that, as society develops, Christian social teaching must develop. To stand still is to become irrelevant. Pope John's *aggiornamento* is always in order in the social field of the modern era. Such constant updating is urgently required in our age of world socialization, today's "daily more complex interdependence of citizens . . . whereby men are impelled voluntarily to enter into association in order to attain objectives which each one desires, but which exceed the capacity of single individuals." If the Church does not constantly update her social awareness and concern, she quickly becomes irrelevant to the modern world of multiplying relationships. In a society of growing, interacting relationships, to become irrelevant is to die.

Society follows laws of development natural to man, of an order different from revelation and the supernatural. Human society embodies a valid life, willed by God for His creatures to bring them to fuller perfection, to enable them to become more nearly themselves, closer to God's image, and thus nearer to Him. Human society, therefore, must minister to the power of man—all men—to know, to act freely, to create, to love truly. The supernatural engrafts itself onto and builds upon these natural faculties—in man as an individual, in man as society.

The Church is the Body of Christ, a supernatural society, a multiplication of relations between God and man, among all men and all creatures with God, souled by His Love. The Church is Christ as *the* Society, assimilating to Himself man as society. To completely cut off the Church on earth from the temporal order is disincarnate angelism. To make of Christ a mere matterless angel is no compliment whatever; to make Christ disincarnate is to destroy Him. The Church must have relevancy to contemporary society to continue Christ here on earth. To the degree the Church relates to society she can continue Him the better.

The Church, then, must know, respect and love human society, as Christ knows, respects and loves man. As Christ understands and respects the mind and will of man, his emotions, appetites, and his whole psychology, so must the Church understand and respect the sound values, aspirations, and valid creations of human society. Despite their natural origin, these are all God's creation and are not to be indiscriminately replaced or distorted by truths, values and criteria derived from another order of things, from revelation and the supernatural.

Further, as Christ knows only too well the evil man is capable of, his sin and hate and pride, so must the Church know the evil which lurks in human society. As Christ distinguishes the physical ills of the body (disease, paralysis, dementia) from the moral evils of the spirit, and perceives their possible interrelation, so must the Church recognize the distinctions and the relationships between social aberrations and the changing environments which embody and nourish them. In short, the Church must know contemporary society *as it is*, not as it was a century or a decade ago; not merely as she would like to see it ideally, based on supernatural judgments alone, without full regard for all that is valid for the natural order which God has created.

The laws, liturgy and pastoral practice of the Church should, in consequence, have relevancy to contemporary society *as it is*, insofar as their supernatural origin and purpose permit. All this requires thorough research and study of society, and some degree of knowledge of the social sciences by theologians, canonists and administrators, in dioceses, religious orders, bishops' conferences and in Rome.

If Church leaders had been more clearly aware of the human and social meaning of the Industrial Revolution, the scandalous loss of the worker which Pius XI bewails could have been mitigated. Paul VI prompts a similar conclusion in a statement referring to the French Revolution: "Though clothed in laicism and protest against the Church . . . the ideas of liberty, equality and fraternity are altogether Christian. . . ." If popes and bishops, clergy and lay leaders had agreed upon these truths and grasped their human and social consequences two centuries ago, history would surely have taken a different course. In hindsight we wonder at this eighteenth-century blindness within the Church. But Pope Paul wants to open our eyes to the present and future, so he continues: ". . . the ideas of liberty, equality and fraternity are altogether Christian, just as are today's social aspirations for justice and freedom."

Within the West these social aspirations of justice and freedom are increasingly met. While the very success of the mixed economy creates new problems, such as automation, creation of artificial wants through advertising, depressed areas and relative poverty amidst affluence, probably the most important social issue is bigness. Man tries to adjust his mind, emotions and spirit—after hundreds of thousands of years of rural aloneness and small-town comradeship—to the suddenly imposed environment of big business, big labor, big government, big cities and the constant awareness of millions of others through the mass media. Something will be said later about the lonely crowd, the organization man, and the dangers of the power concentration now technically feasible and required to meet today's revolutions of equality and this-world betterment.

The broadest issue, which the very affluence of the West's mixed economy accentuates, is that of the rich nations and the poor nations, and the widening gap between them. A hundred years ago class consciousness arose and the class struggle began raging between the have-all factory owners and the have-nothing worker proletariat within the nations of the West. Today a comparable class consciousness is arising between the industrialized nations and the technically underdeveloped nations: between one third of the human family in the West, Russia and Japan, and the two thirds in Africa, Asia and Latin America.

Beginnings of a full-scale class struggle between these haves and have-nots also appear, not only between the West and her former subject territories, but also between Russia and her former subject Communist parties around the world. Certainly basic to the Russia-China quarrel is the fact that the Russians do not want to risk losing what they already have, and the Chinese have so little that they deliberately risk aggression to better their lot. World socialization has reached such intensity that the economy of the whole planet almost becomes one mammoth factory. Assembly-line tributaries flow out from each poor nation, carrying vital raw materials to the rich nations for fabrication into finished products, and return to each nation a fraction of the world's output. But two thirds of the workers now claim that they are getting too little back. Like Samuel Gompers, founder of the American Federation of Labor, they want more.

Labor unions in the Western nations provided the principal countervailing force to win away from property holders many of their absolute rights. What comparable countervailing force can the have-nots of Africa, Asia and Latin America put together to get a fairer share of the world product, a modicum of that more excellent life all men now seek? What is the Christian response to this new class struggle of world dimensions, with nations as the components rather than local unions of factory workers? Will Christian leaders again line up with the status quo of Western supremacy and exhibit the same myopia they showed in supporting the *ancien régime* and absolute property? Or will they declare and strive for the dignity and rights of all the human family?

Chapter Nine

RICH NATIONS, POOR NATIONS

I. The Widening Gap

The amount of goods and services produced in a year by the farms, factories and work force of a nation is called the national product. Gross national product (GNP) is the total output, without subtracting depreciation of equipment or making other careful adjustments. GNP has become an unrefined rule of thumb for measuring standards of living.

All the food and shoes, electricity and transport, laundry, and medical care made available to the whole population of the United States is valued at over $600 billion in 1964. Dividing this figure by the number of people in the nation, about 200 million in 1965, we see that the GNP is $3000 per capita. This does not mean that every man, woman and child receives this much money in hand to spend as they will, because a portion goes into new factories and highways, the repair of old buildings, the training of new teachers, and, importantly, $50 billion, or about 9 percent, goes to armaments and defense. But, on the whole, the annual GNP per capita is a good yardstick for measuring the wealth of a nation, especially for comparing the standards of living in different nations.

The annual GNP of the countries of the industrialized West is about $2000 per capita, that is, about $1300 per person in the Common Market of Europe and about $3000 per person in the United States and Canada.

The annual GNP of more than half of the human family, in the less-developed nations, runs about $150 per capita. In the words of President Lyndon Johnson, "These people have less to spend each day on food and on shelter and on clothing, on medicine, and on all their needs, than the average American spends at his corner drugstore for a package of cigarettes." (Address to editors and broadcasters, April 21, 1964.)

We are rich and they are poor. A great chasm of hunger, disease and ignorance separates us. The great drama of our day is that this gap between the prince and Cinderella, palace and hovel, continues to widen, and that the miserable of the world now realize the disparity between their lot and ours. On the whole, their situation is improving bit by bit. But our stuffed deep freezers and meat twice a day, our schooling for all our children through sixteen years of age, our penicillin and polio shots, our running water and auto for every family, remain for them fantastic luxuries. And the annual rise in our standard of living makes catching up seem for them a futile fantasy.

A nation's standard of living can be increased by putting more and better-trained men to work in more farms and factories, with improved machines and technical methods. An annual increase of 4 percent in the GNP of a nation, over and above the population growth, is considered a high rate of advance. The Alliance for Progress, for instance, aims at a GNP increase of only 2.5 percent per year, and most of Latin America is not even attaining this modest goal. But, nevertheless, let us use the optimistic figure of 4 percent as a measuring rod for the widening gap.

A citizen of the United States who enjoyed a GNP of $3000 per capita in 1964 will benefit by a rise of $120 from the nation's GNP increase of 4 percent in 1965. On the other hand, a citizen of India, Brazil, or Nigeria, who subsisted on a GNP of $150 per person in 1964, will receive a raise of only $6 in 1965. Here is the widening gap in a nutshell. The already rich American receives twenty times more (2000 percent more) in new wealth each year than does the already poor Indian, Brazilian or Nigerian. The rich are getting richer; the poor are getting poorer, relative to the rich, and the poor now know it.

Furthermore, because of an astonishing recent upsurge in population growth, the number of the world's poor is increasing more rapidly than the number of the rich. In Western nations the very wealthy often have fewer children per family than the poor. The word "proletariat" derives from *proles,* a Latin word meaning "offspring." The very poor possess and produce little more than children. This differential now extends on a world scale.

The new population increase of the industrialized nations —North America, Western Europe, Australia, New Zealand, and Russia—is about 1.3 percent a year, that is, thirteen births over the number of deaths a year per one thousand population. The three developing continents have a net population increase averaging 2.1 percent a year: Asia 2 percent, Africa 2.1 percent, Latin America 2.7 percent. The annual population growth of the rich nations is about 13 million. The annual population growth of the poor nations is about 44 million. This means that increased population per year among the world's poor is about 3⅓ times, or 333 percent, higher than that of the rich. There are about 31 million more additional persons in the poor nations each year than there are in the rich nations.

Besides these quantitative disparities, qualitative differences acquire growing significance. One of these is race. The industrialized nations are predominantly Caucasian, with the exception of Japan. The less-developed countries are largely dark-skinned, Negroid and Mongoloid, or, in the case of Latin America, have heavy admixtures of unassimilated colored peoples.

Another complicating differentiation between the rich and poor of the world is nationalism. As the fanaticism of extreme nationalism quiets down in the West, from which it arose in most violent form, ethnic egoism suddenly emerges in nonindustrialized Africa and Asia, and flames anew in Latin America.

A third qualitative difference is religion. The rich third of the earth, excepting Japan, is by and large the heartland of Christianity. The miserable two thirds are mostly Moslem, Buddhist and Hindu. Even if we accept an optimistic figure of 175 million Christians in Latin America, the total number of Christians in the three developing continents account for only about one eighth of the two billion population of the have-not nations. The percentage of Christians in Asia and Islamic Africa is only about 3 percent of that one half of the human family which suffers most from disease, illiteracy and poverty. The dominant Moslem, Buddhist and Hindu religions, now experiencing a renaissance under the stimulus of the new nationalism, often animate the new state with a rallying force and mystique as it strives for self-awareness. This self-identity of the people, prompted by the new national ethos and nourished by their ancient faith and values, easily leads to currents critical of and counter to the Christian faith, brought in from the West and long identified with the colonial powers. Events in Ceylon, Sudan and Vietnam can be fully understood only in this context.

During the nineteenth century, as the Western imperial powers spread their national competition around the world, the Christian churches leagued with them in many instances to obtain security and support for the schools, health and social services which accompanied and undergirded their spiritual apostolate. Christianity made a major contribution to the revolution for this-world betterment, for the "fullness of a more excellent life," in Africa and Asia. Since the Second World War official colonial support has suddenly been withdrawn, and the fifty new national governments now tend toward absorption of the educational, health and social services built up under Christian auspices. This is comparable to the over-all takeover by the state of these basic roles in society which occurred in the West during the secularization following the French Revolution. This major realignment of social roles within the nation will go on for some years, maybe for decades and generations, among the have-not peoples.

Obviously, the ideological and administrative bodies which direct these services will exercise strong influence within the developing nations, because schooling, good health, neighborhood and worker associations touch each family of every slum and village most intimately, offering some tangible surcease for their newly felt, burning aspirations. The degree to which Christian bodies can retain some voice in these society-wide fields depends upon several factors which vary greatly from country to country. It would appear that principal among these, besides mere numbers of adherents, is the degree to which the Church has become truly part and parcel of the new national ethos, and is moving toward local direction by superiors who are citizens of that nation and ethos, and are promoters as well of social progress. A second basic element will be the extent to which the other transcendental faiths have their own *aggiornamento,* an updating to make their truths and values relevant to the new world which has flooded upon them, and are thus able to forge social and political principles, applicable to the fresh fact of socialization, induced by science and its concomitant revolutions.

The hope is that Christian bodies and the Moslem, Buddhist and Hindu faiths will all "open their doors" to each other and find sufficient common ground for basic accord, and even for some collaboration, in these key areas of education, health and social advance. Unless the transcendental faiths of East and West—however different their understanding of God, the Absolute and the next world—can agree on ways and means for helping the whole human family to attain "the fullness of a more excellent life" in this world, they are likely to be eclipsed by the new secular nationalism. If Christian, Moslem, Buddhist and Hindu shatter the spiritual world with another war of religions, fed by theological fury comparable to that which sundered the West after the Reformation, and even if this new religious world conflict remains bloodless, confined to acrimony, suspicion and hate, then assuredly the secularized state will win out. God and things of the spirit will be exiled from the whole workaday world of the here and now.

Religious, racial and national issues, together with class consciousness among the world's proletariat, are stimulated by today's mass media of communication. These were unavailable to Napoleon, and came into full use as a titanic social force only with Hitler. Press, cinema, radio and television stir up the revolutionary urge to equality of races and nations, together with the desire and demand for this-world betterment. The discontent of the have-not nations has risen to fever pitch since the Second World War, much more suddenly than did the discontent of the proletariats of the Western nations during the slow process of industrialization begun in the nineteenth century.

Awareness of themselves as the have-not class, distinct from the have-all proprietors, dawned upon the workers of Europe in the mid-1800s and drew them together in the thousands and millions. Their self-identity smothered regional, religious and national differences, and they coalesced into a self-conscious force to launch the class struggle under the leadership of Marx. In 1850 there was no radio and no television. Milan was then twenty-four hours distant from Paris. Berlin was ten days from New York. Still the workers of the world did unite to a marked degree—psychologically, at first—into the socialist movement in short order.

Today any city in the world can be reached in twenty-four hours. Television not only enables all men to "see it now" and creates the feeling that "you are there"; it gives all the human family the sense that "we are here." The whole world becomes a new "here" which we all share. And, like the "here" of the nineteenth-century factory town, the new, worldwide "here" is divided into the rich and the poor. And the poor now realize it.

At this point another principal actor enters this universal drama: Communism, an atheism which makes this-world betterment a god unto itself, and which makes the secular state that god's prime minister and vicar upon earth, almighty, omnicompetent, infallible. Communism began cultivating the class consciousness of the factory-worker have-nots of the West a hundred years ago. Lenin stated repeatedly and eloquently that the two great inner contradictions which would wreck the nationalist capitalism of the West were the implacable opposition of interests: (1) between have-all proprietors and proletarian workers within each nation, and (2) between the industrialized nations and their have-not colonies supplying raw materials for Western factory systems. A secret of Communism's attraction is that it confidently proffers a complete overhaul of the whole worldwide economic system to cure these mortal flaws in the social body. Of course, painful and radical surgery is required to remove the abscesses and tumors caused by capitalism, and to eradicate the cause itself by collective ownership of the means of production.

The self-confidence of world Communism is now deeply shaken by the Moscow and Peking split—a split caused in great part by Lenin's contradiction number two. The Russian people are now wealthy compared to the two billions in other nations now striving to advance. The Russian rulers already possess much which they desire to conserve, more than they care to risk. In comparison, the Chinese have little to lose by risking war, and much to gain. A conflict has arisen between "Russia, which holds and keeps, and China, which needs to grow and take," in the words of General de Gaulle, February 1964. In the widening gap between rich and poor, Russia is now decidedly among the rich, on the other side, the "right side" of the tracks, a factory-owner dwelling among the great white houses on the hill in bourgeois power and splendor. To Peking's eyes this means Moscow has fallen into decadence, has betrayed the proletarian masses, and has forfeited her world leadership of the Communist revolution.

During 1964 the Chinese Communists formally accused Premier Khrushchev and Russian Communists of revisionism, of abandoning Marxist-Leninist doctrine, and of splitting asunder the world socialist camp. This could turn out to be a charge comparable in import and consequence to Luther's accusations against the Catholic Church in 1517, which launched the Reformation and rent Christianity for four bitter centuries. Peking's indictment against Moscow focuses on national egoism, manifested especially in Russia's international economic policy: "to force those fraternal [Marxist Socialist] countries which are comparatively backward economically to abandon industrialization and become their [Russia's] sources of raw materials and markets for surplus products." In other words, China charges that Russia strives to widen the gap between the rich nations and poor nations. To this end, worst of all,

> They collude with United States imperialism. . . .
> The leaders of the Communist Party of the Soviet Union have completely reversed enemies and comrades. They have directed the edge of the struggle, which should be against the United States imperialism and its lackeys, against the Marxist-Leninist fraternal parties and countries.
> The leaders of the Communist Party of the Soviet Union are bent on seeking Soviet-United States cooperation for the domination of the world.[1]

---

[1] From *Hung Chi*, the ideological journal of the Central Committee of the Chinese Communist Party, reported by Reuters from Peking, February 4, 1964, and reprinted by the New York *Times*, February 7, 1964.

Nailing down further the accusation that Russia is deliberately widening the gap between the affluent third and the proletarian two thirds of the world, the Chinese state that Russia justified its policy "in the name of 'international division of labor.'" Under this policy, poor nations supply muscle labor and raw materials, at depressed wages and prices, for industrialized nations to process through their skilled, high-wage labor and advanced technology. Then the rich nations sell their surplus manufactures to the oppressed nations at high prices, because the poor lack a countervailing force and bargaining power in global trade. In this way the Russians "attempt to turn them [the poor nations] into economic appendages."

> The leaders of the Communist Party of the Soviet Union pursue the policy of great-power chauvinism. . . . [They] obstruct and oppose the revolutionary struggles of other peoples and act as apologists for imperialism and neo-colonialism. . . .
>
> Every remark and every word of Khrushchev's are imperial edicts, however wrong or absurd they may be. All the fraternal parties must submissively listen and obey and are absolutely forbidden to criticize or oppose them.
>
> This is outright tyranny. It is the ideology of feudal autocrats, pure and simple. . . .
>
> Communists of the world, unite on the basis of Marxism-Leninism!

The widening gap becomes such a reality that, next to political survival, it is the major preoccupation of leaders within the poor nations, who are responsible for two thirds of the human family, and is usually the chief determinant in their relations abroad. Building up their national economies to provide basic food, schooling, medicines, transport and jobs to rapidly increasing families—mere sustenance, keeping body and soul together on the most elemental level—becomes the number-one "must." Technical skills, administrative and organizational know-how, machines and equipment to develop local raw materials and human resources must be imported for years and decades, until national development "takes off." Trade and aid must help provide these outside requirements for development.

II. THE CHURCH'S CONCERN

Why should the Church concern herself at all and grapple with these tangled issues? Why not leave these matters, so thoroughly of this-world, to statesmen and economists and engineers? Why does Pope John devote so much space to the rich nations-poor nations theme in his two major encyclicals?

It is because, as he and Pope Paul have stated repeatedly, hunger and human want constitute the number-one problem in the world today. And hunger, like disease and illiteracy, results from the lack of economic and social development, the inability to produce sufficient food, steel, electricity and transport to sustain healthy human life and, *a fortiori*, to realize "the fullness of a more excellent life."

The Pope as universal father must be concerned about all his children, and especially about those in dire need. As Pope John put it, while the Church has the special task of sanctifying souls and of enabling them to share heavenly blessings, as the mother and teacher of nations, "she is also solicitous for the requirements of men in their daily lives, not merely those related to food and sustenance, but also to their comfort and advancement in various kinds of goods in varying circumstances of time." (*Mater et Magistra,* par. 3.)

If the father of a family does not provide for his sick and hungry youngsters, if the pastor of the parish and bishop of the diocese make no effort to assist the needy, then they are roundly and rightly condemned. If the Church as a whole, the Body of Christ continued here on earth today, sent by God to all men, and professedly Catholic and universal, does not concern herself with the miserable of the world, then she too deserves the disdain of the rich and the hatred of the poor. Good Pope John cites the example of Christ, Who, on

seeing the hungry crowd, "was moved to exclaim sorrowfully 'I have compassion on the crowd.'" (Par. 4.)

Indeed, Christ has made our own personal compassion for
the hungry, sick and naked the norm by which each of us
individually will be judged on the Last Day. Saint John puts
the question bluntly: "Suppose that a man has the earthly
goods he needs, and sees his brother go in want; if he steels
his heart against his brother, how can we say that the love
of God dwells in him?" (Knox Translation, I John 3:17.)
Pope John earned the respect of the rich and the love of the
poor by the breadth of his embrace for all God's children:

> Perhaps the most pressing question of our day concerns
> the relation between economically advanced common-
> wealths and those that are in process of development. The
> former enjoy the conveniences of life; the latter experience
> dire poverty. Yet, today men are so intimately associated
> in all parts of the world that they feel, as it were, as if
> they are members of one and the same household.
>
> Therefore, the nations that enjoy a sufficiency and abun-
> dance of everything may not overlook the plight of other
> nations whose citizens experience such domestic problems
> that they are all but overcome by poverty and hunger, and
> are not able to enjoy basic human rights. This is all the
> more so, inasmuch as countries each day seem to become
> more dependent on each other. [Par. 157.]

This passage parallels in marked degree the basic statements by Leo XIII in 1891 on *The Condition of Labor*
(*Rerum Novarum*), and by Pius XI forty years later on *Reconstructing the Social Order* (*Quadragesimo Anno*). The
big difference is that Leo and Pius were addressing themselves to the national economies of the "Christian" West,
while Pope John now opens his embrace to all peoples of the
world. He is concerned with social justice not only within the
nation, but among all nations.

The pastor of a slum parish in New York, Paris or London

knows firsthand that, next to outright hunger, slum living conditions are the most oppressive external affront to human dignity, contributing to many other evils of disease, frustration, promiscuity and crime. He rejoices when his people can acquire improved homes. Diocesan and national Catholic social action departments applaud and support construction of reasonably priced housing, whether publicly or privately financed. The Holy Father considers sorrowfully the slums, not only of New York's Harlem, Rome's Trastevere and Paris' *banlieux,* but of the whole world: Hong Kong and Calcutta, Lima's *barriadas* and Africa's *bidonvilles*. He knows and feels the misery of the dirty, scabby babies, the anxiety of the drained-out mothers, the debilitating apathy or boiling frustration of unemployed fathers.

The Pope praises the efforts of governments, international bodies and private agencies to provide housing, schooling, medicine, work and justice to his hundreds of millions of spiritual children of all nations. Small wonder that Popes John and Paul have moved toward the sharing of pastoral responsibility with the whole college of bishops, so that all pastor-apostles can feed the worldwide flock with spiritual and material bread, concern and care. Consciousness of the pains, tears and wrongs of all the human family has become a cross which no one but Christ Himself could bear alone. And so the popes now seek to share it.

Small wonder, too, that John and Paul VI voice constant encouragement to the agencies, governmental and private, which strive to feed the hungry and care for the stricken, to supply housing for the shanty-dwellers, honest work and just wages to the breadwinners of the world.

However, citizens of the United States show increasing signs of tiredness in the vast task of helping the poor of the world. Foreign aid began as a postwar emergency. Twenty years after the Second World War, rebellion continues in Vietnam and in the new African states. Indonesia threatens Malaysia, India and Pakistan still glower at each other over

Kashmir, the Israelis and the Arabs remain at odds. Castro stays on and penetrates other Latin nations with commando saboteurs and plotters, the *coup d'état* recurs in Latin America. If the prime purpose of foreign aid is the begetting of economic and social improvement to undergird peace, then foreign aid must be failing, because there is no peace. Such is the growing opinion, voiced ever more strongly.

This American frustration is tellingly manifested by many Congressmen, who strive to reduce the annual aid appropriations, with little objection from most of their constituents or, indeed, at their behest. Catholics, while hearing the exhortations of Popes John and Paul to extend help to the developing peoples, follow the same pattern of indifference. Papal teaching on world social justice makes little discernible impact upon the American faithful as a whole.

There was strong citizen support for the Marshall Plan, even great pride in its conception and motives. Perhaps the difference is that the rebuilding of ravaged Europe required only six years, while the upbuilding of the developing nations must go on for many decades. Do Americans lack stamina? or understanding? Europe already had all the technical and managerial skills, patterns and habits of organization needed for its rise from the wreckage. The Industrial Revolution, after all, began in Europe over a century ago. But the fermenting continents lack these technical and administrative skills above all. Revolutionary changes in social structure and psychology must precede their acquisition.

In short, Africa, Asia and Latin America present problems of dimension qualitatively different from postwar Europe, and quantitatively of much greater magnitude. From the angle of numbers alone, the population of the countries receiving Marshall aid was only 350 million as compared with the 2000 million in the developing continents today. We must also remember the 4000 million they will number by the year 2000, the date by which their industrial development might approach the halfway mark. By quantitative comparison alone, today's development demands dwarf those of the Marshall Plan. Still, the exertion by the United States remains much less generous and quite unrealistic.

The Marshall Plan was launched in 1948–51, with economic aid expenditures amounting to 1.7 percent of our gross national product and 11.5 percent of our total federal budget. In 1962–64, economic nonmilitary assistance amounted to only 0.4 percent of gross national product and about 2.2 percent of our federal budget. Today, we are exerting less than one fourth the aid effort we exerted for Western Europe, despite the fact that we must help five times more people, most of whom are beginning from scratch. The current U.S. expenditure for defense and arms is twenty-five times that for economic assistance.

It may well be that we Americans find it easier to make sacrifices for Europeans than we do for non-Caucasians. This is understandable from a narrow, old-fashioned, non-Christian point of view. About 90 percent of the citizens of the United States are of European ethnic origin, and many still have family ties in Europe. Bonds of language, culture, and social and political institutions—and, above all, the bonds of religion, Christian and Jewish—cement Europe and America into the solidarity we call the West. These factors make a visit to Europe, for most of us, a return to the old family homestead.

So, in a very true sense, the Marshall Plan was not *foreign* aid at all. It was all in the family—one member of the family helping a relative to rebuild his burned-down house, a home which we occasionally shared and helped to burn down. Besides these personal motives, American taxpayers could also understand clearly in 1948 the personal threat of a hundred Russian divisions poised in Germany, dramatized by the Berlin blockade, and the calamity of Communist Parties, made ever stronger by hunger and unemployment, taking over West Germany, France and Italy. So, aid to Europe in 1948 was also aid to ourselves, more clearly than can be shown and *felt* with respect to Africa, Asia and Latin America. Europe, after all, was the heartland of our interests and origins.

On the other hand, the peoples and nations of the three developing continents are, by comparison, strangers and outsiders to the extended family which forms the Judaeo-Christian-Hellenic West. This applies even to the one tenth of the United States population who are Negroes, because for two hundred years they have been severed from their African roots and have assimilated the ways of the West, however harsh the refusal of the West to assimilate them.

It does seem hard for most persons to grasp that the interests and destiny of the world outside the West are so closely linked to our own that their betterment and peace contribute significantly to our betterment and peace. So far the case is not yet clear, not sufficiently convincing, to beget feeling, motives, action and *stamina* for a long, hard pull. How few of the Catholics of America and of Europe respond in any meaningful way to the pleas of Pius, of John, and of Paul to realize the new physical reality of one worldwide household, the psychological fact of world consciousness and of one human family. How few, even among the successors of the Apostles, show full commitment to the universal common good and international social justice—at least, judging from the relative apathy toward sacrifices for overseas assistance. But criticism must be restrained; it has all happened so quickly.

The present awakening to the collegiality of the bishops—that with Peter and Paul all bishops partake of the anxieties and cares of the whole Church—will help to open wide their ears to the cries of all. Clergy and laity now awaken to the new world "we," in and out of the Church. Support for more adequate exertions for overseas development, in both the temporal and spiritual spheres, more in keeping with our affluency and the scope of the need and the call of Christ, will surely be generated by Vatican II and its follow-up.

International aid and trade, for social and economic development, is an area of joint concern par excellence in which all Christians can unite—indeed, all Christians and Jews, as well as the other transcendental faiths. But Christians have a special responsibility because of their dominance in the industrial West, where eyes and hearts and purses must be opened. Purses, because ours are so swollen by comparison.

The free nations of Africa, Asia and Latin America number about 1400 million persons. To restate the case, they receive an annual gross national product of about $150 per capita. Based on the gross national product of 1964, citizens of the United States and Canada receive over $3000 per capita. North Americans are twenty times wealthier than the poor of the free world. In Western Europe the gross national product runs about $1300 per capita, and continues to rise.

The moral issue now becomes acute because communications, transport and know-how have attained satisfactory levels to make development feasible. Economic and social development on a world scale is now "do-able." About 1850, European observers, Marx among them, came to see that industrial techniques and production had reached a point where human misery was no longer endurable, that social justice could be realized on a national scale. Catholic leaders such as Harmel, Von Ketteler, Manning, Gibbons, and Leo XIII awoke to the new reality in the 1880s. As usual in the modern world, we were late, but only by a generation. In the 1950s much of the West began to understand that human want must be attacked everywhere—not only within the clan, within the nation, within the West. Pius XII began voicing this moral imperative, which John and Paul have sought, and now seek, to embody through national and international structures, private and governmental.

Perhaps effective Catholic moral support for world social justice will not be quite as tardy as was Catholic moral support for national social justice. Perhaps the *aggiornamento* will indeed begin.

III. Aid to the Poorer Peoples

A. *Governmental Programs*

Basically, the rich nations assist the economic and social development of the poor nations in five ways. First, outright grants of funds, materials, or technical personnel are made by governmental or nongovernmental bodies. Secondly, "soft" loans are provided on noncommercial terms, i.e., at low interest rates and with a long repayment period. Thirdly, "hard" loans on commercial terms are supplied, in keeping with the going world money market, by private lending firms or by governmental bodies.

The fourth basic type of development assistance is by investment for capital formation within the poorer nation. This capital investment provides the equipment and the plant and technical skills needed to build new factories and improve land, to modernize and expand existing plants and transport facilities. This new investment may come from private interests seeking a profit return, or through a bilateral arrangement between two governments, or from investment funds brought together by several governments through multilateral agencies established for this purpose.

A fifth way in which rich nations assist poor nations is by trading with them. Raw products, usually agricultural or extracted from the earth, are sold by the poor countries to the industrialized nations. This trade generates funds with which the less-developed regions can purchase from the affluent nations the equipment and techniques needed to build up their productive capacity by advancing their industrialization.

Development assistance most often entails combinations of these five basic categories. There are many further refinements. For example, certain types of private loans or investment might be insured or guaranteed by the government of the private source against certain risks, like expropriation, civil strife or inflation. If a government or an intergovernmental body makes loans or grants to private business, educational or social groups in a developing country, approval of the government of the receiving country is usually required, or some type of national institute is set up to channel resources to nongovernmental institutions.

An example of such combinations would be a "soft" loan (at 4 percent interest and 30-year payback) of $10 million made by the Inter-American Development Bank (an intergovernmental body whose board of directors represents the United States and all the Latin American countries except Cuba) to the Housing Corporation of Chile (Corporation de Viviendas, CORVI, a national governmental body). CORVI, in turn, makes a loan of $2 million to a savings and loan association, privately owned and directed. This might be accompanied by another loan to the savings and loan association for housing by the pension fund of a United States labor union or business corporation; this loan is insured by the United States Government.

CORVI, the Chilean Government's housing agency, might make a second loan of $1 million to the Institute for Low-Cost Housing (Instituto de Viviendas Populares Caritas, INVICA), which is a nongovernmental organization for promoting housing cooperatives. Then INVICA channels loans of $30–$50 thousand to twenty cooperatives of twenty-five to fifty families each—cooperatives which INVICA has developed and now assists with planning, building and financial services.

INVICA, in fact, functions in this manner in collaboration with CORVI, the Inter-American Development Bank, and many other bodies, private and governmental. INVICA was set up in 1960 with a basic grant of $1 million from Catholic Relief Services, National Catholic Welfare Conference, the official agency of the bishops of the United States for social welfare and socioeconomic development overseas. The $1 million granted INVICA by our American overseas agency became available through a collection taken up in the Catholic churches of the United States for rehabilitation of earthquake victims of Chile in 1960. Food, medicines and services valued at $3 million were made available, with United States assistance, to help meet emergency needs. One million dollars was channeled through INVICA to form and to service housing associations. These now have lending resources totaling $11 million and have already supplied new homes to more than 2000 slum families.

Economic development means an increase in the capacity to produce more food and iron, more shoes, housing, electricity and transport. This advance requires new equipment and plant (capital formation) which can produce these basic items, and more technical and administrative know-how to run the factories and improved farms, as well as the transport facilities (railroads, truck fleets, ports), and commercial and finance systems (wholesalers, stores, cooperatives, banks, credit unions, administration, tax collection, etc.). All this requires ever higher levels of health, education and, above all, political stability.

In the past decade American assistance has gone to 70 countries in which 1300 million people live. Of these, 65 percent are illiterate. Less than one third of school-age children are in classrooms. Less than 2 percent complete high school. Education, therefore, is the largest single component of U.S. technical assistance.

For instance, 40 percent of all American aid to Nigeria has gone into education. Since 1960 the Agency for International Development (AID), through contracts with four universities (University of California in Los Angeles, Michigan State, Indiana, and Ohio) helped Nigeria to reorganize and update the country's educational system. The University of Nigeria was organized into a land-grant institution for research and practical training to prepare agronomists, teachers, public administrators and managers for the nation's expanding business and industry. Enrollment jumped from 220 in October 1960 to 1500 in 1964.

Secondary schools were converted into multipurpose units for vocational and technical training as well as academic subjects. Over a hundred Peace Corps volunteers teach in these schools. The American university teams gave advanced training to 150 faculty members who are now instructing 5000 prospective primary teachers in 35 normal colleges. The American educators also work out of 20 field centers to upgrade experienced primary teachers by in-service training.

In the Philippines, AID also concentrated on education. During a ten-year program ending in 1962, American technical assistance brought about the near doubling of vocational training, from 38,000 to 71,000 trainees. The national budget of the Philippines increased appropriations for vocational education by more than fifteen times, from 2 million to 31 million pesos. AID invested $6.8 million to upgrade 41 agricultural schools, 3 agricultural colleges and 35 trade and industrial schools. To relieve a critical textbook shortage, AID is financing paper imports and technical know-how to print 25 million new textbooks by 1965.

To stimulate classroom construction in Guatemala, AID agreed to supply $1½ million to cover one third the cost, provided the Guatemalan Government paid one third and local communities the other third. Villagers and slum dwellers pitched in with their own labor, local materials and a little cash to provide 48 percent of the cost instead of the expected 33 percent. Between 1961 and December 1963, over 400 schools with 2000 classrooms were constructed at a cost to the United States of $1½ million, or roughly the cost of one high school in our country.

While most AID grants are given to advance public school systems, some assistance is also given to private and church-related institutions. During 1962–64 an AID contract with Saint Louis University provided $396,000 to the Catholic University of Ecuador for laboratory equipment and faculty in order to update the teaching of chemistry and physics. In the same period, grants of $575,000 were made to the Institute for Rural Education (IRE) in Chile, a system of twenty training centers for rural men and women, from which a hundred county agents radiate to supervise adult training groups and demonstration plots in a thousand distant villages. This Institute grew out of the Young Christian Farmer movement ten years ago, and, while retaining its religious inspiration, is now directed by a lay board. A third church-related institution to receive American governmental assistance is Louvanium University in the Congo. Grants of $409,000 have been made to tide over this sole center of higher learning for the Congo's 18 million people during the chaotic years since 1960. To impart technical skills to the Congolese, AID has also made grants of $2¼ million to the Protestant-related training institute, through a contract with an American-based association, the Agricultural and Technical Assistance Foundation, Inc.

AID operates at times through private, specialized organizations like U.S. savings and loan associations, to impart know-how for adapting this well-proven system for housing finance and promotion to underdeveloped areas. AID also works with American labor leaders for trade union development overseas and has contracts of some $500,000 with the Cooperative League in Chicago, and contracts of $1 million with the Credit Union National Association, Madison, Wisconsin, to train co-op leaders and supervisors in a score of countries. Usury pervades the poor areas of the world, making the poor poorer and the rich richer from interest rates of 10 percent a week, 50 percent a year, and more. The fifty cooperative specialists now operating overseas under these AID contracts work hand in hand with pioneers like Father Daniel McLellan in Peru and Sister Gabriella in Korea, and often build upon the beginnings laid down by them. Both are American Maryknollers whose influence in the cooperative field of social development now extends over much of Latin America and the Far East.

Parents want their family to have schooling, better housing, habits of thrift and protection from thievery through usury, and the chance to associate with their neighbors for their joint progress through cooperatives and labor and peasants' unions. AID helps nations to build up national systems, governmental and private, to accomplish just that, as these random samples have shown. Above all, mother and father want their children to enjoy good health, a major component of "the fullness of a more excellent life" that Pope John desires, in the name of the Church and of Christ, for all God's children.

Until a decade ago, malaria was the world's worst illness, as measured in number of cases, degree and length of debilitation, and deaths. In 1955 the World Health Organization initiated a worldwide campaign to eradicate malaria. AID has been a major participant, spending, for instance, in 1962 about half its health budget of $59 million on DDT, vehicles, laboratories and training to help stamp out the scourge. The results come through dramatically in India, which in 1953 recorded 1 million deaths from malaria from more than 75 million cases. Conservatively, these 75 million cases caused a loss of more than 1 billion man-days of work. Illness entails heavy loss in economic production, as well as personal pain and added misery for the family.

In the decade since 1953, about $258 million has been spent on malaria eradication in India. Of this, the Indian Government put up $98 million, the World Health Organization $2.6 million, and the United States $158 million. Of this last figure, $89 million was in rupees resulting from the sale of U.S. surplus food to India under Public Law 480. (This aspect of the Food for Peace program will be discussed later.) The cash contribution in American dollars came to $69 million.

In 1953, malaria cases accounted for 11 percent of all diseases in India; by 1961, this had fallen to 1 percent. By overcoming absenteeism, work output has increased notably in the coal mines, and railroad and irrigation construction, formerly delayed for decades in malarious areas, is proceeding apace. Previously, in tea-growing Assam and West Bengal, 20 to 25 percent of the people reported sick with chills and fever each month during the height of the picking season. Now the disease has all but disappeared. In one large area of 150 million persons, only 2500 cases of malaria were found in 1962, as compared with 25 million before the campaign.

When Guatemala undertook a malaria eradication program in 1957, more than 73 percent of its area was malarious; 300,000 cases, about one tenth the population, were reported annually. In one afflicted area, agricultural output was compared before and after treatment with American assistance. In 1957, more than 30 percent of the people were infected; in five years this figure dropped to less than 3 percent, one tenth the earlier rate. Land under cultivation quadrupled, the value of farm output in the region increased fifty times, terrain formerly uninhabitable was opened to clearance and settlement.

In the Philippines, $5 million of United States aid for DDT, spray equipment and technical services helped reduce malaria in the past decade from 2 million cases and 31,000 deaths to 10,000 cases and 1700 deaths. In Taiwan the toll has fallen from 1.2 million cases in 1950 to only 61 cases and no deaths from malaria in 1961.

Brazil launched its eradication program in 1960 with the spraying of 634,000 houses. In 1964 nearly all homes in Brazil's afflicted areas were sprayed, some 4.2 million family units. In São Paulo, the industrial center of Brazil, and hence the most advanced city, 12 percent of the population contracted malaria in 1960. This figure fell to 1.4 percent after two years of treatment. The U.S. contribution to the Brazil campaign has been $11 million; the government of Brazil contributed $14 million.

Little ones freed of fever, babies' racking chills subsiding, children going to school, fathers able to work, mothers sighing in relief—by the hundreds of millions. This is the heart of foreign aid which mothers and fathers, pastors and preachers in the well-fed, immunized West can easily forget. And understandably so, in the welter of our own concerns, in the anonymity of statistics and graphs, in the counter-charges of partisan political debate, in the deluge of frustrating headlines and TV reports. The issues of the day have broadened to such scope and complexity that the reach of the citizen's mind, the fibers of his heart for feeling and compassion, and the power of the Word to motivate millions to grasp duties and to meet challenges unimagined till now— must all be expanded beyond the boundaries of nation and cultural enclave.

The citizen of this new world must become a new man. The Christian in this new world must grow to new dimensions, fit the size of the new job to be done. Loving one's neighbor does stretch the soul when the world becomes one neighborhood.

Through the control of malaria, the setting up of pure water systems and other health measures, foreign aid has saved the lives of hundreds of millions in the past decade. These now require new housing, additional schoolrooms and teachers by the millions. Cured of chills and fever, and feeling fresh strength, parents can do more work. Overcoming the millennial bonds of chronic illness and near serfdom, they seek more freedom and higher wages. They forsake rural feudalism and flood the cities in search of the better life. They demand jobs which do not exist, because new factories and transport multiply more slowly than do people.

The sinews of economic development—factories, transport, commerce—grow slowly because of lack of sufficient investment for building new plants and equipment. Investment comes from annual savings over consumption. To accumulate savings the citizens of a country, willingly or by governmental control, must refrain from consuming a substantial part of their annual produce. But since the average annual product runs to only $150 per capita, most of this and more must be consumed to sustain life at the barest human level. Savings are necessarily minimal. Since banking systems are primitive, reaching but few people, even these slight savings seldom enter the money channels which buy the stocks and bonds to beget private capital investment. So new factories and transport depend heavily on governmental or foreign investment.

Only meager funds for governmental investment can come from taxes, which already generate so little income that educational, health and normal administrative needs cannot be met. The government and private firms of the developing country derive income from the sale of ores, oil or agricultural produce to other nations; but most raw materials of this primary type now glut the world market, so prices have been falling steadily over the last decade. The hard currency of the West (dollars, pounds, marks, francs), for which the poor nations sell their raw materials, is used to buy machinery and technical services for new factories and transport—new jobs for new people. These manufactures, made by highly paid labor, are sold by the affluent West, Japan and Russia at prices which have been steadily rising. So the ability of developing nations to finance their own economic advance has been falling accordingly. And as more people in village and slum awaken to the promise of a better life and better jobs, which are not forthcoming, riots and demonstrations, *coups d'état* and revolutions ignite and explode.

This political instability and civil strife create a climate of inordinate risk, which not only reduces foreign private investment by the rich nations, but also induces landowners and the wealthy within the poor nations to sneak out their own private investment funds into North America and Western Europe. Over $4 billion of this "flight capital" from Latin America is invested in the United States; between $5 and $15 billion in the affluent West—also making the rich richer.

For these reasons governmental foreign aid increasingly

goes beyond technical assistance and into the much more
complex fields of international trade and investment for overseas development. Education, health, housing, social service
and technical training must synchronize with these more fundamental issues.

At a time when many citizens of the United States have
become frustrated with our aid program and swing the annual
appropriations ax with self-righteous gusto, other industrialized nations, now recovered from the war, are entering the
field. During 1962 alone, five countries set up new organizations for administering assistance. Norway now levies a separate tax to finance foreign aid. Denmark matches government
funds with a national fund-raising drive. Britain, France,
Belgium and the Netherlands, who have long rendered assistance to their former colonies, have radically revamped their
policies and methods to fit the era of African and Asian independence. While Germany, Italy, Japan and Canada lack
similar colonial continuity with the poor nations, they too
have established assistance programs. Germany has recognized the substantial character of this new function of modern government by setting up a cabinet ministry to supervise
activities in some forty countries.

In 1960, these countries of Western Europe, together with
the United States, Canada, and Japan, formed the Development Assistance Committee (DAC). DAC does not have resources of its own. It seeks to influence the level and use of
funds from the member countries. Headquartered in Paris,
DAC is a lineal descendant of the Marshall Plan. Through
it the affluent nations of the free world join hands in the
arduous, far-reaching challenge of helping less privileged
peoples attain in freedom "the fullness of a more excellent
life."

Frank Coffin, now U.S. representative to DAC in Paris
and former deputy administrator of AID in Washington, observes hopefully: "The very countries which were thought to
be lost causes in that remote Senate debate in 1948 [over

the Marshall Plan] have now banded together for a task immeasurably greater."[2]

The nations composing DAC—the United States, Canada, Japan and the countries of Western Europe—provided aid of about $6 billion a year from 1961 to 1964. This is over twelve times the rate of aid from the Russians and Chinese, which ran about $450 million in 1962.

Of the Free World's total in 1962, the United States contributed $3.6 billion for economic assistance and our allies gave $2.4 billion, a ratio of 60 to 40. But $1.6 billion of American aid was in surplus food, and total U.S. funds amounted to under $2 billion. In 1964, Congressional appropriations for the United States aid program fell to $3 billion, a drastic cut from the $4½ billion requested by the Kennedy and Johnson administrations. It must be carefully noted that one third of the $3 billion goes for military aid and armament to our overseas allies, leaving $2 billion for economic and technical assistance. This amount to ⅓ of 1 percent of our gross national product, based on the 1964 GNP of $600 billion. Only 1/300th of America's GNP is spent for economic and social assistance to the 2 billion human beings in the poor nations. This includes the $116 million appropriated in 1964 for international organizations and programs. The United States also gives over $1½ billion annually in surplus food. Though extremely valuable to the hungry receiver, such gifts do not demand great sacrifice from a country with huge stockpiles of grain, the mere storage of which costs over $1 million a day.

France's economic aid, amounting to $879 million in 1962, more than trebles that of the United States on the basis of per capita percent of gross national product. Britain, Portugal and Belgium also carry heavier per capita loads.

[2] Frank Coffin, *Witness for AID* (Boston: Houghton Mifflin, 1964), p. 193. The writer is indebted to Mr. Coffin for insights into AID operations derived from his book and from personal dealings with him and his staff over a three-year period.

British bilateral assistance reached $386 million in 1963 and $500 million in 1964, more than double the figure for 1957. However, the United States citizen carries heavier tax loads for the military defense of the Free World. American expenditure for armament consumes 9 percent of our gross national product, compared to 5 percent among our industrialized partners.

The significant point is that countries other than the United States increased their overseas assistance by 112 percent between 1956 and 1961, and it is still increasing. Frank Coffin, the U.S. representative to Western European nations on foreign aid matters, rightly notes that the long-term upward trend shows "a growing consensus that assistance to developing countries is an essential instrument of modern foreign policy."

Besides these bilateral programs of individual governments, international organizations also engage in aid activities. The United Nations has the broadest composition, with 112 member nations. It helps nations to make surveys of resources and to plan projects through its Special Fund. The United Nations Technical Assistance Program operates through its specialized agencies like the World Health Organization (WHO) in Geneva; the United Nations Educational, Social, and Cultural Organization (UNESCO) in Paris; the Food and Agriculture Organization (FAO) in Rome; and the International Labor Organization (ILO) in Geneva. The two last-named bodies were singled out for special praise by Pope John in *Christianity and Social Progress* (*Mater et Magistra,* pars. 103, 156). The Holy See is represented in the United Nations, New York, and in its specialized agencies by permanent observers, as well as by *ad hoc* delegations as required. The Holy Father makes an annual token contribution to their budgets as a gesture of moral support and solidarity.

The United Nations also supervises the International Bank for Rehabilitation and Development (IBRD), popularly known as the World Bank, which makes "hard" loans for development, and its subsidiary, the International Development Association (IDA), which makes "soft" development loans, that is, at interest rates and payback terms less demanding than those offered in the commercial money market. Ninety member governments are its shareholders.

Between 1946, when it began operations, and 1963, the World Bank made 349 loans totaling $7 billion to 64 member countries and territories. These loans are financing projects in developing nations to increase production, raise living standards and contribute to a better balance in world trade. The four largest categories of World Bank lending are: electric power, $2335 million; transportation, $2260 million; industrial development, $1130 million; and agriculture, $530 million. The World Bank also mobilized $1600 million additional capital from private sources by selling parts of its loans to rich-nation financiers.

The Persian Empire, which Athens turned back at Thermopylae in 480 B.C., was fed from lands irrigated by dams and canals which interlace present-day Iran. By the time of Christ this historic granary of the old civilized world had become largely desert through war and civil strife. A World Bank loan of $42 million completed in 1963 the 600-foot-high Dez Dam. The water, wasted for the past two thousand years, now generates electric power and irrigates a 50,000-acre agricultural pilot project involving 12,000 people in 53 villages. After soil recovery and farming methods prove out, this agricultural development will increase to 225,000 acres.

In Nigeria, Africa's most populous nation, a loan of $28 million has built a 400-mile railroad into the agricultural interior. A second loan of $14 million is now constructing new shipping piers and loading cranes in the main port of Lagos.

The 18,000-foot Andes Mountains have for four centuries cut off Bogotá, the capital of Colombia, from her Atlantic ports of Cartagena and Barranquilla. A World Bank loan of $76 million helped finance the 500-mile railroad which now pierces these geographical barriers, cutting freight rates by half. Additional loans to this key Latin country include $67 million for highways, $10 million to import tractors and earth-moving equipment, and $155 million for power stations which harness the power potential of the Andes torrents. These are some of the best reasons why Colombia, after a decade of civil strife which has claimed 300,000 lives, now enjoys a rate of economic growth which makes it one of the best hopes on that fermenting continent.

Multilateral aid programs, besides those sponsored by United Nations bodies, include the Colombo Plan, drawn up by a committee composed of present and former members of the British Commonwealth, plus the United States. This amalgam of both developed and developing nations handles only technical assistance of modest scope in South and Southeast Asia. It provides principally an annual forum for exchange on common problems and improved planning of the bilateral programs of the associated nations.

The Common Market (European Economic Community, EEC), while composed of six nations each with its own aid programs, has also begun to function like the political unit it will become. The Common Market has established its own Fund for Economic Development (FED), which has provided $730 million for loans and grants, largely in Africa, between 1963 and 1968. This approaches an Alliance for Progress between the old colonial powers of Europe and the new nations of Africa.

The United States and nineteen other American republics established the Alliance for Progress in 1961, with extremely ambitious ten-year aims for economic development and social progress. A net increase in national production of 2.5 percent a year, net above population growth, would be brought about through the massive injection of $100 billion for capital formation and social betterment in one decade. Basic structural reforms of society would be undertaken simultaneously. Latin American sources were expected to supply $80 billion for development. Outside funds were to total $20 billion for investments, loans and grants, about half from the United States and from the rest of the Free World. The Alliance for Progress was forged by the Kennedy administration as the principal response to the human misery and social injustice which spawned the rise of Castroism throughout the hemisphere. President Kennedy gave his fullest official support and much personal attention and prestige to this "New Deal" for Latin America. In like manner, President Johnson committed himself wholeheartedly to the Alliance.

A principal instrument of the Alliance has been the Inter-American Development Bank (IADB), which antedates the Kennedy-sponsored "peaceful revolution." President Eisenhower actually anticipated the Alliance in the last months of his administration with the Act of Bogotá, which in July 1960 promised $500 million for a social progress fund. Having been set up by the United States and the Latin American republics in 1960, largely under the stimulus of leaders like President Juscelino Kubitschek of Brazil, IADB began operations a year later with a capital of $960 million. Of this, $450 million was supplied by the United States, the rest by the nineteen other members, all the Latin American nations except Cuba. By 1963 the Bank authorized development loans of $620 million. It has taken on the added responsibility of administering the Social Progress Fund of the Alliance.

This Social Progress Fund, with U.S. appropriations of $394 million for the first year and $135 million in 1964, gives the Bank powers far different from traditional banking practice. It makes loans in nonprofit fields like education, sanitation, water supply and agrarian reform. These state functions are usually financed in industrial countries by selling bond issues to the public, which are redeemed by taxes during ensuing decades. In the poor countries these public needs cannot be met by such methods. The bonds are not purchased by private investors, principally because the risk of forfeiture looms too great amidst today's social and political strife. So the screaming agitation of mothers and fathers for schooling, pure drinking water, slum clearance, jobs, land reform, health and welfare services frustrates the normal channels for providing this "fullness of a more excellent life." New private finance must evolve. New institutions must be created to satisfy these needs.

The Inter-American Development Bank, in Washington, D.C., is managed almost entirely by Latin Americans, under a seven-man board of directors. Of these, only one is appointed by the United States. He, however, exercises 40 percent of the voting power. The Bank's successful operation under the presidency of Felipe Herrera, a 43-year-old Chilean, has generated such confidence in traditional banking circles that in 1962 bond issues of $99 million were sold to a consortium of Italian bankers and United States private financiers. In 1964 a third offering to the public of $50 million in 20-year bonds at 4½ percent interest was made through a United States syndicate of 102 banking houses, and was quickly bought up. In 1964 the twenty member countries announced that the Bank's authorized capital stock would be increased to $2150 million, more than doubling its original capitalization.

Besides its Alliance aid through the Inter-American Development Bank, the United States appropriated $455 million for development assistance to Latin America in 1964. Formation of a Central American Common Market and a free trade association including most of South America rounds out this ambitious hemispheric undertaking.

The Alliance for Progress, however, has encountered so many difficulties since 1961 that drastic overhauling has been repeatedly called for. Principally, it is thought that the Alliance too often stumbled and vacillated because it lacked an over-all executive body, and that it failed to inspire confidence in Latin America because Alliance authority was too tightly held by the United States. The Latin nations as a whole did not undertake the basic structural reforms of land tenure, tax and profit systems, education and social betterment which the 150 million Latin poor now demand. To redress these defects, a five-man Inter-American Committee of the Alliance for Progress (ICAP) was appointed in 1964, with Carlos Sanz de Santamaria of Colombia as chairman. It is hoped that this broadly based executive authority will generate among Latin citizens, political parties and governments some degree of self-identification with the Alliance, and also will generate a political appeal and ideological *élan* which the far-ranging "peaceful revolution" has lacked thus far.

Despite criticism and the mounting social unrest which brought on the forceful overthrow of the governments in six Latin American countries in 1962–64, the Alliance has made progress. During its first two years, the Alliance has been directly responsible for building 140,000 homes, 8200 classrooms and 900 hospitals and health centers; the installation of 700 community water systems; the granting of 160,000 loans to farmers; the printing of 4 million textbooks. Such concrete achievements have not changed the face of the continent. Far from it. Though these advances are slight, they are nevertheless symbols for millions of poor people—for centuries so lethargic, now suddenly so demanding—that changes are underway.[3]

The most significant of these are basic social reforms. In some countries beginnings are being made toward land-tenure and agrarian reforms, profit-sharing and tax reforms, and other structural changes that will revolutionize the economic system. In most countries a growing number of property holders and industrial and commercial magnates are beginning to admit the need for basic reforms. In all countries the have-not slum dwellers, farm hands and sharecroppers are beginning to forge their own countervailing forces—unions,

[3] See *The Winds of Revolution,* by Tad Szulc (New York: Praeger, 1963), especially pp. 233–81.

neighborhood associations, cooperatives, and peasant leagues —to marshal the power within their nations, until now so divided and weak. And political parties are beginning to mount reform legislative and action programs for all the people. Romulo Betancourt, president of Venezuela until 1964, and Eduardo Frei, leader of Chile's Christian Democratic Party, best personify these advances. With evolutionary changes of its own, the Alliance for Progress offers an acceptable inter-American relationship for the upbuilding of social democracy on a regional scale. This gives reason for guarded hope and for full support of this "New Deal" for Latin America's millions, who must live in misery for the long years and decades required to realize a program of such magnitude and complexity.

Funds and food make up about 90 percent of the dollar value of bilateral aid. The remaining 10 percent pays for personnel who bring skills and administrative know-how into the developing countries. These carriers of technical assistance transmit their professional knowledge and experience to colleagues overseas. After their assigned tour of duty, usually two to four years, they leave behind them trained teachers, administrators, health and other specialists; improved methods for cultivating fields, census taking, eradicating disease, collecting taxes, keeping accounts, and planning for development; new institutions, laws, cooperatives, credit unions, banks, workers' unions, housing associations, schools, hospitals.

The DAC nations—Western Europe, Japan, Canada and the United States—maintain some 65,000 specialists overseas. The Communist countries maintain about 10,000 experts. The Communist nations also receive some 15,000 students into the bloc from the developing continents. The DAC countries officially sponsor some 40,000 students and trainees, with some 100,000 more under the auspices of nongovernmental bodies. Including the 9000 Peace Corps volunteers, the United States supplies only about one fifth of the 75,000 field personnel in development assistance in Africa, Asia and Latin America. France, for instance, in 1962, provided 29,-260 teachers to the fourteen countries of Africa which were formerly her colonies. Britain and Belgium provide proportionate numbers in their old territories.

The Peace Corps of the United States fulfills a unique role, at village and slum levels, in forty-five countries. The volunteers personalize relations between the mighty colossus of the West and flesh-and-blood humans in concrete situations on a people-to-people basis. Their contribution to human understanding and solidarity cannot, however, replace the more impersonal technicians supplied at a higher level by universities, governmental departments and private institutions. These affect the whole structure of the developing nation in a particular field, in a way and of a scope beyond the competence and intent of the Peace Corps volunteer, who is usually young (averaging twenty-four years of age) and relatively inexperienced. For instance, some 1400 volunteers work in agricultural extension and rural community action in Latin America. But their impact is principally at the level of market towns and county seats. To build up rural extension services and agricultural university systems comparable to those of the United States, which account for our superabundant food production, forty-year-old faculty members from Cornell and Iowa State and veteran extension specialists from Wisconsin and Oklahoma are required. Or their peers from other countries. To build up national systems for development these experienced researchers and administrators must deal with researchers and administrators, actual or potential, in the developing countries, and not only with village mayors and barely literate peasant leaders as the Peace Corps does.

In short, the idealistic Peace Corps is surprisingly successful, at the community level, in generating grassroots inspiration, cooperative self-help and broad human solidarity. But it cannot substitute for the more prosaic, institution-building role of the realistic technician among the budding bureaus, business and governmental, of the developing continents.

The application of technology to the production of more food and housing, to the promotion of better health and schooling, requires more industry and commerce, bigger government and better bureaucracies, public and private. In a word, the upper-level aid technician must build up social-ization in the sense intended by Pope John: "the multiplica-tion of social relationships, that is, a daily more complex interdependence of citizens, introducing into their lives and activities many and varied forms of association." Pope John defends the good resulting from these "bureaucracies," pub-lic and private:

> Such an advance in social relationships definitely brings numerous services and advantages. It makes possible, in fact, the satisfaction of many personal rights, especially those of economic and social life; these relate, for exam-ple, to the minimum necessities of human life, to health services, to the broadening and deepening of elementary education, to a more fitting training in skills, to housing, to labor, to suitable leisure and recreation. In addition, through the ever more perfect organization of modern means for the diffusion of thought—press, cinema, radio, television—individuals are enabled to take part in human events on a world-wide scale. [*Christianity and Social Prog-ress,* par. 61.]

This process of world socialization, despite its rapid pace, does not keep up with the more rapid multiplication of hu-man needs—especially the need for food. The provision of "our daily bread" presses heavily upon some 200 million parents every day. As Pope Paul bemoaned in his Christmas message of 1963, about half the world's population suffers from insufficient food and malnutrition.

It takes time and advanced technology to increase the world food supply substantially and steadily so as to match the annual increase of 57 million in world population. As Premier Khrushchev knows full well, even an industrial country like Russia, with steel production second only to the United States and technical know-how to orbit her Sputniks, encounters grave difficulties in meeting its increasing food needs. How much more difficulty India experiences with a population double that of Russia and with industrial capacity and technical know-how many times less advanced.

For these reasons the Food for Peace program of the United States assumes great importance in meeting this number-one problem of feeding the hungry—today, next year, and probably for the next decade. Unlike the development programs already described, Food for Peace helps to satisfy this most basic human need now; while teaching agronomists, improving seeds, and building dams and fertilizer plants require years to fructify into bread and milk.

In 1963 the United States shipped $5.6 billion of food overseas. Of this, $4 billion represented direct commercial sales by American private businessmen, outside government channels. Food for Peace shipments under Public Law 480 totaled $1.6 billion. Of this, $379 million of food was given outright through American voluntary agencies to 71 million recipients in 113 countries. Of these, 36,760,000 were schoolchildren. Through family, maternal and child-care programs, another 23 million were helped. Most of these needy are in the mushrooming slum cities of the poor nations. Another 2½ million are refugees from war and dictatorship, and victims of natural disasters, like earthquake, drought, flood and fire.

Seventeen American agencies are registered with the United States government, through a citizens committee chaired by Charles Taft, to carry out these food programs. The voluntary agencies employed 730 U.S. citizens in overseas posts in 1964, and 7000 additional staff members in the countries of distribution. These are assisted by 100,000 volunteers. The three largest agencies are Church World Service, representing most of the U. S. Protestant churches; Catholic Relief Services-National Catholic Welfare Conference (NCWC); and Cooperative for American Relief Everywhere (CARE), a humanitarian and civic-based operation. These three agencies serve over 90 percent of the 71 million recipients. The U.S. government pays the freight for moving the donated flour, cornmeal, dry milk, shortening and butter oil overseas. In the decade since the inception of Public Law 480 in 1954, over $1½ billion of food has been given to the world's neediest by the American people through the voluntary agencies. Their over-all effort in this and other operations is coordinated through the American Council of Voluntary Agencies for Foreign Service, with headquarters in New York.

The government-to-government programs of Food for Peace are much more extensive, reaching over $12 billion in the first decade of operation, 1954–64. Most of these commodities are sold to governments for their own "soft" currencies, and not for "hard" dollars. By contract between the United States and the recipient nation, these funds remain within the country which makes the purchase. They are then used to finance economic development within that country; to pay local labor and buy materials for building ports, dams, highways, etc.; to make loans to American private entrepreneurs; to develop new industries ($179 million by 1964); to finance scholarships; to pay for American expenses such as maintaining U.S. military forces and supplying embassy needs ($1.7 billion); to finance common defense facilities in 15 countries ($545 million); and similar purposes. The food is also bartered for needed ores such as bauxite, manganese, asbestos, tin, zinc, cobalt and industrial diamonds. Barter transactions amounted to $218 million in 1962–63, helping substantially to stem the dollar flow outside the United States, while simultaneously providing food and work to millions of families overseas.

The Food for Peace program receives strong moral support from religious groups and leaders of the country. Enactment of enabling legislation in 1954 was moved along by a joint report called "The Moral Challenge of American Abundance," put out by the voluntary agencies, most of which are of religious inspiration. This public consensus asserted the existence of a moral imperative to share the abundance of our fertile acres, because, "just as there is no 'surplus' person in the world, so there is no 'surplus' food in the world in relation to the needs of the people." So long as people are hungry and homeless, the agencies state, nothing can be regarded as "surplus." One hundred Protestant, Jewish and Catholic leaders made a similar proclamation on "Food for Peace" in 1961. Clergy and laity of national stature said conjointly:

> Only to preach peace and freedom as Judaeo-Christian principles to people still held by hunger, at a time when we have abundance to remove their bonds, is hypocrisy. The living word must give life to deeds. Abstract principles of justice and charity are not enough. . . . Justice and charity become life-giving through laws and programs, agencies and projects, staffs and tools. . . .
>
> As citizens of the United States, we particularly commend our Food for Peace program, currently receiving new impetus. This great demonstration of the American people for the hungry of the world conforms to our moral responsibilities and demands our continuing support.

In 1963, the Food and Agriculture Organization (FAO) and the United Nations began a World Food Program, which may be the beginning of a worldwide Food for Peace program. So far, however, it is of very modest proportions, having received only $91 million in contributions from sixty nations. Of this, $50 million came from the United States. Our nation, Canada and Australia have become the breadbaskets of the world for cereal grains, while the developing continents have failed to keep pace with growing food needs.

Donations, barter and trade can meet these demands only for a time. Africa, Asia and Latin America must learn to grow more food themselves.

To accent this fact and to spur world concern, the FAO launched the Freedom from Hunger campaign in 1961. By 1964, over $28 million in voluntary contributions was channeled under this campaign to introduce better seeds, insecticides, fertilizers and production methods into the developing nations. But since 75 percent of the world's 2000 million poor are farmers, this addition of $.015 per person to their productive capacity means comparatively little. The more telling effect of the Freedom from Hunger campaign is, rather, the alerting of the world's wealthy, and especially the Judaeo-Christian West, concerning the condition of our next-door neighbors around the world. This admirable FAO endeavor is now being broadened into the World Campaign Against Hunger, Disease and Ignorance, in collaboration with sister agencies in the United Nations.

Many good Christians tire of all this "globaloney." Some good Catholics delight in decrying the waste and boondoggling in governmental aid programs, errors to be expected in an undertaking new to human history, new in its goals, size and complexity. Some warn, with reason, about the dangers of the welfare state, expanded perforce to world dimensions to meet worldwide problems.

Pope John, "mindful of our role as universal father," says in his simple way: "We all share responsibility for the fact that populations are undernourished. . . . As can be readily deduced, and as the Church has always seriously warned, it is proper that the duty of helping the poor and the unfortunate should especially stir Catholics, since they are members of the Mystical Body of Christ." (*Christianity and Social Progress,* pars. 158–59.)

This Christ-given duty to help is fulfilled in part through these programs of governmental assistance, financed principally by the federal income tax. This costs the average

American $12 per person per year, $1 a month, $.03 a day.

Barbara Ward ten years ago proposed the goal that the rich nations of the world should expend 1 percent of their gross national product on developmental assistance. This sum, she says, could be profitably employed. Currently in the Free World the figure runs about 0.4 percent per year, about $6 billion of the $1½ trillion total production of North America, Western Europe and Japan. The United States spends 9 percent of her production on armaments; Western Europe, 5 percent. One of the strong arguments, moral as well as economic and political, for reducing armaments is that part of the productive capacity thus freed could turn out equipment and release technical know-how that would enable the poor nations to attain the take-off level for their own development. Only a dedication and sacrifice and collaboration equal to that evoked by war can motivate the rich of the world to increase their concern for the poor to a level demanded by need. And the need, already high, multiplies much more quickly than does the concern, already low.

So far we Christians, as citizens, are more accomplished in and dedicated to the works of war than we are to the works of peace.

B. *Private Agencies, Religious and Humanitarian*

The Church has sent forth four great waves of evangelization. The first wave came out of Jerusalem and Antioch in the years immediately after the return of Christ to heaven. St. Paul spearheaded this outburst, principally into Anatolia and the Mediterranean basin, the heartland of old Greece and of the Roman Empire.

The second phase of apostolic endeavor came between 450 and 900 A.D. and brought the Faith to the peoples beyond the old Graeco-Roman civilization, notably to the Celts, Franks, Teutons and Slavs. Saints Patrick, Augustine, Boniface and Cyril stand out among the many heroic figures of that era, which transformed the West into Christendom and the East into Byzantium.

The third missionary wave followed the discovery of America and the new sea routes to the Orient. During the sixteenth and seventeenth centuries Christianity approached catholic dimensions for the first time. The American continents were taken over completely—by Spanish and Portuguese Catholics to the South, principally by Protestant Anglo-Saxons to the North, with a sprinkling of French in Canada and the Mississippi Valley. The Orthodox Russians extended this wave northward to the Arctic Sea and eastward to the Pacific. However, the most populous continent, Asia, was hardly affected by this encounter, and the vast interior of Africa was not even pierced. The Hindu, Buddhist and Moslem religions retained their dominance, and primitive animism remained almost untouched south of the Sahara.

Today's great wave of evangelization, the fourth, began about one hundred years ago. Protestant missionaries from Britain and North America, and Catholics from Western Europe, fanned out all over the world in the second half of the nineteenth century. Catholic missionaries from the United States and Canada became numerically significant only in the past generation. They penetrated Africa for the first time, bringing the Faith to about one fifth of the sub-Saharan peoples. Over half the Polynesians became Christians. Admirable apostolic campaigns were waged into the heartland of Buddhism, Hinduism and Islam, but with slight results in the realm of the spirit.

While the Christian apostle carries principally the spiritual message of God's love and man's eternal salvation, he frequently exercises weighty influence in the temporal order as well. Paul and his colleagues brought a dominantly spiritual message to an ongoing civilization, mitigating its cruelty and introducing fresh human values. More telling temporal contributions were made to post-Roman civilization by the monks of the West, in arts and crafts, in learning and philosophy, in the genesis of the universities, the city-state and nation. In the old heartland of the Roman Empire the Church did much to bring about civic order from the chaos which followed the barbarian invasions. And the apostle-monks ranged beyond the pale to win the tribes not only to the spiritual Faith, but also to the new temporal ecumene which became Christendom, the political, societal and cultural framework for a thousand years, until 1500. Catholic and Orthodox missionaries exercised similar cultural influence among the Slavs and nomads of the East. Bishop Ulfilas, for instance, in the fifth century, labored among the Goths along the Danube and rendered their spoken tongue into a written language, complete with grammar and dictionary.

The Catholic missionaries of Latin America performed a similar temporal function in the sixteenth and seventeenth centuries among the Aztecs, Incas and their less-developed blood brothers. The Church introduced schools, more advanced agriculture, arts and crafts into most of the seven thousand miles stretching from California to the Straits of Magellan and also in the Philippines. French Catholic and British Protestant missionaries were less successful with the more primitive Indians of North America, both in spiritual and temporal matters.

In the final wave of evangelization, which began in the 1800s, education, health and social services almost always constituted major adjuncts to the spiritual role of the minister and priest, brother and sister. In fact, a goodly number emphasized these temporal roles by their very titles of medical sisters, teaching brothers, and agricultural missionaries. The Christian missionaries of the past hundred years have been, in fact, among the principal carriers of the four primordial revolutions which now shake the world. To many areas outside the West they introduced especially the ideal of equality among all men and the yearning for this-world betterment, for education and health, human hope and social progress, civil rights in keeping with their dignity as children of God.

This holds especially for Negroid Africa, where the churches encountered no established religio-cultural system similar to Islam.

In 1875 Henry Stanley, the journalist-explorer, wrote from the Congo: "Oh that some pious, practical missionary would come here. . . . Such a one if he can be found would become the savior of Africa." In the next few decades they came in the tens of thousands. By 1964, Christian bodies were operating 60 percent of the primary schools in Negroid Africa, and a large portion of the health and social services.

C. L. Sulzberger, writing from Uganda, said in April 1964:

> The missionaries did come [in response to Stanley's cry] and they did a remarkable civilizing job. They left a visible impact just as colonialism, for all its demerits, left a visible impact.
>
> But the new nations want to run their own churches and they want missionary institutions like schools, but they want them turned over as rapidly as possible to their own clergymen. As with colonialism, they want the products of missionaries and the generosity of their sponsors; they don't want the colonialists or the missionaries themselves. . . . Historically speaking, the age of the missionary is drawing to a close. [New York *Times,* April 8, 1964.]

In India today, the Christian missionary is welcome only if he brings the technical or professional skills needed for developing the nation. The apostle's purely spiritual message is suspect. He is given a visa only as a technician or specially qualified teacher. Even these are shut out of Ceylon and Sudan, and, of course, from Communist China.

The contributions of Christian institutions to economic and social development become, then, of increasing significance to both religious and secular leaders. Church officials are beginning now to reassess the relative import to be given to the temporal and spiritual roles of their apostolate, with special attention to the rapid social and political changes occurring in all developing nations.

In 1964 the Ford Foundation made an initial grant of $98,000 to initiate a survey of contributions to national development being made by institutions of religious inspiration in Africa, Asia and Latin America. The inventory will cover educational, health and social programs. Two widely known social scientists direct this novel study: Dr. Egbert De Vries, Director of the Institute of Social Studies (ISS), The Hague; and Father François Houtart, Director of the worldwide Federation of Centers for Socio-Religious Research (FERES), Brussels. Dr. De Vries is a Protestant. The institute he directs is nonconfessional, being formed by the five universities of Holland, and is in part financed by the government of that country. Father Houtart is a Catholic, a sociologist trained at Louvain and the University of Chicago. FERES, of which he is the principal founder, federates fifteen social research centers of Catholic inspiration in Europe, Africa, Asia and Latin America. These are private institutions, but they work in collaboration with governmental bodies.

During negotiations with the Ford Foundation which led to this grant, it was estimated that Catholic, Orthodox and Protestant churches and related bodies provide goods, staff and services valued at over $200 million annually to the developing nations in the educational, health and social fields. But the outstanding fact is the current lack of reliable data. The church-related groups cannot now supply information on these far-flung operations that is adequate for acquiring an over-all grasp.

Funds and staff derive from scattered mission groups from the West and increasingly from churches indigenous to the three developing continents. Reports, such as they are, usually remain unpublished in the file cabinets of the mission society, congregation or diocese immediately responsible. If sent on to Rome or Geneva, London or New York, the data is often so intermixed with purely pastoral and spiritual concerns that it is difficult to identify as such the society-building operations. Even in cases where schools, hospitals and other social institutions are clearly reported, definitions of function differ with different bodies. A primary school means three grades in one country, eight grades in another. Methodists, Presbyterians and Catholics follow varying concepts and nomenclature in speaking of literacy, adult education, technical training and community development. Jesuits, Salesians and Franciscans use forms which make comparison and collation of totals a hopeless potpourri.

In consequence, until the present, church-related bodies have not been able to tell the world about their endeavors for "the fullness of a more excellent life" for all the human family. In fact, they do not know themselves, in any adequate and professional sense, just what and where and how much they are doing. Nor how well. Nor whether they should be moving into other fields, with new emphases, changed methods and staff.

These questions assume great moment because of the social revolutions now convulsing the developing nation. In many of these, education, health and social services, such as exist, have been provided until now by institutions of religious, usually of Christian, inspiration. Will the new nation-states take over the functions through public agencies, along lines followed generally in Western Europe and North America in the nineteenth century? Will conflicts develop between religious and civil bodies comparable to those bred by the French Revolution and its laicizing principles? Will secularization set in? And, if so, to what degree?

The issue becomes particularly delicate, since the birth of the new nations is often accompanied by a renaissance of Islamic, Buddhist and Hindu self-consciousness and by the tendency to inspirit nationalism with these religio-cultural values and fervor. This awakening easily takes on an anti-

Christian tincture, for reasons perfectly understandable in view of the collaboration of Christian missionaries with Western political and economic power for the past four centuries. In recent generations Islam, Buddhism and Hinduism have not taken an interest in educational and social endeavors in any way comparable to Christianity's wide-ranging efforts. The large question arises as to whether these three great world religions will now seek a significant role in promoting "the fullness of a more excellent life" for their faithful, in conjunction with the new nation-states which now strive to supply food, schooling, health and social organization to all their people. Or will the secularized state take on the whole titanic task, including that of providing social ideology, moving inspiration and moral solidarity?

The larger question still is whether the three great religions of Africa and Asia will join hands with Christianity in the worldwide campaigns against hunger, illiteracy and disease. Or will theological differences keep us apart even in the social field, and at war—ideological and emotional war, if not violence—and thus invite the secularization of the new world society, now in gestation, along paths similar to those that secularized the West following the Protestant-Catholic conflicts of the past four centuries.

In his address opening the Second Session of the Vatican Council in September 1963, Pope Paul addressed the *other* dialogue of Christianity also to "those other religions which preserve the sense and notion of the one supreme, transcendent God, creator and sustainer, and which worship Him with acts of sincere piety and base their moral and social life on their belief and religious practices." On Pentecost Day, 1964, Paul announced the establishment of "the Secretariat for Non-Christians, an organism which will have very diverse functions but an analogous structure to that for separated Christians." (Pope Paul's words, reported by the New York *Times,* May 18, 1964, p. 1.)

The Secretariat for Promoting Christian Unity will, however, treat of problems and with groups which are closely related to the interests of the newer Secretariat for Non-Christians, especially in Africa and Asia. A compelling reason for the ecumenical movement among Christians is the necessity of bearing witness to the whole world of one Lord, one faith and one baptism, in and through the one Church of Christ. The two dialogues—among Christians themselves, and by Christians-as-a-whole with non-Christians—are closely intertwined, especially in the social fields. In Tanganyika, for example, Protestants and Catholics have for the past decade worked together to build up the country's educational system. Now that Moslem leaders show increasing interest in schools, Christian groups, acting in unison, are in dialogue with the Moslems in order to seek acceptance for Moslem educational aspirations and due support among governmental leaders and national opinion.

After the initial survey of educational, health and social contributions made by religious bodies, being financed by the Ford Foundation, several case studies in depth are projected. Among those under consideration are the Tanganyika school system, technical training in India, health services in Nigeria, welfare and emergency assistance in the Congo, universities in the Philippines, basic and literacy education via radio in Colombia, and rural workers' movements in Northeast Brazil. A consultative committee of Protestant, Orthodox and Catholic leaders advises the technical team which directs this survey, and enlists the collaboration of mission-sending bodies and of national churches through the survey offices which have been set up in Rome, London, New York, Bogotá, Brazzaville and Mwanza. Among the members of this consultative committee are Monsignor L. G. Ligutti, Permanent Observer of the Holy See to the FAO, Rome; Bishop Lesslie Newbigin, Associate General Secretary of the World Council of Churches; Bishop J. Blomjous of Mwanza, Tanganyika; Rev. Dr. Paul Abrecht, Executive Secretary, Department on

Church and Society, World Council of Churches; and this writer.

Until recently, the educational, health and social activities of Christians have been undertaken principally by specialized mission groups from the West. About a decade ago the churches of the West began showing a more general concern for "the fullness of a more excellent life" for the whole human family, but often without direct relationship to spiritual evangelization. This activity has given rise in the West to scores of voluntary agencies for overseas service, supported by a broad spectrum of national churches and by humanitarian civic leaders with strong religious motivations. Corresponding counterpart agencies have taken form in the developing nations, under the direction of local citizens and with increasing dependence upon their own resources.

Many of the voluntary agencies in the United States were developed during and after the Second World War to meet the subsistence needs of refugees and displaced persons in Europe, North Africa, the Middle East and East Asia. Church World Services, Catholic Relief Services-National Catholic Welfare Conference, Lutheran World Services, Cooperative for American Relief Everywhere (CARE), and American Joint Distribution Committee (Jewish) are among the largest and best known. The last named is by far the oldest, with antecedents going back to the turn of the century. While they began with geographically limited, emergency goals, in the past ten years these agencies have spread over the globe to meet chronic misery in ninety nations and territories. Most significantly, they have evolved from merely welfare and emergency activities into long-term technical assistance and institution-building operations. These are closely dovetailed with programs of social reform and the development of socioeconomic structures now being undertaken by their national counterparts in Africa, Asia, and especially in Latin America.

Voluntary agencies based in the United States received telling impetus in 1954 through the enactment of Public Law 480, under which the superabundant foods of America's fertile acres are channeled to hungry peoples overseas. During the past decade, 15 billion pounds of flour, cornmeal, powdered milk, shortening, beans and other commodities have gone to schoolchildren, nursing and pregnant mothers, hospital patients and other needy persons through the voluntary agencies. This private and governmental partnership accounts for about 15 percent of the Food for Peace program of the United States.

Catholic Relief Services-NCWC administers the largest among the voluntary agency programs. In 1963, this agency distributed foods valued at $104 million to 26,250,000 persons: 17 million individuals in family groups; 6½ million schoolchildren; 2¾ million in hospitals, leprosaria, orphanages, etc. The U. S. Government paid $27,127,000 for ocean freight to ship the food to 74 countries. Funds, medical supplies, clothing and other supplies in the 1963 program amounted to $44.8 million, bringing the total annual value of the Catholic Relief Services-NCWC operation to $176 million.

An overseas staff of 130 Americans stationed in 74 countries, assisted by another 400 local agency personnel, supervise this vast program of welfare and socioeconomic development. These expenses and other operating costs are paid by annual grants of about $5 million from the Bishops' Relief Fund Collection, taken up in the 17,000 Catholic churches of the United States, usually on Laetare Sunday. A sum, roughly equal, is provided by the counterpart agencies of the 74 recipient countries, from private and public sources, for their own staff and domestic operational costs.

American voluntary agency programs are valued at over $500 million a year, of which about 60 percent is United

States food. These agencies supply resources to about 100,000 slum and village centers overseas. These centers are staffed by 500,000 volunteer workers, who are trained and directed by provincial and national community service organizations which have developed in the past ten years, often in direct response to the Food for Peace program carried out by U.S. voluntary agencies. These community service organizations are comparable to those financed in the United States by the United Fund or Community Chest, and by church-related bodies. Since public welfare is often barely existent, some governments now subsidize these private associations and rely upon them to initiate countrywide programs for dependent children, for the tiding-over of rural workers now flooding the cities, for resettling tenants on new lands, and for the aged, ill and unemployed. Many of the new national social organizations are of religious inspiration, in keeping with the culture of the area—Christian, Moslem, Hindu, Buddhist. Food for Peace, given by the people of the United States, is distributed without regard to race or creed.

The overseas volunteer committees, brought together to manage the 100,000 local distribution centers, under the direction of a salaried professional staff, are rapidly becoming nuclei for community and economic development within their own slums and villages. La Playa, a forlorn fishing village of a hundred families on the Caribbean coast of Colombia, provides a good example of this process, observed by this writer personally. Caritas, the Colombian counterpart organization of Catholic Relief Services-NCWC began, in 1960, to give milk to children, pregnant and nursing mothers under the direction of a local committee. The need for water to reconstitute the powdered milk brought to the forefront the need for a pure water supply for the whole village. The daily gathering of children and mothers, so many of them weak with malaria and amoebic diarrhea, highlighted the need for a medical dispensary. So the village leaders began working together on these projects. This led to child care and home hygiene courses; to a community center for storing food, medical and other supplies; and, to accommodate the necessary meetings, to the first assembly hall in village history. These changes were followed by a night school for adult literacy classes, a carpenter shop with tools for the use of all, and projects for draining malarial mud pits and beautifying the village streets and plaza. A credit union and fishing cooperative are now under discussion.

This evolution from direct relief to cooperative self-help and long-term development, by village and slum dwellers themselves, now repeats itself in thousands of faraway places. But this process of social articulation does not end at this grassroots level. The microcosms of local nuclei join into city, province and nationwide movements for social and economic betterment. These diversify into agricultural and technical training centers, credit unions, savings and loan associations, and cooperative federations, radio and television literacy and basic education systems, and medical and community development programs. This social fabric is not imposed from without. Private leaders of the respective countries, in conjunction with public agencies and planning authorities, conceive and direct these creative initiatives, which increasingly draw from their own local resources for funds and technicians. In Venezuela, for instance, top industrial executives have banded together to collect and administer a self-imposed tax, a dividend for national progress of 2 to 5 percent of their annual profits. In 1963–64 this brought in over $5 million, which was used to finance socioeconomic development at the grassroots level in a coordinated nationwide operation.

Many of these national voluntary movements now federate into multination regional associations. In 1963 the first Latin America-wide conference for literacy and basic education systems was held in Bogotá. A regional federation was organized, and Carlos Acedo Mandozo, executive director of the Venezuelan businessmen's movement for social development, was elected president. In 1964 the first continentwide meeting of Caritas and nongovernmental housing cooperatives was held, resulting in continuing federations for all Latin America.

Voluntary agencies based in the United States have become keenly aware that they must not impose their own preconceptions upon this new growth of private associations in the developing continents. Theirs is the role of a catalyst, offering funds, equipment and technicians to help the take-off of development programs under local leaders of each nation. These must be indigenous to their own land, people and culture, without the artificial impress of cultural imperialism. Still, each nation and culture can learn from other nations and cultures, so the voluntary agencies form international channels of people-to-people communication.

This growing world family of private bodies concretizes the concern of people for other people—*as people, as human beings, as brothers in the human family,* not as nationalist groups or power blocs. People-to-people projects can be more flexible and experimental than government-to-government programs. As pioneer pilot programs, they can be proven out before they are expanded by government assistance. Such has been the case with radio and basic education, credit unions and cooperatives, savings and loan associations, agricultural and technical training, agrarian reform, farmers' and workers' organizations. In some countries private programs are more stable than the governments themselves; these provide continuity for the generations of effort required.

To the extent that they are people-to-people and operate at slum and village levels, voluntary programs marshal the most important ingredient for national progress: the people themselves. They articulate the amorphous mass of individual atoms, in the broken-down village and the mushrooming slum, into the small primary groups and common-interest tissues required for a living, organic social body. Many development efforts wrongly expect social and economic advance to proceed solely or dominantly from the top to the bottom: from national capital to provincial city and market town, to village and slum; from government officials down to the man in the furrow and the housewife at her washing.

National development does not truly move ahead until the so-called "little people" start to change. These millions of peasants and slum dwellers have little or no property, little or no voice and power. For centuries they have subsisted outside the main current of the modern world; a proletariat, in Arnold Toynbee's phrase, *"in* but not *of* the society." Before a nation can develop, these villagers and slum dwellers must first feel their own needs and determine to band together to satisfy them. They must experience what Marina Bandeira, director of the radio schools of Brazil, terms "conscious-ization," the acquiring of an awareness of themselves as persons living in concentric circles of interacting social groups: the family and neighborhood, the village and town, province and nation, region and world. They must become conscious as well of their nonpolitical identities as farmers and workers, believers and heirs of a cultural tradition. They then begin their own simple voluntary undertakings, of their own free will, breaking with tight patterns of kinship and community tradition, to devise together new ways of meeting needs newly felt.

As these collaborative strivings link up over fences and valleys and jungles to become organized movements, we then perceive a nation in true development. A market economy, savings accumulation, capital formation—in short, economic development—becomes more feasible and fruitful. Only to the degree that a nation is an organic body of nongovernmental intermediate groupings, each with its measure of self-autonomy under freely chosen leaders—as opposed to an amorphous mass of inarticulate human atoms, directed only from above—does it become a resilient and free society. A developing nation must have a developing people.

During the Second World War the voluntary agencies of the United States associated themselves into the American

Council of Voluntary Agencies for Foreign Service (ACVA). While the 38 member agencies retain their operational autonomy, they strive through the American Council to coordinate their goals and methods of operation, to share technical knowledge and experiences which are mutually helpful, and to provide concerted approaches for collaboration with governmental and other bodies at home and abroad. Reflecting the growing emphasis on technical assistance and training programs, the American Council, since 1960, has entered into contract with the Agency for International Development of the United States to operate a Technical Assistance Information Clearing House (TAICH). This office collects and circulates data on the overseas development work of private nonprofit groups based in the United States. The 759-page TAICH directory of 1964 gives profile reports on 242 agencies, including 80 Protestant and Catholic missionary societies, and details the operations of 181 agencies by category of work, country by country.

Despite Church-State problems and the fear of becoming too closely identified with American diplomatic policy expressed by some voluntary agency leaders, the partnership of public and private endeavors in overseas social and economic development continues to mature.

The foreign assistance arm of the United States, the Agency for International Development (AID), has set up an office to treat specifically with voluntary agencies. The Latin American Bureau of AID has appointed a special officer to promote people-to-people aid between cities and community organizations of the United States and similar groups south of the border. The Pan-American Union Development Foundation, American Freedom from Hunger Foundation, and numerous other private assistance programs have mushroomed since 1960. Labor leaders, physicians, nurses and other vocational and professional groups have banded together to provide training, equipment and personnel overseas.

Among personnel-sending programs formally sponsored

by the Catholic Church is Papal Volunteers for Latin America (PAVLA). By 1965, over 300 teachers, medical workers, journalists, social workers, agronomists, cooperative experts, radio specialists and other technicians from the United States had answered Pope John's call to help out. Other lay missionaries are in Africa and Asia. This American Catholic awakening was preceded by several decades of activity by European confreres. Protestants, both American and European, have antedated Catholics in this field by generations. Accompanying this lay apostolate on a world scale is the increasing readiness of clerical mission-sending societies to enter into social economic development as such, in addition to providing traditional school and health services.

Since 1960, United States voluntary agencies begun in the aftermath of the Second World War have been emulated, and in some ways exceeded and improved upon, by fresh voluntary initiatives in Europe, Australia and New Zealand. The Oxford Famine Relief Committee (OXFAM) of Britain, the Freedom from Hunger Campaigns of Australia and New Zealand, *Entre-aide Catholique* of Belgium and MISEREOR of Germany are outstanding examples of this latter-day flowering of social concern on a world scale.

The German program, inspired by the Catholic bishops, is particularly noteworthy. Its free-will collections total over $12 million annually, and this sum is matched by a similar amount from the Federal Government. German Lutherans conduct a comparable program.

To assure optimum results, part of MISEREOR's funds are spent to finance development institutes in the respective countries overseas. These employ staffs of economists, sociologists, agronomists and other specialists to make technical surveys and to prepare projects which fit into the long-term development plans of the nation. In Latin America these professional institutes and programs are conjoined into a continental network through the Center for Economic and Social Development (DESAL) in Santiago, Chile. DESAL is directed by Father Roger Vekemans and lay leaders like Ramon Venegas and Sergio Ossa Pretot.

Since 1962, OXFAM has quadrupled its annual free-will collections to some $4 million a year, and has moved beyond its original famine and emergency aims into training and development programs. While several OXFAM leaders have been affiliated with the Quakers, the organization itself is strictly nonconfessional. Its funds are collected principally through an army of volunteers of all faiths, and some of no faith, in the neighborhoods, factories, and offices of Britain. And these monies are distributed through voluntary agencies and religious groups of every persuasion, including Catholic Relief Services-NCWC, in all three continents.

The past five years have brought such a sudden mushrooming of nongovernmental social operations on a world scale that international coordination has not yet taken definitive shape. The older American and European agencies with joint refugee and welfare experience have formed the International Council of Voluntary Agencies (IVAC), with headquarters in Geneva. Some of these agencies and newer development-minded bodies, including many of the mission-sending societies, met in 1964, formally and informally, to foster establishment of a coordinating center, or at least of an information clearinghouse. The FERES-ISS study, being financed by the Ford Foundation, will greatly help in this direction.

The philanthropic foundations of Europe and North America have also entered increasingly into overseas social development and training during the past decade. The Rockefeller Foundation has a long record in these fields, especially in Latin America, where it began public health work in 1917. By 1926, thirty-seven Foundation staff members were already stationed in fourteen Latin countries, and hundreds of Latin technicians had come to American universities through scholarships. Rockefeller grants to Latin universities have been principally in the fields of health, agriculture and science. For example, the University of Valle, Cali, Colombia, is receiving $2 million over a five-year period to develop a graduate school of medicine. The Catholic University, Santiago, Chile, is receiving $85,000 for graduate centers in neurology and nuclear medicine. Grants of $85,000 are helping to improve corn in Nicaragua and agricultural training in Honduras. Comparable grants made in Africa and Asia emphasize research and training. The Foundation's overseas contributions amount to about $11 million annually.

Of all private sources, the Ford Foundation makes the largest financial contribution to the developing continents. In 1962 it substantially increased its overseas commitments with appropriations of $40 million to help these nations to provide "the trained leaders, skilled persons, and enlightened citizens essential to their national development." These grants go principally to educational centers such as Allahabad Agricultural Institute in India and Louvanium University in the Congo. Training for civil administration and teaching receives heavy emphasis. Until 1961 the Ford Foundation concentrated its overseas development in Africa and Asia. But in the past three years it has set up offices in Latin America with budgets of $2–$4 million per year.

Many other North American and European foundations have recently entered the global campaigns against hunger, disease and ignorance. Private trust funds and industrial corporations are also lending a hand. But these, together with the mission societies and voluntary agencies financed by free-will offerings, and the tax-supported governmental aid programs, cannot do the whole job. Even if they are all multiplied many times over—as indeed they must be, in the name of justice and love and world peace—the decisive role must be played by the developing nations themselves. To become truly themselves, they must take their destiny into their own hands, within their own frontiers, and in concert with other lands.

They must develop themselves, through their own striving, by work, organization, and trade, as well as by aid.

IV. COUNTERVAILING FORCES, INVESTMENT AND TRADE

A. *The Competing Blocs*

Until 1960 the flow of aid and trade between rich and poor nations divided rather clearly into two distinct streams. The Western bloc strongly favored those countries which hewed closely to the political policies of the Western allies. The Russian-dominated bloc dealt almost exclusively with the Communist satellites and nearby party-liners. But now this "two bloc" world concept is changing radically. The proposition of Secretary of State John Foster Dulles, that neutrality is immoral, has been abandoned by both the United States and Russia.

Poor nations now accept aid and trade from rich nations wherever they can be found. They strive always to reduce the attached strings which would impede flexibility and impugn national sovereignty. Vigorous assertion of nationalism is still necessary for home consumption, to keep the government in power and to wring more authority and effort from citizens and workers. It proves profitable also as leverage in bargaining between East and West. Neutrality has come to mean playing one bloc against the other, thus forging each side, polarized until recently around the United States and Russia, into the countervailing force which the weak nation has till now completely lacked. Attempts by the have-nots to associate into a neutral bloc continue, but with no clear success thus far.

President de Gaulle launched the concept of a third force, a Europe of fatherlands, French-dominated, shortly after assuming power in 1958. And now China breaks with Russia to rend the Eastern bloc, and cultivates anti-Soviet adherents in Africa, Asia and Latin America—significantly, without much success among the Communists of the industrialized West—to form a bloc of her own. France and China, coyly and realistically, play off each other against their erstwhile allies, at least tentatively. In a direct military confrontation,

France would quite certainly again back up the United States and free-world defense, on one hand, as she did in the Cuba missile crisis; and, on the other hand, China and Russia would collaborate in a military showdown with the West.

Theoretically, it would seem that if a poor nation has three or four blocs to treat with, instead of two, or only the one to which it has committed itself, then its bargaining power vis-à-vis the great powers increases proportionately. The larger the number of competing sellers the buyer can deal with, the more advantageous are the terms he can probably obtain. This seems borne out by some aid and trade developments of recent years. The United States began serious assistance, trade and commodity price adjustment programs with Latin America, only after the Russian bloc began threatening this American sphere of influence, especially through Castro. France now carries on much more generous aid and development programs in its former African territories than she did before their independence, chiefly in response to Communist inroads. (French foreign aid is more than double American foreign aid, in relation to gross national product. United States economic assistance in dollars in 1964 was less than 0.4 percent of her annual gross national product, compared to about 1.8 percent for France, which selects her beneficiaries more cautiously, concentrating on those former colonies which promise better returns.) Russian aid commitment to wayward China has suddenly reversed itself. The Chinese complain that Russia has "made a unilateral decision to withdraw 1309 Soviet experts working in China, to tear up 343 contracts on the employment of experts and to cancel 257 projects of scientific and technical cooperation, and pursued a restrictive and discriminatory trade policy against China." Possibly China and France will now enter into trade and technical aid pacts, conceivably to include even nuclear technology.

Poland, Yugoslavia, India and Egypt (for her Aswan Dam and control of Suez) have been especially adroit at obtaining aid by playing off East and West against each other. Brazil and Congo are among the countries of their respective continents which have most profited from the neutralist stance. Panama's chances of eroding American absolute claims to, and *de facto* total control over, the Canal are much improved by the fact of Communist presence in Latin America. Middle East and Venezuela oil contracts and African and Latin American mining concessions are being revised to the advantage of the poor nation, and to the disadvantage of Western, Russian and Japanese developers, due in great part to competition among the world blocs. In short, the have-not nations are striving, with some success, to build up a countervailing force to improve their bargaining power with the affluent nations, and they are doing so by capitalizing on the struggles and differences among these rich Westerners and Russians.

This tactic, while it may obtain better trade arrangements for the have-nots and more control over their oil, ores and canals, does inspire, at least in the United States, a deep and widespread disillusionment with the whole concept and apparatus of aid to underdeveloped countries. This reduces citizen support and Congressional appropriations, and endangers the whole assistance program in the form it has taken since the Marshall Plan.

The attempt to draw a parallel between the two historic processes—have-not class consciousness against proprietors within the industrializing West of the 1800s, and class consciousness by the have-not two thirds of the world against the industrialized nations in the 1960s—breaks down at this point. In each Western nation the worker was physically present. He could strike and demonstrate, picket and close down the factory itself. And he could vote: therefore, Congress and state assemblies passed reform legislation. Today, on the other hand, while the miserable of the world may be psychologically aware of the wealth and the good life pouring from Western and Russian factory systems, they are not physically present in Pittsburgh, the Ruhr and Smolensk.

They can only picket and burn faraway embassies and consulates. They cannot close down rich-nation ports and plants, nor pressure effectively for less armaments and more consumer goods. They cannot elect congressmen and senators who would pass antitrust and New Deal and civil rights legislation on a world scale. They have only the forum of the United Nations. And for that reason the United Nations and all its works are of much greater import and are held in much higher esteem by the poor nations than they are by the rich.

In short, workers and peasants of the West could and did develop a countervailing force within their respective nations: labor unions, farmer and consumer associations, broadly based political parties. They gave flesh and muscle to the idea of social justice and the common good of all the nation's people. The Church gave doctrinal and moral support to these strivings—belatedly, however in many areas. Today, on the other hand, it is not yet clear how workers and peasants of the poor majority of the world can develop a telling countervailing force to confront the affluent, technically advanced third.

While the United Nations and regional systems, like the Organization of American States, remain mere forums for debate and permissive accord without effective sanctions, no reform of the world economic and political forces, sufficient to meet the widening gap, seems possible. To complete the vicious circle—in view of the power blocs, of racial and cultural differences, and of the inability of many poor nations to forge their own inner consensus required for stability and mature, long-term action—it is difficult for the United Nations, at today's pace, to become that "public authority, having worldwide power and endowed with the proper means for the efficacious pursuit of its objective, which is the universal common good in concrete form." Pope John expresses this desire and hope nevertheless in *Pacem in Terris*. Perhaps the world's moral and political thinkers and leaders will

move at last in this direction. Otherwise, strife and conflict—
hopefully, short of early nuclear holocaust—will intensify as
the gap between wealth and misery, already so wide, continues to spread.

B. *Investment*

Three key issues enter at this juncture: first, the workers
and the peasants of each developing country must themselves
form a countervailing force within their frontiers in order
to acquire a voice in the economic, political and social life
of their homeland; second, new investment for capital formation for economic and social development must be marshaled
from domestic and foreign sources—but foreign investment is
being frightened away by political instability and threats of
wholesale collectivization, and by ideologies fostering such
policies, which is especially true in Latin America, where
domestic capital is fleeing to the United States and Western
Europe; third, trade must be combined with aid, investment
and reform as instruments for development.

The first point, internal social reform, including peaceful
society-wide revolution, will be discussed in the next chapter.
The second and third issues, investment and trade, must now
be introduced, despite the assurance of oversimplification for
the sake of brevity.

Eduardo Frei, the Chilean leader of the Christian Democratic Party, recently noted that 35 million additional new
workers will enter the labor force of Latin America by 1975.
But, he warns, only 5 million new jobs will be open to them
at the present rate of economic growth.

New jobs are created by new businesses and factories, by
new transport and utilities systems. These new installations
must be financed by new capital, by new investment funds
from private or public sources, from within or without the
developing country. We have already noted that a major reason for Latin American economic stagnation is the flight of
local capital to countries outside the region, especially to the
United States, Switzerland and the Common Market coun-

tries. The Department of Commerce reported that over $4 billion of Latin American funds were invested or deposited in the United States in 1964. Estimates of total Latin American monies abroad run as high as $15 billion, although this is probably an exaggerated figure. A more realistic estimate might run $8–$10 billions. No one can arrive at a definite figure, because many of these transactions are secret.

The Alliance for Progress aims at an increase of economic production at the rate of 2½ percent per year. This is to be a net gain, that is, over and above the annual population increase of 2 to 3 percent. So the national economies must produce, on the average, about 4½ percent more each year over the preceding year. This would require new social and economic investments of about $10 billion a year from all sources, public and private, Latin American and foreign—a goal much in excess of the present rate. When the Alliance was launched it was hoped that private investment from the United States would total $3 billion during the present decade, about $300 million new investment per year. Since United States business firms had invested $500 million in a single year, 1957, this goal seemed feasible.

But with the advent of Castro, the political strife and *coups d'état* in many Latin American countries, private investment from the United States fell catastrophically. In 1961 the figure reached a low of $173 million. In 1962 there was a net *outflow* of capital from the nineteen Latin American republics of $32 million. From the viewpoint of the private investor, this reversal is easily explained. Since 1960, United States-owned firms, especially in the extractive and utilities sectors, have been expropriated or gravely threatened in several countries. Brazil took over properties of the International Telephone and Telegraph Co. and the American and Foreign Power Co. Argentina and Peru canceled oil concessions. While negotiated settlements may prevent total loss to the investor, and sometimes even permit continued operation, these and similar moves undermine confidence in American and other foreign private-funding sources. The rising flame of nationalism and xenophobia, often exploited by demagogues and Marxist political movements, still makes the future uncertain.

However, with the victory of the reform government of President Romulo Betancourt in Venezuela, in December 1963, over nationalist extremists and saboteurs armed by Castro, the investment climate has improved considerably. This Venezuelan victory for structural reform within the democratic process, together with advances in Mexico, Colombia, Peru and Argentina, has reversed the investment outflow. Southbound capital reached a net inflow of $78 million in 1963.

While this is far from sufficient in view of the need, it revives hope that a formula for activating new industries in Latin America and the other developing countries with the help of foreign private investment can be worked out. Private capital ventures from the Common Market are also playing large development roles, especially in the new nations of Africa and Asia, and increasingly in Latin America. Methods of insuring private investment against expropriation and civil strife are being tried out on a restricted scale. And consortiums of American, European and Japanese corporations often combine for joint ventures with investors within the developing country.

The Atlantic Community Development Group for Latin America (ADELA) was formed in 1964, under the leadership of Standard Oil of New Jersey and FIAT of Italy. Their aim is to gather $200 million in development capital from free world corporations. Among the participants are International Business Machines, Petrofina of Belgium, the Swiss Bank Corp., Ford, First National City Bank, W. R. Grace Co., Pfizer, Chase Manhattan Bank, Socony-Mobil, and a Japanese consortium. They are seeking new investment opportunities in Latin America. It is of special interest that a principal promoter of this international business venture is

Senator Jacob K. Javits, Republican from New York, strongly seconded by Senator Hubert H. Humphrey, Democrat from Minnesota. Both these men have striven creatively to transform the Alliance for Progress into a broadly based, long-term, undertaking in which all segments of society participate, public and private, Latin American and foreign, the United States and its free world allies.

C. *Trade and Development*

"Trade as well as aid and investment" has become, of late, another formula for development advanced by many economists and political leaders. The poor nations are now making a strong case for realigning the world's economic forces so that trade favors their own development. At their insistence, the United Nations Conference on Trade and Development (UNCTAD) was held March–June 1964 in Geneva. For three months they sought out ways of forging a unified countervailing force from the disparate streams of trade which flow in all directions among the nations of the world. They made a beginning. The industrialized, factory-owning nations —the West, Russia and Japan—did give a little ground.

Thinkers and moralists in the world social field, whether of Christian or other ideologies, must rethink their positions on social justice and the common good as applied to world trade and development. The great breakthrough of Catholic social thought was categorical rejection by Leo XIII of the laissez-faire theories of the free market. He declared that workers could and should associate to defend their rights to obtain a just share of the joint product of capital and labor, and that the state must intervene with legislation and market regulation toward these ends. Piux XI went on to elaborate the right to bargain collectively over the exchange of work for wages. He espoused social justice in which the very structures of the economy and society itself—property-holding, worker and farmer organizations, state activities, tax systems and other basic relationships—work together for the common good of the entire nation.

Now Pope John extends these principles on a world scale. He espouses international social justice and the "universal common good in concrete form." Can these high-flown principles be concretized through proposals like those initiated at the United Nations Conference on Trade and Development? Will new concepts of justice and law induce trade to depart from free market rules and thus realign bargaining power between the affluent and proletariat on a world scale?

In the raw capitalism of the 1800s the factory owners tended to coalesce into monopolies. They could muster great power in the free market of individual workers (from a hyperplentiful labor pool) and of individual, unorganized consumers. The worker possessed no comparable countervailing power to bargain on even terms for his wages and conditions of work, or for the prices he paid as a consumer for finished goods. He had minimal—indeed, almost no—control over the input and output of the factory system.

The poor nations now complain that they are in a comparable position in the worldwide production system. They supply raw materials—food, fiber, ores, crude oil—from their primary, extractive economy. They purchase finished manufactures and technical services from the industrial nations. These latter, the poor nations complain, can manipulate to lower the prices they pay for the crude output, mostly with hand labor, of the unorganized poor nations. Simultaneously, the have-nots charge, the rich nations exercise full control over the finished products and expensive technical skills which the developing nations must obtain in order to advance.

Since the Second World War, world trade has been regulated by the General Agreement on Tariffs and Trade (GATT). The 75 developing nations increasingly voice complaints that the GATT system grossly favors the industrialized West. Some attack it as an active remnant of colonialism, of might over right transferred to the economic field. They allege that GATT is a rich man's club exploiting the major portion of mankind who are in a weak bargaining position.

Isaiah Frank, who headed the United States delegation to the preparatory meetings for the United Nations Conference on Trade and Development, summarizes this subjective feeling of poor-nation class consciousness:

> In order to understand the drive and fervor of the less developed countries for this Conference, it is not enough to examine their trade problems in terms of statistical trends. The problems are serious; there should be no question about that. But beyond any objective level of analysis, the leadership group in these countries is fired with a sense of injustice, a feeling that the international trading system is stacked in favor of the advanced countries. . . . What they want is to change the system, and the U.N. Trade Conference is viewed as a vital step in that direction. ["Aid, Trade and Economic Development: Issues Before the U.N. Conference," *Foreign Affairs*, January 1964, p. 212.]

Dr. Raul Prebisch, the noted Latin American economist and Secretary General of UNCTAD, is the principal spokesman for the less-developed nations in advancing the new trade-and-aid formula for development. In the UNCTAD documents he shows that prices for the farm and ore products which the poor nations sell to the rich have fallen 12 percent since 1957. At the same time the machinery, transport and technical equipment which the industrial nations sell to the poor have risen in price. This has caused a 16 percent decline in the balance of trade of the poor nations during the last decade, which means that the payments received by them for their products has fallen 16 percent, in relation to what they must pay for their purchases from the rich countries. And purchases of machinery and technical skills from the rich are a necessity for the developing poor nations.

In ten years this has caused a drop of over $13 billion in the earnings received by the poor nations for their exports.

And this decline of income has nullified half of the $26 billion in aid and investment made by the United States and other developed countries. For instance, the 1964 cocoa crop of Ghana brought in 60 percent less money than it did ten years before, although the crop is now larger than it was then. This is due to the sharp fluctuations in commodity prices which seem endemic to the completely free market. Between 1950 and 1962, coffee prices fluctuated between a high of $1431 per ton and a low of $657. Cotton ranged from $1000 to $447. Natural rubber, from $1024 to $432. The rubber production in one Asian country increased by 18 percent in the past seven years, but the value of the crop dropped by 14 percent. A drop in the price of rubber of one third of a cent caused an anual loss of $5 million to the nation.

Most of the economically underdeveloped countries depend upon one or two crops or ore exports for the bulk of their overseas trade. Chile, for instance, projected 1964 exports valued at $520 million, of which $450 million was copper ore. In other words, 87 percent of Chile's annual income depends upon this one item. If the price of copper drops 10 percent, Chile loses $45 million in purchasing power. When the United States decided to stop stockpiling copper, the whole national economy of Chile was badly shaken. It is against such heavy dependence upon the tender mercies of rich nations and their unilateral decisions that the poor nations are now uniting.

Such realities have led to priority for price-stabilization agreements through international commodity agreements. Already agreements have been negotiated, under United Nations auspices, for wheat, sugar, tin, coffee and olive oil. Consideration is being given to the refinement and extension of these agreements in order to guarantee the purchasing power of primary commodities, and to maintain their parity with the prices of manufactures. UNCTAD has also proposed the stabilization of each poor country's total earnings from exports through compensatory payments. Tariffs preferential to young industries and a development insurance fund are among the other new approaches which would give greater voice and advantage to poor nations trading in the world market, and would lead to their more rapid development.

Pope Paul showed his interest in the UNCTAD meeting by sending a delegation to represent the Holy See. The instructions to these delegates were published by *Osservatore Romano* (April 3, 1964). The papal letter expressed warm support for the aspirations of all the world's peoples for a higher standard of living. It asserted that the grave problems of world trade cannot be solved by simple application of a completely free international market, nor by the opposite extreme of a totally planned economy. Applicable principles advanced in *Mater et Magistra* and *Pacem in Terris* were cited on the great issue of international cooperation to support an openness for restructuring the world's trade system. The document stated:

> It is necessary to work resolutely during this period of transition for the establishment of proper channels and efficient organizations capable of bringing about full satisfaction of the more legitimate human aspirations within the framework of national independence.

The papal instructions to the UNCTAD delegation concluded that mankind will find its way to cooperation and peace by recognizing the demands of international ethics and by utilizing the physical and human resources of the countries concerned in keeping with their dignity. The Holy See's delegates were instructed "to stress the moral implications of the problem of development and the importance of finding a lasting solution, even if it requires time."

So we see that international ethics do exist and the issues of trade and development do have moral implications, in the judgment of Popes John and Paul. The principles of Christian social teaching on international social justice must be applied day by day to concrete programs like those which have come out of UNCTAD, in much the same way as social principles are applied to concrete programs within a given country on the right to organize, farm price supports or civil rights. In this way we can help the have-nots of the world marshal their countervailing force.

The UN Conference launched such a vast undertaking that it was foreseen that it could only initiate changes in attitude and lay the groundwork for the restructuring of world trade over a period of several years. It is instructive that the 112 participant nations voluntarily divided themselves into three groups—the Western countries, the Communist bloc and the underdeveloped countries, the last-named group numbering 75 countries. Each of the three blocs appointed a committee of representatives to treat with the other blocs. In the midst of this "constitutional" assembly, the New York *Times* reported how United States' fears that Russia would steal the limelight by propaganda plays were allayed, because "The Russians, for their part, find themselves *coupled with the rest of the industrialized world* in statements by the poor countries on what the rich countries should do for them." (May 24, 1964, page F 1. Italics added.)

The analogy with organization efforts of the proletariat in the early days of Western industrialization is again brought to mind. They forged their countervailing force as have-nots by confronting the whole gamut of absolute property rights, and often they sought to bargain collectively not merely with each factory, but with the whole of an industry in a given area. Now the "proletarian" nations are adopting a comparable strategy vis-à-vis all the industrial powers of the world, lumping together "free enterprise" and mixed economies with the Russian collectivist system, because they all share the common trait of this-world affluency.

Father Louis Lebret spoke in the name of the Holy See's delegation to UNCTAD on two points of particular importance. First, fair trade on a global scale is a basic means not only of development, but also a necessary step toward human solidarity and world peace.

> Our delegation [of the Holy See] takes the view that the problem is one not only of trade in the strict sense, but of the entire gamut of international relations and intercourse. While not underestimating the efforts so far made by all the richer countries or by associations of countries or by international organizations—to which we give all due credit—we must nevertheless stress that only radically changed attitudes will engender a deeper and more effectual altruism, and open up wider prospects for trade and commerce, toward the day when a truly interdependent civilization emerges.
>
> That is the great revolution this Conference must initiate, a long-term bloodless revolution, whose first phase will be marked by the resolutions and decisions here adopted. [International Catholic Migration Commission, Press Release No. 19, April 20, 1964.]

The second point stressed by Father Lebret is that measuring development growth in statistical totals of gross national product can be very deceiving. Because, so measured, growth may be merely a veil cast over the *human* reality, covering the fact that the small but powerful privileged class of the nation benefits principally, while the "vast urban or rural majority derive little benefit at all, where their incomes are not actually declining. . . . Development is in fact indivisible [from social reform], and progress must be achieved for every section of the population."

This great issue of society-wide reform and peaceful revolution within the respective nations must now receive at least brief attention.

Chapter Ten

REFORM, REVOLUTION
AND IDEOLOGY

Father Louis Lebret's statement to the United Nations Conference on Trade and Development opens the eye to a few fundamentals which too many leaders of poor nations blithely pass over, in their fulminations against the privileged nations of the world.

The injustices of today's system of world trade, which they so roundly, and at times soundly, criticize, are matched and exceeded by social injustices deeply entrenched within their own national borders. How often the very leaders of the have-not nations who self-righteously arraign the world's factory-owning sector for gouging the poor on a global scale and fattening on their sweat and labors, are themselves guilty of like injustices to their own people at home. Some crusaders for world justice seem strangely blind to the self-perpetuating feudal system of their own landed aristocracy and commercial oligarchy. Their lamentations for the weak of the world too often evoke crocodile tears. They would reform the wayward rich only on a global scale, without curbing their own extravagant indulgence of self, made possible by the sweat and labor of their own countrymen, workers and share-croppers at home.

Too often it also happens that portions of aid grants and easy loans, made available by rich-nation largesse, find their way into private pockets. Graft and corruption, of the type made notorious by the big-city bosses of the United States, sometimes occur on a national scale.

Probably, however, this has been exaggerated by some American critics including businessmen and lawmakers who eagerly dip into our own domestic pork barrel. Some indiscriminately attack most foreign assistance as "money down the drain." Their allegations against "operation rathole" become easy excuses for reducing aid appropriations and taxes, and maybe to fatten the pork barrel here at home. Nevertheless, it is unfortunately true that foreign aid has at times helped to maintain poor-nation bosses, dictators or military juntas quite beyond the requirements of internal security or regional stability.

A goodly number of the poor nations do need drastic reform within their own borders in order for development aid, foreign investment and the reorganization of world trade to have the required effect. This reform within the poor nation is of two types: that which replaces the self-serving bosses and their pocket-lining cronies with honest public servants, as in our own cities and states when we seek a "reform administration"; and that which is much more drastic and difficult to achieve, the substantial reorganization of social, economic and political structures—management-worker relations, wage and profit levels, tax and educational systems, political and civil rights, and other institutional changes that enable the proletariat to enter the mainstream of society. This high ideal, which Christian social teaching terms "a just social order," promotes the common good of all. To be effective, such substantive reform must be led by reformers of the first type, honest men who have the true concerns of all the people at heart.

Sometimes this structural reform is so far-reaching and drastic, so society-wide and sudden, that it is properly called a "social revolution," albeit peaceful in the main, with a minimum of violence. The old order folds up, a new order unfolds—but at an accelerated pace, and almost always, if it is to be successful and enduring, under the inspiration of an ideology, a rationale, a mystique. Social revolutions such as these may alter the face and form of a nation and change world history, if a sufficient proportion of mankind is affected, at a significant depth, and for an adequate number of years.

Social revolutions of this nature are now occurring in all three developing continents.

To be successful these societal transformations require also transformations in the engrained customs and personal characters of individuals. Economic and social development require the application of technology and rationalized processes to production, work and human relations. The constancy and regularity of the machine, the assembly line and the office impose constancy and regularity upon mechanics, workers and clerks. Whims, personal habits, and passing appetites must be controlled. Coordinated group action and punctuality are essential. Human powers of creativity must be concentrated on impersonal goals, aroused by new motives. Face-to-face and kinship relations, of paramount value for many thousands of years, must give way to "organization man."

At the onset this demands an asceticism which is best, and perhaps only, motivated by a deep grasp of, and strong commitment to, an ideology concerning man and his destiny, society and its values, creature and Creator. Ideologies of such depth and attractiveness are the major contenders in the arena of world issues today.

Three of the areas most vitally engaged in a societal transformation of unprecedented proportion are Latin America, Africa, and Asia. A consideration of developments in these evolving sections of the world will present a most revealing picture of the ferment and agitation racking many of the have-not nations.

I. Latin America

Mario Lopes da Silva works on a banana plantation in Northeast Brazil. I met him in December 1963, while visiting

the office of the farm workers' unions in Natal, the hub city
of Brazil's fermenting sharecropper area.

As I entered the office, Mario Lopes and two other members of the local union were in agitated discussion with officials of their state federation. A fresh crisis for their three-
year-old organization had occurred the night before. Mario
Lopes and 150 fellow workers who form the local *sindicato*
on five neighboring plantations had gone on strike, the first
full-fledged work stoppage in the short history of the Christian-inspired peasants' movement. Its leaders have been
formed by the social training center set up in Natal in 1960
by Bishop Eugenio Sales.

"Why did you go on strike?" I asked Mario Lopes.

"Because we get so little that we have to become thieves
to feed our children," he shot back without hesitation.

"What are your wages?"

"Three hundred cruzeiros a day. And we work only three
days a week on the average."

Three hundred cruzeiros equaled twenty-five U.S. cents at
the time, and the current inflation spiral of 5 percent a month
was eroding this daily pittance by a penny each month.

"But that isn't the whole story," Lopes went on. "The plantation landlord won't allow us to graze a couple of goats on
his lands to get milk for our little ones. That's why we organized our union, so all of us can stand together for a
little justice."

"Well, what does the proprietor think about all this?"

"Oh, he doesn't like it at all. And especially he doesn't
like me, because I head up the union. That's how the strike
actually began yesterday. The landlord told me I was fired,
that I must vacate my shack and get off his land in twenty-
four hours."

"Then what happened?"

"I took a stick in my hand," Lopes gesticulated. "I told
him that he and I had better draw a line on the ground to
show where *his* land ended and *mine* began, because I would

only leave my place a dead man. The landlord walked away. The thirty men who work with me held a meeting. They decided to stand with me and have a showdown. Then the hundred and twenty workers on four neighboring plantations, who are fellow members in our local union, they also voted to back us up. So now we're all on strike."

José Martins da Cruz spoke up at this point. He is vice-president of the peasants' federation, which covers the entire state of Rio Grande del Norte. He explained the over-all goals of the state's sixty thousand sharecroppers and farm workers who had formed forty-six local unions since 1960 under his leadership.

"We want an 80 percent increase in wages [from twenty-five to forty-five U.S. cents a day]. We want a family subsidy of thirty-five cruzeiros [three cents] a day extra for every child in the worker's family. We want the plantation owners as a whole to recognize our right to form a union, that they must bargain with us all together.

"We're really part of a big movement," Martins went on, with Mario Lopes nodding proud agreement. "We're spreading over all the state and country, even joining with other nations of Latin America and the world."

Mario Lopes, José Martins and their sharecropping brothers personalize the great fresh reality which is the new Latin America. Their new-found comradeship and emerging ability to lead and to organize give flesh and sinew, spirit and hope to the drive for reform, for political, economic and social transformations. These society-wide changes in structure are so far-reaching, global and interrelated that they deserve the term "revolution."

This revolution is now actually happening, with spasms of violence in some places, with peaceful changes in others. The old feudal structure is being overturned consciously by the oppressed peasants and slum dwellers themselves, who are joining hands with sincere intellectuals and students, as well as with demagogues and paid agitators. Leaders of business and political parties here and there are beginning to realize that they cannot hold back the tide which threatens to engulf them and their privileges. So they, too, awaken to the need for radical reform—revolution, in fact. As the old regime totters and starts to fold up, a new economic and social order is conceived and unfolds. However, in today's embryo tomorrow's fresh creation cannot yet be fully discerned. The struggle and tension will continue until the major goals of social justice and broad human welfare are attained, or until chaos or totalitarian tyranny takes over.

The high degree of social justice and welfare which now obtains in Western Europe and North America is the slow-maturing product of two centuries of conflict and change. This process was highlighted by the American and French Revolutions of the late 1700s, by the popular movements of Jefferson and Jackson, the communes and British Chartists, by the civil wars and antitrust legislation of the 1800s, the struggles of labor and farm organizations, the New Deal of the 1930s, and the racial strife of our day.

For the past century North America has enjoyed political stability and economic progress to a degree unmatched in any other part of the globe. The Catholic migrants to the United States found here a flourishing natural life, a civic and economic community within which they could build up their young Church. As a spiritual body the Church was nourished and supported by the strong, progressive society of our nation. Quite the opposite has obtained in Latin America. The Church there for two centuries has been battered and weakened by ideological and political strife, by social immobility and economic fossilization. In her human and social manifestation the Church has shared the ills of the civic body, whose outmoded feudal structures are at last collapsing to produce the crisis of the hemisphere.

The Church as a whole, inside and outside of Latin America, has awakened to these new realities only in the past five years or so. Now, at last, the Church is stirred by this travail.

In terms of Church membership, our Latin American confreres account for one third of our 550 million baptized adherents. We refer to the Latin American Church as one third of the visible Body of Christ. Speaking to the region's bishops in November 1963, Pope Paul called Latin America "a continent with a Christian tradition, yet a menaced continent."

Bishop Manuel Larrain of Chile, for twenty years the continent's most forward-looking prelate, and now president of CELAM, the council of Latin America's 640 bishops, took up this theme in an address in 1964. "What we have to face," said Bishop Larrain, "is the hard, painful birth of a new civilization. The danger arises if we do not become aware of this event, and if we cannot give guidance to all the dynamic drives stirring up in our continent." (First Latin American Meeting of Caritas, Santiago, Chile, February 1964.)

Bishop Larrain attributes this "hard, painful birth of a new civilization" to two major causes. One he calls quantitative, the other qualitative. First, Bishop Larrain cites the "demographic explosion. We are at present 200 million inhabitants. In 1980 we will be over 350 millions. Toward the close of the century, we will be about 600 millions. This means that we must get all these rapidly increasing masses of people incorporated into educational and social channels, so that the rapid changes brought about by the demographic explosion can really find the fair and adequate solutions which are necessary."

The qualitative cause, which the presiding bishop of the Latin American hierarchy adduces, refers to "modifications in social and cultural structures. Latin America is undergoing a rapid, overall transformation; changes take place in the cultural, social, political and civic fields, giving the continent a new physiognomy upon which we must focus for the future." Bishop Larrain explains how these structural changes become especially apparent. Until a few years ago, he states, the region's rural population, 60 to 70 percent of the people, were excluded from the cultural and social, economic and civic life of their respective nations. In very recent years, however, "the rapid spread of communications media, of radio, television and roadways, has suddenly incorporated these huge marginal masses into the life of the nation, thus causing deep structural changes."

Along with these exterior facts of population growth and fundamental structural change, Bishop Larrain points to a new phenomenon within the human person himself: "Active participation of the whole population in the life of the nation, and most of all, the extraordinary desire for human betterment manifest among all strata of society." To this Latin American Church leader the troubles afflicting his region are comparable to strong currents of a river seeking to change its course, "and we must give our continent the course it requires." The Bishop concludes:

Many a time we have—let us be honest!—erroneously described these troubles by simply calling them revolt, the agitation of Communists. While really at bottom they are but a desire for improvement, for human advance, for finding a just and humane solution, a solution which allows men to fulfill that longing for betterment and perfection which lies at the core of all their spirits.

We see then that Mario Lopes, the dollar-a-week banana worker, and Bishop Larrain, son of an old Chilean family of the landed aristocracy, and now head of Latin America's Catholic hierarchy, for four centuries one of the most arch-conservative bodies in the world, today agree closely on their society's ills. And together they seek drastic remedies.

This new accord, this growing understanding and joint action of the high and the low within the region, and of clergy and laity within the Church, may well turn out to be the most telling transformation of all Latin America's intertwining revolutions. The Church, as a whole, is no longer to be identified with the landed aristocracy, with the political oligarchy and the oppressive status quo. Bishops and priests, religious and lay leaders, both men and women, provide much of the new ferment for institutional reform and peaceful revolution. This hopeful and dramatic change among Catholics manifests itself in many ways.

First, a Christian-inspired ideology of social revolution now appears. Webster's Collegiate Dictionary defines "ideology" as "the integrated assertions, theories, and aims constituting a politico-social program." But in today's common usage, ideology means much more. It connotes not only intellectual assent, but also emotional and determined commitment to fulfillment of an *action* program based upon ideas about man and society. Sometimes ideology also suggests the distortion of facts, conscious or unconscious, to fit a doctrinaire position.

Ideologies, with and without distortion, are a fact of life in the Latin American crisis. Communism, other breeds of Marxism, varying interpretations of socialism and laissez-faire capitalism are in daily, often deadly, competition, in a manner and to a degree never experienced in North America. During the past ten years another political, social and economic program has gradually evolved, that of social democracy. This ideology can be divided into two major branches: that which is personified by Romulo Betancourt, President of Venezuela from 1959 to 1964, through his Party of Democratic Action; and that which is advanced by Eduardo Frei, President of Chile, and Rafael Caldera, heads of the Christian Democratic Parties of Chile and Venezuela, respectively. While Betancourt bases his program on humanist concepts, Frei and Caldera draw from Christian social teaching for many of their root ideas. But all three come up with a practical program which is similar enough to invite cooperation. This social democracy, shared among them and a growing number of Latin American political leaders, is often called the "democratic left."

Eduardo Frei's view of the Latin American crisis accords with Bishop Larrain's. Frei says: "The great mass of the people do not participate in the real life of the country. The democratic system has not been faithfully expressed. The fact that privileged groups control the land, the banks and the journals [newspapers and magazines] has permitted the democratic system to conserve structures as they are. These groups can perpetuate the system by obtaining representation in Congress." (*Look,* June 2, 1964.)

President Frei makes clear that the term "capitalism" denotes monopoly control in Latin America, a reality much different from the democratic capitalism of the United States and Western Europe. In Latin experience, capitalism has simply not worked; "as a system [it] dehumanizes the economy." Frei deeply fears socialism, because when ownership of the means of production "is a monopoly under the sole control of the state, there results as a consequence a concentration of power in the bureaucracy that is as merciless and more merciless in its operation than the private businessman."[1]

Eschewing both socialism and laissez-faire capitalism, Frei and his associates envision a program in which the workers participate as part-owners of the industry which employs them. This would come about by enforced profit-sharing and property-spreading. Workers would elect company directors and would invest part of their profits in other industries to broaden their base of security and property holding.

Leonard Gross, senior editor of *Look,* concludes his article cited above:

> Frei is a deep challenge to our thinking. But the evidence indicates that he represents an emerging South American synthesis. While some of his radical-Christian ideas may take some getting used to, his integrity, his competence and dedication are properly a cause for celebra-

[1] Paul Sigmund, Jr., *The Ideologies of the Developing Nations* (New York: Praeger, 1963), p. 312. This book gives forty-four statements by leaders of the developing continents. Several are used in this chapter, especially concerning Africa and Asia.

tion. Chile is moving left. So is South America. We can only hope it will move left with the likes of Frei.

In 1862, Lincoln called the American idea "the last best hope of earth." In 1964, radical democracy appears to be the last, best hope of Chile. That it is the single alternative to Marxism is the most significant lesson available in South America today.

The ideology of Christian democracy inspires political, labor and managerial groupings, which are under the control and direction of laymen and of non-Christian associates. These autonomous social movements, despite the occasional confessional tag, are by no means Church-controlled. They are *of, by* and *through* the laity as civic leaders striving for the common good in collaboration with other men of good will.

The principal role of the official Church is to teach and to inspire. Until ten, or even five, years ago this responsibility was ineffectively carried out. Reactionary forces, in and out of the Church, soft-pedaled Christian social doctrine. In some places papal encyclicals did not get to the public. But today the most advanced teaching of the Church on social issues reaches the people through pastorals and public statements of national conferences of bishops, through newly written catechisms, liturgical services and preaching campaigns with heavy social content, and through hundreds of intermediate and grassroots training centers. These are usually directed and manned by lay leaders.

The 1962 pastoral of the Chilean bishops on "Social Reform and the Common Good," and the 1963 statement by the Brazilian Bishops' Council on "Basic Reforms for a Just Social Order" stand out among the episcopal documents of our day. Both apply Pope John's *Mater et Magistra* and *Pacem in Terris* to the concrete realities of their countries. The chapter headings of the Brazilian statement offer a good "feel" of its content and spirit: Transformations Can No Longer Be Postponed, The Rural Question, Reform of Business, Tax Reform, Electoral Reform, The Presence of the Church Through Laymen.

A principal author of the Brazilian statement and of the social apostolate over the whole continent is Archbishop Helder Camara of Recife. He is also Executive Secretary of Brazil's Council of Bishops and Vice-President of the Council of Latin American Bishops (CELAM). Archbishop Helder Camara has attracted worldwide attention and admiration with his fresh ideas and activities. In 1963 he circulated his personal thoughts in a twenty-four-page letter entitled "Exchange of Ideas with Our Brothers in the Episcopate in the Course of the Second Vatican Council."

Archbishop Helder Camara is one of the Latin leaders of the movement known as "The Church of the Poor." This voluntary grouping of bishops, priests, religious and seminarians seeks, in his words, "to study the mystery of the Poor One [Christ] and to discover practical ways to help the Church find again the lost paths of poverty." He suggests that the titles "Eminence," "Beatitude" and "Excellency" be abandoned, and that "we [bishops] lose the obsession to be of the nobility and drop our coats of arms and mottoes.

"It seems like nothing," the Archbishop continues, "but how this creates distance between our clergy and our faithful! It separates us from our century, which has already adopted another style of life. It separates us especially from the workers and from the poor."

During the fear-filled weeks following the Brazilian military coup in April 1964, Archbishop Helder Camara, joined by Bishop Eugenio Sales and a score of other prelates, made repeated public appeals to the rightist junta to reduce unjust jailings, harassment and worse. The bishops asserted that all radical reformers were not Communists and Marxists. They personally intervened to rescue sincere social revolutionaries of the democratic left from political liquidation and exile. But principally these bishops have insisted that reactionary repression will not cure Brazil's social and economic ills. Drastic reform and peaceful revolution are required.

Raul Cardinal Silva is another recognized leader of the Latin American social apostolate. This writer first met Father Silva in the slums of Santiago in 1957, where he first gained attention for his work among the poor as founder and national director of Caritas, Chile's social welfare agency. A few days before our meeting, this priest had led by night a thousand squatters, newly arrived from their rural serfdom, onto the military drill field adjoining the capital city. There they were building their hovels, of odd pieces of zinc and thatch, cardboard and packing cases. Meanwhile Father Silva fended off the police and negotiated long-term payments for the land so that each family could acquire title to their home-site.

Finding a place to squat upon by invading a public parade ground represents a signal improvement over gutters and garbage dumps. But even today the housing among the slums (*callampas,* meaning mushrooms) of Santiago, and of all Latin cities, is abominable beyond North American powers of imagination. The 200,000 poor in Santiago's hovels average over five persons per room. Proceeding far beyond land invasion by night, Father Silva and his coworkers, in collaboration with the Alliance for Progress, set up the Institute for Low-Cost Housing (INVICA). This agency has developed 120 housing cooperatives and savings and loan associations, which provided 1500 new homes in 1964.

Another indication of the transformation which is now occurring within the Church of Latin America is that, in 1960, this simple padre of the slum dwellers was appointed Archbishop of Santiago and was named Cardinal Silva by Pope John. In 1962 the New York *Times* reported:

> Chile's Roman Catholic Church is trying to help solve critical political and economic problems here to improve the lot of the common man. The move is under the leadership of 55-year-old Raul Cardinal Silva, . . . who calls for drastic social reforms. . . .

Despite some gains, there is general agreement here

[Santiago] that there are gross social inequalities. But the meat of the latest message from the Catholic hierarchy is that reforms are going entirely too slowly and that too many so-called faithful Christians in Chile are showing cold indifference to problems of the masses that have now reached the emergency stage. [International edition, November 5, 1962, p. 7.]

In 1962 the present writer arrived, after a four-hour jeep ride, at the residence of Bishop Silvio Haro of Ibarra, on Ecuador's altiplano. A formal committee of lay leaders had prepared a reception. These committee members were not the hacienda owners, not the affluent merchants of the town, nor the beplumed Knights of St. Gregory in battle array. Rather, Bishop Haro had gathered around him truer representatives of his flock and those closest to his heart, delegates from the festering slums and scrubby mountain farms. As can happen so readily among the unlettered, ceremony was overcome, not to say crushed, and they spoke out spontaneously, "giving testimony" from the heart.

The change within the Church of their area, as manifested by their own bishop, was a principal theme. The afflicted themselves recognized the Church as mother of the poor, champion of the oppressed, promoter of a new social order based on justice and human dignity. One mother, weary with worry, malaria and a nursing baby at her breast, broke up the meeting. "This *palacio*," she exclaimed, "the Bishop's palace, is no longer reserved for the rich from the big haciendas. Now it has become *our* house, *my* house, the home of the poor." This weary mother broke up the meeting, because Bishop Haro burst into tears and left the room. And so did the North American visitors.

It is truly a humbling experience for us of the affluent U.S.A., the Colossus of the North, to encounter in our brothers south of the border this new incarnation of the Christ of the Gospels, as the poor Nazarene Who had not whereon to lay His head. Down there Our Lord is becoming visible in

His Church, in ways which we Americans in our suburban-parish complacency find difficult to understand.

Nourished by Pope John's encyclicals and Paul's pressing insistence upon the social apostolate, strengthened by the spirit of *aggiornamento* and by the new regional and world solidarity fostered by the Vatican Council, the Latin American Church goes about her newly grasped, complex and dangerous task of redeeming the temporal, the things of this world. Amidst bitter strife and near chaos she seeks to humanize the social order, so that all men might realize and live the dignity which is theirs as children of God and brothers in Christ.

By no means must we conclude that this transformation within the Church has achieved completion, that a vigorous social apostolate is launched in every diocese and parish, slum and village. This is certainly not the case. These reports tell of beginnings only, young initiatives of the past five to ten years. But these beginnings seem destined to become the wave of the future. The immensity of the continent and the complex structure of the Church must be appreciated. There are 640 bishops in Latin America's 510 dioceses and prelatures. All of these do not become Johannine pastors and enlightened social leaders overnight.

Ten years ago it was difficult to name ten bishops of strong social consciousness and vision on the whole continent. In 1965 Cardinal Silva, Archbishop Helder Camara and Bishops Larrain, Haro, and Sales are among some 50 bishops with an exceptional grasp of, and active dedication to, the social apostolate. These are supported by another 200 or so brother bishops who, while less vigorous and creative, offer dependable collaboration to the more active leaders. In each country a nucleus of progressive bishops now carries weight in the new national conferences of the hierarchy. There is every indication that in a short time their forward-looking views and social programs will prevail in the continent as a whole, as they already do in several countries. For instance, of

Chile's twenty-seven ordinaries, only five are now regarded as conservatives. This is a far cry from the day when social encyclicals did not always reach the public, and when, only five years ago, bishops and lay leaders supporting the social reforms of Frei's Christian Democracy were denounced to Rome as "pinkoes" and "fellow-travelers."

So, while the social apostolate and inner renewal are not yet universal, they do increasingly enter into the mainstream of Church policy and Christian life. Bishop Larrain of Talca, Chile, the 65-year-old veteran social apostle of Latin America, and the object of threats and rebuffs for his "leftism" during his twenty-five years as a bishop, received belated but strong ratification for his *avant-garde* position in November 1963. He was elected president of CELAM by the delegates of the region's twenty national conferences of bishops. The position of Pope Paul in these matters is indicated by his appointment, in 1964, of Archbishop Helder Camara, until then only an auxiliary without diocesan jurisdiction of his own, to the Archdiocese of Recife, the leading post in Brazil's Northeast, the troubled area where Mario Lopes, the banana peasant, and 15 million of his brothers in Christ subsist in subhuman misery.

Clergy and lay leaders have set up technical centers for the survey and planning of socioeconomic development, notably in Chile, Colombia, Venezuela, Mexico and Northeast Brazil. These professional institutes, unlike any operation under Catholic auspices in the United States, have been partly inspired by European economists and sociologists like Fathers Louis Lebret of Paris, François Houtart of Brussels, and Roger Vekemans, the Belgian Jesuit who heads the social science department of Chile's Catholic University. These development services are strongly supported by MISEREOR, the overseas social program of the German Bishops, which supplies some $8 million annually to Latin America. This program is supervised by the Center for Economic and Social Development for Latin America (DESAL), located in Santiago, acting through national development institutes which DESAL helps to establish in the respective countries.

These regional and national centers have in the past three years brought together economists, sociologists, agronomists, and financial, research, cooperative and educational specialists. These technical teams analyze their nation, dioceses and provinces, villages and haciendas, cities and slums. Taking into account illiteracy, disease, land tenure, housing, unemployment, and revolutionary movements other than Christian, they plot out the reforms to be promoted by social action of Christian inspiration, conjointly with all men of good will. Programs already functioning are strengthened. Needed movements are initiated. National and local specialists are trained. Others are sought abroad. Funds are raised, locally and by loans and grants from MISEREOR, and from foundations, the Alliance for Progress and European governmental and private sources.

The various categories of national organizations for labor and rural leadership, radio and basic education, cooperatives, agrarian reform, rural extension, housing and technical schools call upon the professional services of the development institutes to grasp their own situation and goals more clearly. These specialists help them to systematize their operations, to establish budgets and to obtain the kinds of personnel their particular category of work require. They test model organizations and techniques from other countries—savings and loan associations from the United States, radio education from Colombia, community action from Venezuela—adapt them to local realities, and devise new mechanisms to attain their social and economic goals.

The development centers correlate these programs with the national plans of the respective governments and regional bodies, and with Alliance for Progress and Common Market initiatives. DESAL in Santiago and the Center for Social Investigation (CIS) in Bogotá are now requested by governmental agencies like the Inter-American Development Bank and the Institute of Agrarian Reform to make surveys and plans for them under contract.

In the United States, Catholic intellectual centers have played only a slight role in the conception, planning and staffing of the New Deal, New Frontier and affiliated social advances. Our Catholic universities have made little creative contribution to the labor and farm legislation of the past thirty years. Nor have they done much for the preparation and implementation of the social security and tax systems, the reform of banking and monetary structures, and the great international undertakings like the United Nations, the Marshall Plan, Point Four and the Alliance for Progress. Catholic leadership in the labor and racial fields, modest as it has been, came on the whole from specialized movements without close connection with our universities. We and our nation have been the beneficiaries of intellectual initiatives and creativity from Harvard, Columbia, Princeton, Chicago and other universities, state and private, and from foundations and institutes of social study like the Brookings Institution. To a large degree, it can also be said that in Europe, until the Second World War, Catholic intellectual centers made but modest contributions to the structural reforms required for technical, economic and social progress in their respective nations. Louvain in Belgium and Nijmegen in Holland, however, have come forward in recent years.

Implementation of the social teaching of the Church has belatedly attached itself to an ongoing economic and social system in Europe and North America. We had little to do with setting it up. We have been tinkerers and remodelers rather than the architects and builders of today's Western industrial, welfare society, which now impinges upon the whole world.

While the new development centers and social movements of Christian inspiration in Latin America already show surprising accomplishment and greater promise, it must be stressed that these are young endeavors, still subject to the vagaries of history and judgment of the future. Nevertheless, for the first time in the modern era, Christian social teaching has entered the temporal arena during the formative period of democratization, industrialization and urbanization, instead of tardily attaching itself as a critic external to an already established social system, as in the democratic and technical development of the North Atlantic community of nations since 1776.

For these added reasons, Catholics, and indeed many other Christians and men of good will, are paying increasing heed to the new role of the Church in the social revolution of Latin America. Catholics in the United States have established the Catholic Inter-American Cooperation Program (CICOP), which is educating North Americans on these issues through publications, conferences and seminars which feature all of the Latin social leaders cited above and scores of their associates. Since 1960, Latin American and northern specialists in the cooperative, labor and managerial fields have come to know each other and to begin to work on numerous programs at all levels.

One of the most promising of these initiatives at the European-American level is the International Christian Union of Business Executives (UNIAPAC), with headquarters in Brussels. This association of employers and managers, which promotes application of Christian social teaching within their own milieu, is especially strong in Holland, Belgium and France, where the movement began after World War I. After the Second World War, UNIAPAC spread through Western Europe, notably in Germany and Italy, and since 1960 its leaders, most of whom are identified with Christian democracy, have devoted much energy to Latin America. The world congress of UNIAPAC was held in Santiago, Chile, in 1961, and in Mexico City in 1964. It also sponsored two forums on Latin American economic development in 1962 and 1963, in Brussels and São Paulo, Brazil.

The five hundred corporation executives who attended

these sessions, and the scores of specialized workshops which have followed, are concerned with the concrete aid, trade, investment and training programs which are the bases of development, as seen in the previous chapter. They strive to implement the reform of tariff and trade laws, to promote joint investment ventures, to supply technical assistance, and to support other international measures which would advance social and economic progress in Latin America. Within their respective countries the Latin leaders of UNIAPAC have become a nucleus within the business community who recognize the need for radical structural reforms and who back up concrete political and social movements to implement peaceful social evolution through democratic processes.

Business and industrial leaders as a group are under severe criticism in Latin America. In some countries their very existence is threatened. They must reform their nineteenth-century labor and profit policies in order to avoid collectivization. One of the main charges alleged against foreign investors is that they collaborate with local laissez-faire capitalists and continue them in power. Foreign firms are in this way also blamed for the unjust economic system of the nation. For this reason, among others, it is imperative that the business leaders of Europe, Japan and North America who have Latin American interests, confer with their Latin colleagues not only concerning trade and investment, but also on internal reform for a just social order. Within the business community of the world some men now have vision enough to see that social justice must obtain among all peoples before world peace can reign. They begin to recognize the new world "we."

Paul VI spoke on the role of businessmen in June 1964 to the leaders of UNIAPAC's Italian affiliate, the Christian Union of Industrial Managers (UCID). The Holy Father expressed to them "real respect for what you are . . . producers of wealth, organizers of modern enterprises . . . generators of work, of employment, of professional training suitable for giving employment and bread to an enormous mass of workers and collaborators." For these reasons Paul recognizes that business managers are among the principal tranformers of society. They exercise great influence on the conditions of modern life and open up for society new and unimagined developments. This they accomplish "by means of the deployment of the operative forces which science, technology, industrial structure and administration place at the disposal of modern man."

Paul sees this power to transform society and this "magnificent development of human faculties," which characterize today's industrial managers, from a spiritual and creative viewpoint. For him these "immense and superb capacities . . . have revealed the divine reflection in the face of man and have discovered further the traces of a transcendent and dominating Thought in the cosmos, opened up by scholars for new explorations and by you for new conquests."

Their position then, Pope Paul states, is eminent and strategic. For all that is good in their managerial endeavor he gives "the tribute of our gratitude, our praise and our encouragement. . . . This testimony of ours is a sign of the attitude of the Church toward the modern world, an attitude of attention, understanding, admiration and friendship."

While these laudatory phrases might sound at first a bit fulsome, Paul clearly redresses such an impression. He expresses acute concern for the ideology of today's Western-style industrial society, and for the ideas and motives of capitalism in particular. He grants that today's Western capitalism is not the capitalism of the nineteenth century, so roundly condemned by Leo XIII. "But the fact remains that the socioeconomic system generated by Manchester liberalism [in the European sense of laissez-faire individualism] and still persisting in the conception of the unilaterality of the possession of the means of production, and of an econ-

omy directed toward paramount private profit, is not perfection; it is not peace; it is not justice."

For Pope Paul, this capitalist system, motivated by private
profit and built upon unilateral ownership of the means of
production, must be criticized further "if it still divides men
into irreducible opposing classes, and if society is marked by
the deep and wounding differences which torment it." These
deep and wounding divisions in human solidarity, the Holy
Father laments, "are barely held in check by legality and by
the temporary truce of some agreement in the systematic and
implacable struggle which should lead to the domination of
one class over the other."

Paul urges upon industrial managers the necessity "to
emerge from the primitive stage of the industrial era," based
upon the selfishness of "the one-sided profit economy."
He calls this a materialistic orientation of life which bases
human well-being predominantly on economic goods and
temporal happiness. He likens these materialistic ideologists
of the profit economy with "those who make antique dialectical materialism the fundamental dogma of a bleak sociology . . . , who put the golden calf in the place which belongs
to the God of heaven and earth."

A new sociology is being elaborated, Paul affirms,
"founded on the Christian concept of life and on the effective
remaking of the economic structures in accordance with this
concept." This new sociology favors the common good and
opposes the old individualism. He lists the effects of this outmoded selfishness which opposes "one's own advantage to the
advantage of human brotherhood." This devisive individualism now opposes capital to labor, private profit to the common good, the class concept to the organic concept of society,
the private to the public economy, private initiative to ration-
ally planned enterprise, national autocracy to the international market.

"It is necessary to have new visions, wide and universal,
of the world," Pope Paul concludes. "You businessmen have

been the pilots of the formation of modern industrial, technological and commercial society. You Christian businessmen still can with new ability and new virtue be the pilots in the formation of a more just, more peaceful, more brotherly society. . . . With the strength of Christian love you can do great things."

This is the vision of a new national, regional and world society which guides and animates the Christian leaders of the democratic left in Latin America. Through worker, farmer and slum-dweller organizations, through political, intellectual and managerial groups, these leaders and their ideology are beginning to make significant impact.

Among the growing number of American leaders who grasp and appreciate this new Latin American reality, Vice President Hubert Humphrey stands out. In his report to the Senate on the Alliance for Progress in 1963, the then Senator Humphrey stated: "One of the most hopeful signs in Latin America in recent years is the renaissance of the Catholic Church and a new awakening on the part of Church leaders to the shocking social and economic problems of the continent." The Senator noted with resounding approval that the social-reform aims of the Alliance for Progress coincide with those promoted by national pastoral letters from the bishops of Chile, Panama, Venezuela, Brazil, Argentina and Colombia. (88th Congress, First Session, Senate Document No. 13.)

On the floor of the Senate in July 1963, Humphrey recounted that he, colleagues of the Senate Foreign Relations Committee, and Alliance officials had just come from a luncheon meeting, which he hosted, with Cardinal Silva of Santiago, Chile. The Senator asked for unanimous consent to print in the *Congressional Record* the 1962 pastoral letter of the Chilean bishops, "advocating basic structural reforms in Chile. It is a model document for all Latin American countries to follow in implementing the aims of the Alliance for Progress."

In the scholarly quarterly, *Foreign Affairs,* Senator

Humphrey returned to this theme in July 1964.[2] He first shows that the Alliance must not be merely pragmatic and economic, but must also have social content and ideological animation—"a mystique all its own, capable of inspiring a following." The Alliance and the United States, Humphrey insists, must identify themselves with "conscious, rapid change in the socioeconomic structure, a process that can correctly and precisely be called a revolution. If used not as a slogan but in its precise sense, the policy of peaceful social and economic revolution is a correct characterization of Alliance policy."

The Senator stated that he was impressed "by the fact that the two fastest-growing political movements in the larger countries of South America today are the two most intensely ideological movements—the Marxist and the Christian Democratic movements."

Turning then directly to the Church, Humphrey alerts readers of his *Foreign Affairs* article that "we should be aware of the renaissance of one of the traditional institutions found in all Latin American societies—the Catholic Church." This rebirth, to his mind, comes in great part from the "far-sighted social and economic philosophy of Pope John's recent social encyclicals *Mater et Magistra* and *Pacem in Terris* . . . strongly pushed by the Vatican. Men who once would have been 'promoted' to mountain parishes for their advanced views are now being appointed bishops and cardinals."

Humphrey sees the Church as filling other important roles, besides promoting drastic reform and peaceful revolution. The upbuilding of a just society requires rapid change, and sometimes the destruction, of old institutions. The Senator observes that, in a revolutionary era, there is a pressing temp-

---

[2] "United States Policy in the Western Hemisphere," *Foreign Affairs,* July, 1964, Vol. 42, No. 4, pp. 585–601.

tation for the state to absorb total responsibility in the social and economic order. The state feels compelled to eliminate all institutions which it cannot directly control, to create an atomized society of mere individuals. Humphrey cites history as the teacher, and Cuba as an objective lesson, that an atomized society is the easy prey of totalitarianism. This is because mass society eliminates all the intermediate groups between the individual and the state.

During the next decade, when revolutionary change will be the order of the day in many countries, Humphrey foresees "times when a brake is needed on the action of the state if social pluralism and individual political liberty are to be preserved. In some Latin American countries, it may be the Church that will be called upon to play that role."

Finally, Senator Humphrey points out that the Catholic Church, together with Roman law and language, "is one of the principal unifying forces in this vast continent. In an age of rampant nationalism, the common bond which the Church provides may have a powerful impact in overcoming the separatist tendencies of the age and in achieving hemispheric unity."

Christian social teaching in Latin America now reverberates over the horizon with the suddenness of thunder. Outward historic forces, social and economic, political and technical, give peculiar timeliness and help to motivate the social apostolate which this doctrine inspires. But it would be an error to conclude that this new life is effervescent, only the mushrooming product of the crucial events since Castro, without roots in time and theology.

Serious effort to apply Christian social teaching to Latin American realities became noticeable in the 1930s, due in great part to the stimulus of Pope Pius XI. University chaplains, a few professors, seminarians and a few priests, most of whom pursued part of their studies at Louvain, Paris and Rome, awoke to the "incarnational" theology then fermenting in Europe before the Second World War. Bishop Manuel Larrain, president of the Council of Latin American Bishops (CELAM), was among the young leaders who began forty years ago to pioneer today's Christian ideology of the temporal. Monsignor L. G. Ligutti, for years executive director of the National Catholic Rural Life Conference, Des Moines, Iowa, and now permanent observer of the Holy See to the UN Food and Agriculture Organization, was one of Bishop Larrain's earliest collaborators.

Jacques Maritain, through his books, especially *True Humanism,* and through lecture tours (most Latin American intellectuals speak French), has exercised telling influence. This writer has encountered high officials in Brazil who avow that their "conversion" to Christianity, from rationalism and Comte's positivism, dates from Maritain's stay in their country in the 1930s. Eduardo Frei openly acknowledges his own ideological debt to the French Thomist, whose ideas he first met as a university student in Santiago. With his schoolmates Frei formed a social-study circle, which exerted influence in university politics and, in time, grew into today's Christian Democratic Party. For the future, however, Frei foresees that Christian social ideology will draw much nourishment and *élan* from Teilhard de Chardin, who has already developed a large following throughout the continent.

Among present-day theologians of the temporal, forty-year-old Bishop Marcos McGrath of Veraquas, Panama, stands out. Before his elevation to the episcopacy, Bishop McGrath was Dean of the theological faculty of the Catholic University, Santiago, Chile, filling a chair made notable by Father Gustave Weigel, the Jesuit ecumenist. The young Panamanian-born prelate serves with distinction on the theological commission of the Vatican Council, a post to which he was nominated by his progressive confreres in the Latin American hierarchy.

Bishop McGrath has become a continental exponent of "incarnational" theology, which seeks to incarnate Christ

constantly and everywhere in time and place, by projecting
Him into the warp and woof of daily life, work and worry,
tears and joy. "The Church is the divine leaven working in
the mass of society," the Bishop says.[3] "And we believe that
Christ is more active in His Church today than when He
walked visibly over the hills of Galilee. Literally, in His own
words, it was better for the Church that Christ should go
away so that He could send forth, infuse the Holy Spirit into
the souls of all believers."

It is God Who acts through Christ in His Church, Bishop
McGrath continues, and the mission of the Church is specifically religious. "But she strives to make man and his whole
life religious. . . . Quickly, Christianity touches upon the
temporal order—the world of work, of art, of science, of
education, of business, of politics: of all that is not specifically
religious." All human relations involve basic human values,
doctrines and moral principles, the Latin American theologian
insists. But the application of these principles rests mainly
with the Christian layman himself, "whether it be in settling
a family quarrel or launching a union into a major strike."

The Church as a religious society is distinct from the temporal order, the Panamanian prelate concludes. But Christian
men, fathers and citizens, who compose by far the greater
part of the Church, "live deeply imbedded in the temporal
order."

The Christian active in the temporal order finds himself rubbing shoulders and convictions with men of very
diverse creeds. In all honesty of purpose he must strive for
a serious cultivation of temporal values in themselves, material well-being, culture, science and the like, and in their
proper relation to peace and spiritual progress. In this he
will link arms with all men of good will wherever possible,
with never a need to impose his religious creed on others.

[3] From "The Role of the Church in the Temporal Order," a paper given at
the first annual meeting of the Catholic Inter-American Cooperation Program (CICOP), Chicago, January 1964.

II. Sub-Saharan Africa

From the viewpoint of Christian presence, Africa and Asia must be sharply distinguished from Latin America. Christians number 90 percent of the population in Latin America, but only about 5 percent in the rest of the underdeveloped world. In this diaspora, by far the highest concentrations of Christians are found in Negroid Africa, south of the Sahara, where the figure runs about 20 percent, and as high as 35 percent in the Congo. This compares to less than 1 percent in the Islamic, Buddhist and Hindu regions. In Asia, only the Philippines (which should really be classified with Latin America) and Vietnam have significant numbers of Christians. But these 30 or so millions are isolated islands among the 1800 millions who form Asia's sea of massed humanity.

So in sheer numbers of Christians, Sub-Saharan Africa should be treated apart from the continent's northern half, and this Islamic area is best combined with Asia as another great world division.

Another important reason for this division is that the leaders of southern and central Africa have been much more frequently the beneficiaries of Christian education than have the leaders of North Africa and Asia. Very often the reformers, revolutionaries and ideologists of the Negroid nations are now, or at some time have been, Christians themselves. However, it is noteworthy that Christian social doctrine usually does not stand forth clearly as an important component of their own formulations of national goals, policy and ideology. One reason for this lack could be the fact that most of these leaders received only elementary, and in some cases secondary, schooling under Christian auspices. Further, the curricula of these schools under the colonial regimes were purposely deprived of social content which might have accelerated dissatisfaction with the ruling European powers and fomented reform and revolution. Civil rights, the right to organize, collective bargaining, national self-determination and local cultural values were understandably seldom proclaimed in Christian pulpits, pastoral letters, press, classrooms and training centers before the Second World War and the wind of revolution which ensued.

Nevertheless, men originally trained to be country school-teachers, plantation foremen, army sergeants, and petty bureaucrats quickly acquired greater authority and became the founding fathers and leaders of their nations. They now play heightened roles in the world arena. Christian or not, their ideologies are remarkably alike. The main thrust of them all focuses on overcoming internal tribal disunity and external threats from the world powers to build up their people and territory into a modern nation-state.

Having secured identity as an independent nation in the past five to ten years, they strive toward a political, economic and social system which will assure and enhance this national identity and will provide "the fullness of a more excellent life" to their people. Some of the methods they espouse, however, are not always compatible with the ideals of most Western nations. Among these are African Socialism and one-party rule. Both these approaches, which have such vital impact on the economic and political orders of Africa, have sound roots in their tribal and chieftain systems of hallowed tradition. But they also involve rejection of capitalism as morally unjust and of the parliamentary party system as an invitation to chaos and weakness, particularly since national self-consciousness is shredded by tribal enmities centuries-old and still erupting.

A dominant factor which affects all African ideologies is that of speed. Strong centralization and state control of the economy are justified as means of catching up with the industrialized nations, of narrowing the widening gap. As President Kwame Nkrumah of Ghana, a principal pioneer of African Socialism and one-party rule, puts it: "What other countries have taken three hundred years to achieve, a once dependent territory must try to accomplish in a generation if it is to survive. Unless it is, as it were, 'jet-propelled,' it will lag behind and thus risk everything for which it has fought. Capitalism is too complicated a system for a newly independent nation. Hence the need for a socialist society."[4] President Nkrumah draws the conclusion that, during the period following independence, even a system based on social justice and a democratic constitution may need backing up by emergency measures of a totalitarian kind. Because, he asserts, without discipline true freedom cannot survive.

Nkrumah was baptized a Catholic and attended mission schools for eight years. A German priest sent him to a secondary school near Accra. Then he went to Lincoln University in Pennsylvania, where after graduation he taught political science. Concentrating on "finding a formula by which the whole colonial question and the problem of imperialism could be solved," he studied Hegel, Marx, Engels, Lenin, Gandhi and Nehru. "The writings of these men did much to influence me in my revolutionary ideas and activities, and Marx and Lenin particularly impressed me, as I felt sure that their philosophy was capable of solving these problems." It must be noted by partisans and critics of Catholic education that the determining ideas of President Nkrumah's political and economic ideology were gained after his grade-school years.

The socialism and "emergency measures of a totalitarian kind" of Nkrumahism, inspired in part by Marx and Lenin, do not result in the exclusion of private enterprise, even that financed and directed by foreign capitalists. Kofi Baako, Leader of the House and Minister of State in Ghana, and for years a trusted lieutenant of Nkrumah, shows that African Socialism still provides a large role for private investment. This ideology of a mixed economy to accelerate economic development is characteristic of most African and Asian leaders. Baako asserts that a large proportion of the productivity

[4] Paul E. Sigmund, Jr., *Ideologies of the Developing Nations* (New York: Praeger, 1963), p. 186.

of an industrial company remains in Ghana in the form of wages to employees. These wages create tax revenues and purchasing power, which encourage further investment and plant expansion. "In good companies, of which there are many," the Nkrumahist spokesman continues, "a share of the profits is plowed back into the company for development of its enterprises. This is, in fact, further investment. If there are fears of permanent foreign domination in the commercial and industrial field of our economy, these fears should be immediately and permanently abandoned." Baako reassures that the government controls this danger by forbidding ownership of land by foreigners and by limiting the duration of leases and concessions. But, Baako continues, in a statement which summarizes the over-all bargaining dynamic between rich nations and poor, "the duration of leases and concessions must be balanced against the encouragement of overseas capital in such a way as to guarantee a reasonable return for the investment."[5]

Another mark of African Socialism which distinguishes it from Marxism is its attitude toward religion and things of the spirit. Baako states that "Nkrumahism as a philosophy" recognizes, among the natural rights of man, those in the religious sphere. He lists the specific guarantees in Ghana, among them the right of all "to practice their religion in private and public without suffering any disadvantage in their civil life; the right of parents in the religious education of their children." Baako concludes: "In fact, atheism is foreign to Africa, and religion is the basis of all our culture."[6]

President Leopold Sedar Senghor of Senegal is another proponent of the African Socialist ideology who is strongly critical of Marxism, for both its social and religious content. He is also another product of low-rung Catholic schools who later developed his key ideas during higher studies abroad

[5] *Ibid.*, p. 192.
[6] *Ibid.*, p. 190.

and through his own soul-searching. He was much stimulated by the intellectual ferment at the Sorbonne in Paris and by socialists like Saint-Simon, Proudhon, Fourier, and Léon Blum. Senghor, probably Africa's most respected thinker and poet, directly confronts the accusation leveled against himself and other African Socialists "of being atheists, Marxists, and of outlawing religion. Though this smacks of propaganda, it poses a fundamental question. Can we integrate Negro African cultural values, especially religious values, into socialism? We must answer that question once and for all with an unequivocal 'Yes.'

"We are not 'Marxists' in the sense given the word today," Senghor asserts, "in so far as Marxism is presented as atheistic metaphysics, a total and totalitarian view of the world, a *Weltanschauung*." He accuses the Communist countries of having made the state "an omnipotent, soulless monster," of stifling the natural freedoms of man, and of drying up "the sources of art, without which life is not worth living."

With other African Socialists, Senghor attacks the materialism and selfish motives of capitalism with a vehemence approaching his condemnation of Communism. He states that "a third revolution is taking place, as a reaction against capitalistic and Communistic materialism—one that will integrate moral, if not religious, values with the political and economic contributions of the two great revolutions." The two former revolutions referred to are, of course, the French Revolution of 1789 and the revolution of Marx and Lenin in 1917. In today's third revolution, the Senegalese leader says, "the colored peoples, including the Negro African, must play their part. They must bring their contribution to the construction of the new planetary civilization."[7]

Senghor is the most articulate exponent of "Negritude . . . the whole complex of civilized values—cultural, economic, social, and political—which characterize the black people."

[7] *Ibid.*, pp. 240–47.

These values are the product of "intuitive reason . . . which comes to grips, expresses itself emotionally, through that self-surrender, that coalescence of subject and object; through myths, by which I mean the archetypal images of the collective soul; and, above all, through primordial rhythms, synchronized with those of the cosmos." Senghor opposes Negritude "to European racialism, of which the Nazis were the symbol." Europe's racialism, with its hatred, violence, weeping and shedding of blood, is "foreign to our continent's genius: our *need to love* . . . the sense of communion."

In a statement remarkable for its global cultural implications, Senghor says that, "Seen within this prospect of the civilization of the universal, the colonial policies of Great Britain and France have proved successful complements to each other, and black Africa has benefitted." In his judgment, British policy reinforced traditional native civilization, while French policy forced Africans actively to assimilate European civilization. "This fertilized our sense of Negritude. Today, our Negritude no longer expresses itself as opposition to European values, but as a *complement* to them."

The African philosopher says that his people no longer disagree basically with European values, with the exception of capitalism. But Africans are utterly opposed to the presumptuous theory that European civilization is the one universal civilization, "to be imposed, unmodified, on all peoples and continents. . . . Actually, our criticism of the [European] thesis is that it is monstrously antihumanist . . . that they [Europe and North America] have no idea of the *pre-eminent dignity of the human person.*" Senghor concludes:

Our revised Negritude is humanistic. I repeat, it welcomes the complementary values of Europe and the white man, and, indeed, of all other races and continents. But it welcomes them in order to fertilize and reinvigorate its own values, which it then offers for the construction of a civilization which shall embrace all mankind. The neo-humanism of the twentieth century stands at the point where the paths of all nations, races, and continents cross, "where the four winds of the spirit blow."[8]

Julius Nyerere, President of Tanganyika, is another African leader who was educated in Catholic schools. He also taught in them for several years. He received his bachelor's degree from Makerere College in Uganda, and his M.A. from the University of Edinburgh. He has remained a practicing Catholic.

Nyerere has bravely stood for moderation in his struggle for national independence. Following the motto of freedom and work, he has avoided demagogic promises and has championed multiracial harmony which allows Europeans, Indians and other minorities to participate freely in Tanganyika's development. But Nyerere's ideas on the single party, a socialized economy, the relationship of workers to political organizations, and positive Pan-Africanism, resemble those of other national leaders already surveyed.[9]

Nyerere is convinced that Africa must unite in order to avoid becoming the prey of a "second scramble for Africa" by the powerful capitalist and socialist blocs. The Tanganyikan president denounces both these economic and political systems as practiced in the Western and Eastern blocs.

"What is wrong with capitalism? To my mind, capitalism went wrong when it divorced wealth from its true purpose . . . to satisfy very simple needs: the need for food, the need for shelter, the need for education, and so on." Nyerere affirms that competitive capitalism whets the appetite for power and prestige as ends in themselves:

So what happens? There is then ruthless competition between individuals—not to get wealth to feed themselves, or to clothe themselves, or to house themselves, but to seize

[8] *Ibid.*, pp. 248–50; from an address, "What Is Negritude?" given by Senghor at Oxford University, October 1961. Italics in the original.
[9] *Ibid.*, pp. 196–211.

enough wealth to give themselves more power, more prestige than their fellows, i.e., wealth that exceeds their real
needs and will enable them to dominate other individuals.
When that stage is reached, one millionaire is prepared to
spend millions simply in order to destroy another millionaire.[10]

Nyerere then asserts that socialism arose in the West in
order to remove "this sin of capitalism" and to return wealth
to its original use—the satisfaction of simple human needs,
the banishment of poverty. He believes that capitalist countries are hypocritical if they refuse to recognize the relative
attainment of these goals within socialist countries. But, showing his openmindedness toward both systems, Nyerere
charges that the socialist nations "are now committing the
same crime that was committed by capitalists before. . . .
Internationally, they are now engaged in using wealth in ex-
actly the same way as the capitalist countries—for power
and prestige."

> And socialist countries, no less than capitalist countries,
> are prepared to behave like the millionaire—to use mil-
> lions to destroy another millionaire; and it need not neces-
> sarily be a capitalist millionaire—it is just as likely to be a
> socialist millionaire. In other words, socialist wealth now
> tolerates poverty—which is an even more unforgivable
> crime!

With his eyes fully open to the sins of both capitalism and
socialism, the Tanganyikan president embraces socialism. He
believes that no underdeveloped country can afford to be anything but socialist, and that socialism arose to remedy the
mistakes of capitalism. Since the socialist nation can fall into
the same crime of using wealth to acquire power and prestige, Nyerere wants correctives to these present-day socialist

---

[10] *Ibid.*, pp. 205–11; from "Nationalism and Pan-Africanism," an address by
Nyerere to the Second Pan-African Seminar, World Assembly of Youth,
1961.

sins: "Let us make sure that it [wealth] is used solely for raising the standards of our people. Let us not allow the wealth that we are creating to live side by side with poverty, and tolerate that poverty."

Nyerere applies Marx's theory of the inevitable class struggle of the rich and poor within a nation to the world division between the have and have-not nations. "This division is not between capitalists and socialists, or between capitalists and Communists; this is a division between the poor countries of the world and the rich countries of the world." He warns that the rich countries are both capitalist and socialist. "The poor countries of the world should be very careful not to allow themselves to be used as the 'tools' of any of the rich countries of the world, however much the rich countries may seek to fool them that they are on their side." For these reasons, Nyerere fervently espouses African unity. This leads him to seek federation with Zanzibar, Kenya, Uganda and other English-speaking neighbors. This accounts too for his proposal of an African army to deal with unrest within the continent, whether internal strife or conflict introduced into Africa by the competing world powers, be they Western, Moscow, Peking, or some combination thereof.

The African Socialism of Nyerere is viewed favorably by Catholic spokesmen of Tanganyika. Among these are Bishop Joseph Blomjous of Mwanza and vice-chairman of the Secretariat of African Bishops at the Vatican Council. Another is Lady Chesham, born Marion Donoghue in Philadelphia, Pennsylvania. She and her husband, Lord Chesham, settled on a Tanganyikan coffee and cattle plantation in the 1930s. She became an early supporter of Nyerere's movement for independence and is now the only white woman member of the young country's national parliament. Since 1958 she has been re-elected annually to the executive committee of the Tanganyika African National Union Party; Lady Chesham is the only non-African who serves on this governing body of the Party, which has a virtual monopoly in Tanganyika.

A third endorsement of African Socialism comes from Father D. W. Robinson, who is secretary general of Tanganyika's National Conference of Catholic Bishops. Father Robinson, an American Maryknoll priest, explains that the concept of Nyerere's brand of socialism, known locally as Ujamaa, derives from "the traditional African way of life as expressed in the extended family . . . [and] the inherent dignity of the human individual, simply because he is human, a member of the human race with spiritual value, and a brother, not a servant, in the human family."[11]

All citizens share the family responsibility of being concerned about each other's welfare, of making a positive contribution to the common good, of enjoying the security, the help and the feeling of belonging that comes from family life. According to Father Robinson's interpretation of Nyerere's socialism, all citizens have a right to share in the profits and benefits of such a society, not equally, but in proportion to the effort and skill of the individual's contribution to the common good. Within this framework, personal ambition and competition are good, so long as exploitation of others for selfish gain is avoided. Pure speculation with land or wealth is considered unlawful exploitation of others.

Labor unions are permitted, but unfair demands and irresponsible strikes are closely controlled by arbitration and negotiation processes under which only the government can determine true grounds for a strike. Father Robinson observes that, "Although some felt that such legislation would be a death-blow to the trade unions, in fact the same legislation gave legal recognition and strong support for the labor movement . . . which is daily winning better wages and terms of service for the workers through agreements with employers."

Since land is considered the chief natural resource of Tanganyika, the law prevents land speculation and does not per-

---

[11] From "Ujamaa—Socialism and Tanganyika," *World Campus*, October 1963, pp. 3–6.

mit absolute ownership in fee simple. As Father Robinson phrases it, the law "puts the stress on the right to use the land. . . . Thus the proprietor can be compelled to put idle land to productive use under threat of losing his right over the land. In which case, the land can be turned over to others for development."

In the view of this American Maryknoll priest, this social-istic society of Tanganyika offers the Church a most favor-able opportunity for fulfilling her divine mission. "Ujamaa [Tanganyikan socialism based on the extended family] seems to be in complete conformity with the principles of natural law applied to society . . . in complete conformity with the social teaching of the Church."

The general secretary of the National Council of Catholic Bishops concludes that there is no need for confessional trade unions and political parties in Tanganyika's pluralist society. The ghetto must be avoided.

Rather the work of the Church is to integrate itself with society, becoming co-extensive with it, making itself pres-ent in society through its members in all the organizations, functions and aspects of society. Thereby it ensures the continued existence of policies based on the natural law and in conformity with Christian social principles.

III. Asia and North Africa

This vast land area, with over three fifths of the world's population, is the home of so many diverse nationalities and tongues, cultures and ideologies that generalization involves serious risk of misunderstanding.

One characteristic shared by all the nations, except Japan, is economic underdevelopment and poverty. Fully 1200 mil-lion persons have incomes of less than $100 a year. A system of mixed economy obtains in most countries, but anticapital-ist socialism, similar to the African type, is fervently preached and strongly influences planners and political leaders. China, of course, has become the practitioner and exporter of Communism in its most violent form.

Neutralism in the Cold War was first advanced by Nehru of India and Sukarno of Indonesia. Nasser of the United Arab Republic (Egypt) has practiced nonalignment with great finesse and profit, enabling him to obtain the Suez Canal from France and Britain and the monumental Aswan Dam from Russia. Nationalism, on the whole, is not as vehement as in Negroid Africa, but is often appealed to as a means of justifying greater sacrifices from citizens and workers, and to cement internal unity against foreign aggression —political, economic and cultural, real or imagined. Most of the countries were under European or American domination for a century or more, and only gained their freedom since the Second World War. Remarkably, however, only Algeria had to fight a full-fledged war of liberation. The United States has taken over many of the peacekeeping burdens formerly carried by Europeans. Moscow and Peking vie for position and power in this period of flux and readjustment.

From the viewpoint of the Church, three characteristics stand out: the paucity of Christians, usually less than 1 percent; the pervasive presence of the ancient religions and culture systems of Islam, Buddhism and Hinduism; and the growing pressure of the population spiral.

Only in the Philippines and Vietnam is the number of Christians appreciable. Small islands of Christian faith are also found, as in Goa and Kerala, India and in the Middle East. In recent years Christian conversions have mounted in Korea and Taiwan, but this is due to extraordinary circumstances and effort.

On the whole, Christianity is now on the defensive, often under attack as an appendage and ally of the Western colonial powers. The three ancient religio-cultural systems of the area are being stimulated into new and enlivened expressions by technology, nationalism, and the social upheavals which accompany today's human progress. In some countries, like

Sudan and Vietnam, the Church is under active attack. In China, North Vietnam and North Korea she has been liquidated.

In the areas where the Church is free to function, no great advance is being made, with the very few exceptions already cited. In today's realities, no notable improvement can be expected, within the power of human foresight, from the mission techniques and attitudes in use for four centuries.

This missionary crusade, often heroic and saintly, was marred by a heavy admixture of cultural imperialism. Western styles of conduct, legalism and formulas of thought clothed the Faith in its liturgical, moral and intellectual expressions. The Word of God made Man was never permitted to take on the oriental dress He had once worn in Galilee. Latin and Nordic cultures, myths and manners, music, literature and architecture—great but transient human creations—became overly identified with divine truths, commands and counsels. Asia and North Africa normally regarded these Western forms as merely human—and foreign—interlopers. Secure with their own more ancient cultures, they were neither impressed nor attracted by a Faith made Western. In the mystery of grace and divine salvation, there are undoubtedly other explanations, more profound and supernatural, for the failure of the Christian apostolate among the Moslem, Buddhist and Hindu peoples. But we cannot comment upon, much less change, what we cannot know without divine enlightenment.

The Vatican Council has already authorized liturgical changes which can correct four centuries of obvious cultural imperialism in the field of public worship. It has also begun to mitigate the legalism of Roman law, which had so pervaded the Church, and to replace this with the pastoral approach incarnated by Pope John. Pope Paul now commits the Church to sustained dialogue with the great non-Christian religions by the establishment of a new and special secretariat. Undoubtedly this will multiply and give added prestige to earlier efforts at dialogue, as distinct from conversion, like those pioneered by Father Bede Griffiths among the Hindus, and by the French Benedictines of Toumliline among the Moslems of Africa. Certainly we shall also see more intellectual interchange among philosophic and religious thinkers, similar to the conference cosponsored by UNESCO and Pax Romana in Manila in 1960 on the impact of the world's great religions on the modern world.

It is in the temporal field that the dialogue and new relations with the Eastern religions are most likely to find early meeting ground, and in time, perhaps, considerable common ground. The dignity of man, his equality and rights, national and international social justice, the universal common good and world peace are fast becoming the concerns of all men. Moslem, Buddhist and Hindu leaders, as well as Christians, show increasing awareness that the Other World of the Absolute cannot be reached without dealing with the complex relations of this-world. And that the God of all is Lord of both worlds *in continuum*.

The universal acclaim which Pope John aroused with his two social encyclicals was not a passing outburst. World leaders—Moslem, Buddhist, Hindu, Jewish and Christian, as well as nonbelievers—continue to quote these basic documents. They even gather formally and publicly to search *Pacem in Terris* for common ground and blueprints for bridges which can lead to peace on earth. The World Council of Churches sponsors similar meetings of religion and the new world society. The dialogue among Christians and the other great religions has indeed begun.

It is in Asia and North Africa that poverty is greatest and that the numbers of poor are mounting most rapidly in relation to land area, natural resources and potential economic production. It is in this same area that the most drastic programs of birth prevention have been initiated. The government of India has launched a program of artificial control and of sterilization of men and women. Japan has added the even more Draconian method of widespread legal abortion for nontherapeutic reasons.

These facts point to another great issue for the Church which would speak to all man. It is an issue of particular gravity because it involves intimately the family and the life-giving processes which the Church has for nineteen centuries guarded and ennobled in Western civilization. As the world takes on one universal civilization, the Church's role therein will be greatly affected by her views on responsible parenthood and population growth.

Chapter Eleven

POPULATION GROWTH AND RESPONSIBLE PARENTHOOD

Father Bernard Häring, the authoritative Redemptionist theologian, stated in June 1964 that the principle that family regulation may be a necessity in the modern world was included in a draft declaration for the Vatican Council. "While recognizing the principle of responsible parenthood and the limitation of family size that that implies," Father Häring said, "the declaration is silent on means toward this end. It would thus represent no relaxation of the Church's ban on contraceptive devices."[1] However, the *Times* story goes on, if approved, this Council declaration "could serve to extend discussion on birth control . . . and provide new ground for theological work on the issue." Father Häring was discussing the latest of some five or more versions of Schema 13, on "The Church and the Modern World."

It could well be that this theological issue arouses the attention of more people, and at a deeper level of personal concern, than has any other doctrinal discussion in the Christian era. The discussion will probably go on for some time, even after the Council ends. And it is likely that it will become more public, and even more confused and confusing, despite the well-meant desire of many Church officials to keep the affair within the family and to avoid further disturbance of consciences.

[1] New York *Times,* June 12, 1964, p. 1.

All this is not surprising. The problem affects directly most Catholic families at some time or other. Furthermore, as a world social issue, population growth has importance which may well override all the other great issues, both for the human family in general and for the Church in particular. Also, it is a relatively new social and doctrinal concern. Only since the Second World War has it aroused great public interest in the nation and the world at large. Only in the past fifteen years has the Church begun to consider the subject outside the narrow context of personal and marital morality, and in the wider context of the whole family in the economic and social order, actual and future. Only in 1951 did Pius XII open up the limits justifying the use of the rhythm method of periodic continence, as a means for avoiding conception and spacing births, for medical, eugenic and social reasons.

Pope John brought the issue decisively beyond personal moral considerations, and set it squarely in the framework of the common good, national and international. He did this in a special section of *Mater et Magistra*, entitled "Population Increase and Economic Development." John says that some persons, "consequent to statistical reasoning, observe that within a matter of decades mankind will become very numerous, whereas economic growth will proceed much more slowly. From this some conclude that unless procreation is kept within limits, there subsequently will develop an even greater imbalance between the number of inhabitants and the necessities of life." (Par. 186.)

Recent advances in public health and medicine, Pope John admits, have lowered death rates in less-developed countries, while birth rates have remained high. "Meanwhile the productive systems in such countries do not expand as rapidly as the number of inhabitants. Hence, in poorer countries of this sort, the standard of living does not advance and may even deteriorate." In consequence, some persons propose the avoidance and curbing of conception and birth "by every possible means . . . lest a serious crisis occur." (Par. 187.)

Pope John asserts that on a global scale the relationships between births and resources are such that "grave difficulties in this matter do not arise at present, nor will in the immediate future." He considers the arguments, pointing to such grave difficulties, as so controversial and inconclusive that nothing certain can be drawn from them. (Par. 188.) "Besides, God in His goodness and wisdom has, on the one hand, provided nature with almost inexhaustible productive capacity; and, on the other hand, has endowed man with such ingenuity that, by using suitable means, he can apply nature's resources to the needs and requirements of existence."

Accordingly, John warns against proposed solutions "whereby, contrary to the moral law laid down by God, procreative function also is violated." He recommends, rather, that man should acquire an intimate knowledge of the forces of nature and control them ever more extensively. He believes that advances "in science and technology give almost limitless promise for the future in this matter." (Par. 184.) Moreover, to promote needed economic and social advances, "international cooperation is necessary, so that, conformably with the welfare of all, information, capital, and men themselves may move about among the peoples in orderly fashion." (Par. 192.) Pope John then speaks of marriage and the family, through which human life must be transmitted "in accord with the most sacred, permanent, inviolate prescriptions of God."

Procedures which are permissible for checking the life of plants and animals cannot be used to interfere with human life, because the life of man is sacred, "since from its inception it requires the action of God the Creator." Those who depart from this plan of God offend His divine majesty and dishonor themselves and the human race. They also weaken the inner fiber of the community and nation. Pope John concludes by repeating his assurance that, while the task might be difficult and even impossible due to human perversity, "the provident God has bestowed upon humanity sufficient goods wherewith to bear with dignity the burdens associated with the procreation of children." (Pars. 193–94.)

Pope John takes a giant step toward reality by placing the issue of birth regulation squarely in the context of population vs. resources. At least he opens the door to the extent of talking about the delicate affair in terms of the whole human race, taking it outside the walls of the private family, the national community and the affluent West. But having finally posed the problem in its true dimensions, Pope John then differs strongly with almost all commentators who are not visible members of the Church, and with some within as well. He does this by refusing to admit that on a global scale grave imbalances between the number of births and available resources arise at present, or will arise in the immediate future.

This position goes directly counter to that advanced by most non-Catholic authorities on the subject, private and governmental, Christian and non-Christian, Western and non-Western. Many of those concerned with the population issue would normally be regarded among the men of good will with whom Popes John and Paul seek dialogue and cooperation. But, in this instance, Pope John appears adamant and uncharacteristically abrupt. He calls their arguments "so inconclusive and controversial that nothing certain can be drawn from them." (Par. 188.)

Never does Pope John recognize that the principle of family regulation, at some time in the future, or in some places at present, may be a necessity, as now reported by Father Häring. In this matter, it must be admitted frankly, John disappointed many, while still positively advancing the debate toward reality, within and without the Church.

Dating from his years in Rome, much progress is in evidence. Research into the physiological, social and related aspects of the population issue is now encouraged under Catholic auspices. Scientific demographic institutes are at last being set up in Catholic study centers and universities, which had been either blind to this global issue, or artlessly dodging it, for some years. Theologians and bishops are beginning to take a deeper, longer look, especially at new developments in the fields of endocrinology and synthetic steroids which can affect ovulatory patterns. Medical doctors and physiologists are engaged in serious work on the biology of reproduction. Family-life groups and pastors are now re-examining non-doctrinal, cultural commitments to pro-natalist and largest-family-possible ideals. The moral acceptability of the rhythm method has become widespread, and current studies are seeking precise data and indices on the menstrual cycle, to make periodic continence "safer" and more conducive to a full expression of human love.

There are many persons, however, Catholics included, who wonder about the applicability of the rhythm method in the less-developed areas of the world. They recognize the possibility, and even desirability, that periodic continence can be perfected and become acceptable in the affluent West. But the illiteracy, housing conditions, familial patterns and human yearnings among hundreds of millions in the poor nations seem to dim the hope that rhythm can be effective on a world scale. It requires knowledge of the calendar and record-keeping, as well as a certain level of human conviction, control and commitment—all of which may be outside the intellectual grasp, contrary to the religious principles, and beyond the moral strength of those who can least afford large families. The world's thousand million neediest find themselves in a condition where dire want frustrates their struggle to free themselves of indigency.

Some Catholic leaders of the social awakening in Latin America are especially skeptical about the practicability of periodic continence on a meaningful scale amidst the slums of their expanding cities. They point to the illiteracy and lack of Christian conviction. They point to the statistic that, typical of all Latin American slums, the 200,000 inhabitants in the *callampas* of Santiago, Chile, average five persons to one room, and a small, ten-by-ten room at that. As leaders and pastors who know that their people are more than statistics, they point out that in this one room parents and children, cousins and friends eat and drink, live and sleep. They point also to the cultural and character trait called *machismo* (maleness), manifested by many Latins, which exalts the physical prowess of procreation. Under this influence the man must prove his virility by siring numerous children, and by maintaining liaisons with more than one woman. The father's duty in caring for the child is minimized. All this leads to rates of illegitimacy which exceed 50 percent in some countries. Why, ask some Latin leaders, pretend that rhythm can work in the face of such concrete realities?

Still, experiments, approved or acquiesced in by Church authorities, are now beginning to test the applicability of the rhythm method among the poor, in the United States and abroad. The movement for family regulation sponsored by the Church on the island of Mauritius arouses particular interest, both in Catholic and non-Catholic circles. This tiny island of 720 square miles, alone in the Indian Ocean 1000 miles east of Africa, has become, indeed, something of a test case in the world issue of population vs. resources. This is because it epitomizes in intelligible dimensions, based on sound British Colonial Office statistics, the dilemmas posed by today's dramatic drop in death rate and upward spiral in population growth. It holds special interest for Catholics, because the Church occupies a pre-eminent position there, both by law and tradition, and because of the leadership of Bishop Daniel Liston, an Irish Holy Ghost missionary. Naturalists remember Mauritius as the home of the celebrated dodo bird, now extinct. When discovered 350 years ago, the island was uninhabited by humans.

Today there are 1000 Mauritians per square mile, about twenty times the population density of the United States, and about equal to the density of Belgium and Holland, the most populous and, economically, among the most advanced countries in the industrial West. Farming, principally sugar, supports the island of Mauritius.

Reliable statistics, because of British dominion which goes back a hundred years, make Mauritius almost unique among the less-developed countries, and especially prized by demographers. Until the middle of the nineteenth century, the high birth rate of the island (about 40 new babies each year per 1000 population) was just about balanced by a high death rate of almost 40 deaths each year per 1000 population. Immigrants from India, China and Africa accounted for some population increase.

Then—roughly 1870 through 1946—the death rate slowly declined to about 30 to 35 deaths each year per 1000, while the birth rate remained steady, giving a net increase of about 5 to 10 persons per 1000, or ½ to 1 percent annually. Suddenly, due principally to malaria control and other public health measures, the annual death rate dropped from 36 to 14 in the four years following 1946. Simultaneously, the birth rate rose from 38 to 50 per 1000. By 1950 the annual rate of natural increase was 3.6 percent, or 36 additional persons per 1000 each year (based on a birth rate of 50, a record high, and a death rate of 14 per 1000).

Before 1946, the annual net population increase ran about 4000, in a total population of 400,000. By 1950 this annual net gain had jumped to 13,000. Since 1950, both the birth and the death rates have fallen to about 40 and 10 respectively, giving a current annual increase of about 30 per 1000, or 3 percent. The net population increase is now over 20,000 a year, five times the 4000 gained annually twenty years ago. By the end of this century, the number of people on Mauritius will almost triple to over two million persons, if today's growth trend continues. And there is no known reason why it will not.

This will give the rural island a density of 2800 persons for each of its 720 square miles—over fifty times the density of the United States which is supported by a level of industrial technology and capital which Mauritians have no hope of attaining by 2000 A.D., if ever.

That is why officials of the Church, there, as well as lay and civic leaders on the island, are seriously concerned. In 1963 the rhythm method was introduced in a program of family regulation that attempted to deal with realities of the Mauritian social and economic community, not merely the needs of the individual family as an isolated unit.

Mater et Magistra states that on a global scale the ratio of population to resources does not create grave difficulties at present, nor need such arise in the immediate future. Providence assures us that the almost inexhaustible productive potential of nature, exploited by man's technical ingenuity, "gives almost limitless promise for the future in the matter." A good many Mauritians, Catholics included, regard the coming generation as the "future." Looking at their own problem, which they grant is not planetary in scale, they foresee some grave difficulties, for the solution of which they must, under the providence of God, exercise foresight and prudence.

Technicians and researchers find no "almost inexhaustible productive capacity" on Mauritius through the science and organizational ability which are applicable in the near future. It is all very well to assert that, in developing places like Mauritius, "international cooperation is necessary, so that, conformably with the welfare of all, information, capital, and men themselves may move about among the peoples in orderly fashion." But will this outpouring of technical assistance, foreign aid and capital investment be forthcoming? Who in the United States or Europe is going to buy stocks and bonds, or vote taxes to build a factory in the Indian Ocean? Where are the raw materials, the power, the fuel, the customers? And as for the freedom of men to move about among the islands and nations of the world, what Western country will admit a million Afro-Indo-Chinese immigrants in the next thirty years? James Norris, president of the International Catholic Migration Commission, and the first lay auditor at Vatican Council II from the United States, makes the point that transport and resettlement of migrants costs about $1000 a person. Who, he asks, will pay the $1 billion required to move a million Mauritians?

The more realistic and reasonable hope, for the benefit of Mauritius in the next few decades, is that the world price of sugar might be stabilized by international agreement, as discussed in Chapter Nine.

The true drama of Mauritius is, of course, that it gives a preview of the imposing dilemma our children will face. In two or three generations, the problem of transplanting a million Mauritians will have spiraled into the problem of moving a hundred million Indians, Javanese, and Chinese into new living space. All of this presumes, of course, that nuclear cataclysm will be avoided and that the behavior of men and women will continue along the general patterns set by Adam and Eve. These are expectations well within the possibilities of God's providence. They must be foreseen and planned for, within the limits of human prudence and intelligence. And, always, within the norms of the moral law.

For these reasons, Catholic leaders on Mauritius and in most other parts of the world, and many persons not members of the Church, have watched with deep interest, and have participated in, the present discussion on family regulation. But, from the first, there has been a tendency to expect too much from the Vatican Council, and from Schema 13 in particular.

There are many issues which the Council will not solve, but toward the solution of which it will only prepare the ground and provide the momentum. The Council should be likened to a "constitutional assembly." It does not produce simplist solutions to the most complex and far-reaching problems of human history. Rather, the Council begets a new oneness in Christ, a broader and deeper consensus, new theological perspectives, new pastoral guidelines, and new organs and institutions to come to grips with the new issues, in harmony with old roots and traditions. All this will take time, much study and prayer, and never ceasing inspiration of the Holy Spirit, Who breathes when and where He wills.

The issue of population growth and family regulation is new in many respects, as we have seen. Only in the last decade has "the pill" come into physical being—posing theological questions never faced before, and depending in turn upon human knowledge of physiology and psychology that is still inadequate. Our present knowledge of the whole realm of reproductive biology is meager. Answers to questions that are basic to the rhythm method, such as the length of the "normal" fertility cycle, are only now being seriously sought. Positive research on the processes of conception and birth has been woefully neglected. We have concentrated, understandably, on disease and death, with thumping success. In 1963 the tax-supported National Institute of Health in Washington reported an annual expenditure of some $700 million on the control of mortality, broadly defined, and only $3 million on subjects related to fertility.

The public debate over population growth and family regulation will continue via press and television panels, convention talks and pulpit pronouncements. It will generate some enlightenment, and a great deal of misunderstanding and premature expectations. But this great issue will be solved, in God's good time, principally in the quiet of research centers and theological discussions, and in the depth of prayer and of consciences well formed by Christian truth and grace.

Chapter Twelve

FREEDOM AND PEACE

The Center for the Study of Democratic Institutions, presided over by Robert M. Hutchins, is among the secular bodies which have fully welcomed the Church's entry into the other dialogue. The Center, which has no religious identification whatsoever, undertook sponsorship of the international convocation on John's encyclical, *Pacem in Terris,* February 1965. Some 700 national and world statesmen, business and professional leaders, scholars and churchmen were invited to attend. They represented all the major economic, political and cultural systems of the globe. They were asked to tackle some of the world's thorniest issues:

How to achieve universal acceptance of the idea of the co-existence of nations with differing ideological and social systems;

How to assure sufficient flexibility to settle international conflict by negotiation, and how to devise mechanisms for peaceful social and political change;

How to obtain recognition of the urgent need for rapid progress toward disarmament;

How to take action and develop understanding to create mutual trust among nations;

How to achieve the elimination of racism in all countries;

How to achieve international cooperation in assisting the developing countries in the interests of the prosperity of the world, and how to make full use of science and technology for developing cooperation among nations;

How to encourage further development of the United Nations, so that its means and structure may become equal to the magnitude of its tasks.

That the leaders of the world should turn to Pope John for inspiration—or, at worst, as an excuse—for holding such an assembly on the theme of peace on earth, is striking proof that the other dialogue has indeed progressed. But the fact of this convocation points to a more arresting reality. When the powers of this-world—including those with close non-Christian religious connections, as well as those officially of atheist ideology—turn to a pope, as they have, then we have startling evidence that peace on earth is, indeed, in a fragile state. Things must be extremely precarious, if they go to such lengths. Perhaps fresh new opportunities for peace on earth will now open up to mankind. On the other hand, the importunities of the balance of terror may have become so frightening that every avenue must be explored, even the way pointed out by Christ's Vicar on earth.

It is a gauge of the rapid pace of today's social changes that the Church, only recently attacked as the oppressor of human liberty, should suddenly provide inspiration for freeing mankind from the tyranny of fear, hatred and suspicion on a global scale. While the issue of Church-State relations will certainly recur in particular applications here and there, it is fast losing the urgency it assumed but a few years ago. Popes John and Paul, and the bishops of the world as a body, have accepted fully the fact of a pluralistic society. The granting of full religious liberty, and the removal of more insidious disabilities in heavily Catholic areas will undoubtedly still meet occasional obstacles. But the amelioration is so apparent that formerly sensitive minorities have quieted most of their cries for redress. They all seem heartened by the work of the Council, heralded by Pope John's reassuring words: "Every human being has the right to honor God according to the dictates of an upright conscience, and therefore the right to worship God privately and publicly." (*Pacem in Terris,* par. 14.)

But freedom of religion, important as it is, is not enough for Pope John. Catholics must not only allow persons of differing religious convictions, and of none, to go their separate ways in peace; they should also "weigh the opinions of others with fitting courtesy and not measure everything in the light of their own interests. They should be prepared to join sincerely in doing whatever is naturally good or conducive to good." Since the principles of Christian social doctrine derive, for the most part, from requirements inherent in all human nature, they provide a vast field in which all men—Christians and those professing other religions or no religion—can meet and arrive at a consensus on the social order.

Thus, Pope John, with Paul and the Council following in his wake, goes far beyond the rather negative principle of mutual passive tolerance among social and national groups of conflicting ideologies or of differing religious convictions. He reverses dramatically the contamination phobia which tried to justify the defensive stance assumed by the Church since the Counter Reformation. By urging Catholics to collaborate sincerely with men of good will, whatever their beliefs, "in doing whatever is naturally good or conducive to good" in the social, civic and economic fields, Pope John breaks out of the ghetto mentality. North American Catholicism has been particularly scarred by this separatist obsession, and for historical and sociological reasons this is easily understood. Fortunately, for some years now it has been quite outmoded.

But the vision of John and Paul reaches far beyond the horizons of particular nations or regions. They think in the context of the whole world. Pope Pius XII had already reset the whole Church-State issue within the context of the new world community as a *pluralist* society, in his oft-quoted address to Italian Jurists, December 1953. It appears that Pius XII was moved, at least in part, by the United Nations discussions on the Declaration of Human Rights, which were then in progress. Full liberty of conscience and of worship is among the basic rights guaranteed by the UN Declaration. Having affirmatively analyzed the movement toward world unity and having noted the pluralist nature of this new international community, Pius affirmed that throughout this-world territory the citizens of member states must be allowed the expression of their own beliefs and ethical and religious practices.

Perhaps Pope Pius was also influenced by the debate on "the separation of church and state" then gathering steam in the United States. The practical American issue became the hub of the related doctrinal controversy which was stirring in Rome. Soon students at the venerable Gregorian University were hearing about the "static school," whose leaders were identified as Monsignors Joseph Fenton and George Shea, and the "dynamic school," led by Fathers John Courtney Murray and Gustave Weigel. In 1959 the present writer attended a series of lectures on the Church and religious freedom by Father Raul Cereceda, a Chilean Jesuit, in the Institute of Social Sciences of the Gregorian University. Father Cereceda developed the subject in terms of the debate between the "static" conservatives and the "dynamic" progressives. He openly embraced the school of Murray and Weigel.

This gave a preview of coming events in the Council, where the issue of religious liberty became, in the words of Father Murray, "the American issue at the Council." The Murray-Weigel school of thought was strongly supported by the bishops of the United States as a body through the intervention of Cardinal Spellman, Cardinal Ritter and others. The New York Cardinal brought Father Murray to Rome as his personal theologian for this issue.

It is in the field of religious liberty that the American Catholic Church has made its greatest contribution, so far, to the other dialogue, despite the ghetto pattern which has so marked our Catholicism. Father Cereceda, in his 1959 lectures, purposely prefaced his treatment of today's world pluralism with an analysis of American pluralism—because, he explained, this social and ideological reality, so significant politically at national and world levels, first appeared in the United States as a major factor.

In 1959, Father Cereceda manifested no anxiety or reticence toward the "static school" conservatives of the Roman Curia, physically so close at hand. He volunteered that if the question were put to him, as to whether he agreed with Cardinal Ottaviani, his response would be another question: Does the Cardinal agree with Pope Pius XII? If the Cardinal does agree with Pius XII, asserted the Chilean Jesuit, then he, Father Cereceda, agrees with the Cardinal.

The presence of this type of professor in the Pontifical Gregorian University in the 1950s helps to explain the roots which so quickly nourished Pope John's *aggiornamento* within Rome itself.

In *Pacem in Terris* John goes beyond tolerance and liberty, as the merely negative removal of political inhibitions, to the much more positive promotion of intergroup and interideological communication and collaboration. We still cannot grasp adequately the depth, scope and future implications of these giant steps on the whole human stage, and up the fragile ladder toward peace and that sense of solidarity and brotherhood which must support world understanding.

John does not base Christian openness on a spurious relativism, which would dilute all doctrinal convictions. Having denatured all truth into mere opinion, the epistemology of relativism would then accord all "truths" equal status as mere opinions, all more or less false. John, in keeping with the mainstream of Thomist concepts, directly embraces the reality of truth on one hand, and the fact of error on the other.

The two *are* different. They are not to be equated or accommodated with each other philosophically as a basis for civil tolerance. Error does exist as error, and as error does not possess "equal rights" with the truth. We Catholics *are* doctrinal absolutists. We are not doctrinal relativists, and will not become so for the sake of dialogue among Christians or with the modern world, nor for the great goals of world peace and human freedom. We Catholics freely embrace and stand for some things knowable by natural reason, and for the Something shared with us erring humans supernaturally by Christ.

Pope John distinguishes between error and the one who errs. The two must never be confused, "not even when there is question of error or inadequate knowledge of truth in the moral or religious field. The person who errs is always and above all a human being, and he retains in every case his dignity as a human person; and he must be always regarded and treated in accordance with that lofty dignity." (Par. 158.) In short, whereas error, in the theory of knowledge, may not have any rights, the human being who holds and propounds error does have rights. He has rights because of the dignity of his origin and nature and destiny, of the highest value in the natural order of things, and because of Christ in the supernatural order.

But John does not profess a static theory of knowledge, or psychology of error, in which the erring mind rests, immovable and complacent. The human yearning to know—to grasp and to identify with reality—surges constantly within the human mind, ever reaching, searching, deepening. "Besides, in every human being, there is a need congenital to his nature and never becomes extinguished, compelling him to break through the web of error and open his mind to the knowledge of truth. And God will never fail to act on his interior being . . ." Because the one in error is still a human person with dignity, value and rights, and because he can at a future date learn and believe the truth, he is not to be condemned and ignored and avoided. Men who believe they possess truths must talk and associate and collaborate with men whom they conceive as being in error.

This attitude of openness should be applied not only by dogmatists, but also by relativists. These, by their own theory

of knowledge, regard the view of "absolute truth" as erroneous and presumptuous, and quite often hold the absolutist
himself, especially if he is Catholic, in mild contempt, or as
not worth bothering with.

Beyond the philosophical realm, this attitude of openness
should be cultivated and practiced not only by all Christians,
but by all who believe in "the one supreme, transcendent
God, creator and sustainer, and [who] worship Him with
acts of sincere piety and base their moral and social life on
their belief and religious practices."[1] Christians, who hold
convictions of truth, must communicate deliberately with
those whom they regard as being in error, or as lacking a full
grasp of the truth—particularly with those who do not acknowledge Christ as God incarnate, Redeemer and Savior.
Christians do not seek dialogue with Jews, Moslems, Hindus
and Buddhists, primarily because they are in error, but because they are fellow human beings. And conversely, Jews,
Moslems and others who regard Christians as being in error
must seek converse and association with the "gentile" and
"infidel" Christians, as brothers in God's family.

In his herculean study of the birth and growth of civilizations, Arnold Toynbee reaches the conclusion that the score
of civilizations which man has created in the past five thousand years are not, as he had first thought, the basic intelligible units of, and actors in, human history. This role is
reserved rather to the world's higher religions. They alone
generate higher species of society, of a self-sufficiency, inner
integrity and over-all influence adequate for Toynbee's concept of the basic intelligible units of human history.

The Oxford philosopher of history suggests that, until now,
much of the world's tension and strife has been generated by
nations and civilizations vying with each other for supremacy,
driven by their respective prideful convictions regarding their
own particular view of man and way of life, to the intolerant

[1] Pope Paul to Second Session of the Council, September 1963.

exclusion of others. This fostered a sense of manifest destiny which led to war and aggression, accounting for many of history's catastrophes. This idolization of self often became so enflamed that it overreached itself, forging that nation's or civilization's prideful, driving hubris into the weapon of its own self-destruction.

This conviction of being the bearer and carrier of exclusive truth, Toynbee suggests, lies at the heart of the problems of war and peace. Consequently, convictions so absolutely held as to inspire this sense of messiahship must be mitigated or degermed, exorcized or exiled from the human mind, heart and society. Only then can man live in peace.

Toynbee applies this thesis to the world's four higher religions—the Christian, Moslem, Hindu and Buddhist faiths. (He has riled our Jewish brothers by placing the Hebrew religion in a lesser category.) The Oxford professor wants the four higher religions to overcome the idolization of self which, to his mind, is implicit in their respective claims to a supernatural revelation from God which is unique and exclusive. This is required, Toynbee insists, to achieve peace in the future world society which is now in travail.[2]

This is the sort of philosophical relativism and religious irenics which the Church emphatically rejects. Despite the worthy social goals for all mankind which motivate such a proposal, the weighty erudition that bolsters it, and the supreme priority assigned it, the Church cannot accept Professor Toynbee's thesis. Pope John bases the other dialogue on a firmer, deeper grasp of reality and truth, both natural and supernatural, and an unpatronizing recognition of the existence of error. But the error is different from the man who errs. *He does have rights.* That is the truth through which peace is to be found.

[2] Arnold Toynbee, *The Study of History* (Oxford University Press, 1954), especially Vol. VII, Part VII, "Universal Churches," pp. 425–49; and *An Historian's Approach to Religion* (Oxford University Press, 1956), especially pp. 131–44.

Furthermore, John asserts, from the viewpoint of the men already convinced of certain truths, the dialogue with persons believed in error can be positively beneficial. It can lead to the discovery of greater and deeper truth: "Meetings and agreements in the various sectors of daily life, between believers and those who do not believe or believe insufficiently because they adhere to error, can be occasions for discovering truth and paying homage to it." (Par. 158.)

The Church today goes on to open the dialogue not only with Jews, Moslems, Hindus and Buddhists, but also with Communists. Pope John does not mention atheistic materialism or Communism expressly. However, these surely fall within the "false philosophical teachings regarding the nature, origin and destiny of the universe and of man," and the "historical movements that have economic, social, cultural or political ends," which originated from the false philosophical teachings. (Par. 159.) John distinguishes the false philosophy (atheistic materialism) from the historical movements which the false philosophy inspired. "These teachings, once they are drawn up and defined, remain always the same, while the movements, working on historical situations in constant evolution, cannot but be influenced by these latter and cannot avoid, therefore, being subject to changes, even of a profound nature."

In other words, atheistic materialism is one thing, a false doctrine fully condemned. But the historical movements, like Marxist Socialism and Lenin's Communism to which this doctrine originally gave rise, and to which this doctrine imparts a certain inspiration even today, must be viewed on their own merits, because they are in constant evolution and have undergone changes, even profound changes. (It must again be noted that *Pacem in Terris* does not use the words "Lenin's Communism" and "Marxist Socialism." But the meaning is unmistakable, and has been so accepted by many authoritative interpreters of Catholic social teaching.)

Pope Paul in *Ecclesiam Suam* returns expressly to this

problem of dialogue with Marxists and Communists. He certainly pulls no punches. He cites the reasons "which compel us . . . to condemn the ideological systems which deny God and oppress the Church, systems which are often identified with economic, social and political regimes, amongst which atheistic Communism is the chief." Pope Paul points out that it is not so much the Church which condemns these systems, as that it is they which express their radical opposition to the Church and the cause of Christ. "Our regret is, in reality, more a sorrow for the victim than the sentence of a judge."

Nevertheless, Paul opens the door for dialogue, however difficult this might be. In line with John's fatherly approach, he distinguishes the ideological and political systems from the human beings who embrace and direct them. "We have no preconceived intention of excluding persons who profess these systems and belong to these regimes. For the love of truth discussion is always possible."

Recalling Pope John's analysis in *Pacem in Terris,* Paul acknowledges, too, the difference between the doctrines which give rise to social and political movements and the movements themselves. "The doctrines of such movements, once elaborated and defined, remain always the same, whereas the movements themselves cannot help but evolve and undergo changes, even of a profound nature." For these reasons, Paul leaves ajar the door opened by Pope John: "We do not despair that they [the movements and the men who uphold them] may one day be able to enter into a more positive dialogue with the Church than the present one which we now of necessity deplore and lament."

Further, in *Pacem in Terris,* John finds something in these movements which is positively good. "Besides, who can deny that these movements, in so far as they conform to the dictates of right reason and are interpreters of the lawful aspirations of the human person, contain elements that are positive and deserving of approval?" (Par. 159.) In consequence, cooperation with these movements for concrete goals now becomes possible, and perhaps even praiseworthy. "It can happen, then, that a drawing together or a meeting for the attainment of some practical end, which was formerly deemed inopportune and unproductive, might now or in the future be considered opportune and useful." Great prudence and special experience are needed "to decide whether this moment [for cooperation] has arrived, and also to lay down the ways and degrees in which work in common might be possible for the achievement of economic, social, cultural and political ends which are honorable and useful." Ultimately, the Church has the right and duty to intervene if necessary in such decisions. (Par. 160.)

At this point, Pope John cautions those generous souls who become so enkindled with zeal for justice and change that they might "have recourse to something like a revolution." He asks that they proceed gradually and warns against destructive violence. (Pars. 161–62.) The violent revolution spoken of in this context is, of course, to be distinguished from the peaceful social revolution, through nonviolent methods, discussed in Chapter Ten, and espoused by Martin Luther King in the South of the United States and by Christian democracy in Latin America.

The immense task of restoring peaceful relations within the human family, Pope John concludes, falls on the shoulders of all men of good will. These relations necessary for peace are fourfold: "between individual human beings; between citizens in their respective political communities; between political communities themselves; between individuals, families, intermediate associations and political communities on the one hand, and the world community on the other." (Par. 163.)

As a concerned father, John exhorts all men, and especially Christians, to do their part in restoring peaceful relations at these four interdependent levels of world society. It is an imperative of duty and, especially for Christians, a requirement of love. "This is a most exalted task, for it is the task of

bringing about true peace in the order established by God."
(Pars. 163–64.)

It is a dialogue of this dimension, penetrating even the Iron
Curtain, which offers hope to a world too often on the brink
of nuclear holocaust. Such interchanges, actual and possible,
are of a mixed nature. Some are cultural and ideological,
some involve trade or the movement of persons. In time they
can lead to meaningful disarmament, and in the age of over-
kill, every step forward, even the tiniest, like the test-ban
treaty, is a good step—maybe a giant step, because it begins
to thaw out the Cold War.

Christopher Hollis, the Catholic English historian, correctly states that security is possible only if we can find a way
by which frontiers between nations are made less important.
"We must throw our weight behind movements for international freedom of trade and international freedom of migration. But beyond that it is clear that there is little hope of preserving permanent peace if the doctrine of absolute national
sovereignty is maintained."[3] Like Popes John and Paul, he
sees the need for an international authority. The United Nations must be strengthened and brought, as quickly as possible, to the maturity which its role demands.

This is true, as far as it goes, but we must look behind and
beyond the fact of national sovereignty. We must promote
communication among the ideologies which animate the na-
tionalisms and the other fuels of world tension. World peace
among the nations is closely related to human freedom within
the respective nations. The great majority of every nation's
citizens do not want war, and they particularly fear nuclear
war. But the power structure in some lands is such that the
people at large lack voice or the social instruments for wield-
ing the power to support their convictions.

Through today's technology and mass communications
media, power—the ability to move reality—can become fear-

[3] Christopher Hollis, "War in the Nuclear Age," *Religious Education*, May–
June 1964, pp. 227–33.

somely concentrated in the hands of the few, to be used at the discretion of the few. Some ideologies foster the authoritarian or the totalitarian state, not in theory but as a practical result of the concentration of economic and political power. Modern technology, in itself, tends in the same direction, because it enables man to focus enormous physical energy on mammoth tasks involving tens of thousands of humans. Each worker makes but the most insignificant contribution to the whole undertaking, usually without understanding, or having any voice in, the plans or outcome. He is not unlike a cog in the machine he tends, or a punch hole feeding into the computer data he knows and cares nothing about.

The technological revolution, and the other revolutions of equality and material betterment, geometrically multiply human relationships, bringing about the new environment of socialization. In the "sociosphere" thus created, the individual can easily lose control of his personal destiny, and forfeit his freedom and creativity to the will of the few, the power élite. We have already seen that, despite the dangers of technology and socialization, Pope John holds them justified as advanced expressions of man's creativity, from which many positive goods and rights can result.

In the decade of the 1950s Romano Guardini became the principal Catholic thinker on the complex problems of human freedom and modern power (technical, social, economic and political) within the nation and on a global scale. Reinhold Niebuhr is the best-known Protestant philosopher and theologian to have written extensively on the phenomenon of power and the moral ambiguities it begets for men of all faiths and of none.

Guardini views power in a positive, creative light, resembling the affirmative stand of *Pacem in Terris*. Indeed, Pope John is probably indebted to the German priest for some of his philosophical concepts and much of his pervading confidence, while still recognizing the real dangers of power.

For Guardini, power is not a "dirty word" or principally a

threatening temptation. Power is ontologically proper to man; the exercise of power is essential to his humanity. "Man cannot be human and, as a kind of addition to his humanity, exercise or fail to exercise power." To be human is to wield power.[4]

And power is a religious fact: "Man's natural God-likeness consists in this capacity for power, in his ability to use it and in his resultant lordship. Herein lies the essential vocation and worth of human existence." All human work, every act by which man purposefully moves and transforms reality— every exercise of power—is the consequence of man's participation in God's sovereignty. Man is that extra-special creature who has dominion over other creatures, and a certain physical, but not moral, independence of the Creator. Every man is lord—by the grace of God—over nature and of himself. And, like the Lord's power, the power of man is universal. It is not limited to a unique and separate department of human existence. "Every act of doing and creating, of possessing and enjoying, produces an immediate sense of power."

Guardini knows from bitter firsthand experience under the Nazis the abuses and tyranny which today's concentrated power can be put to by sinful man. In conversation with him in 1958, the present writer saw and heard him express the threat he feels from Communist power, "even now only a hundred miles away," as he pointed out of the window of his Munich home. For these historical and experiential reasons, and not only from a philosophical impulse, Guardini seeks to understand the implications of modern power and to reorient its uses. He sees that in our epoch, due to techniques and socialization, power over nature and over man will continue to accumulate. Consequently, the "core of the new epoch's intellectual task will be to integrate power into life in such a way

---

[4] Romano Guardini, *Power and Responsibility, A Course of Action for the New Age* (New York: Regnery, 1961). Also, *The End of the Modern World, A Search for Orientation* (New York: Sheed and Ward, 1956). Both are short, pithy studies, only 104 pages and 133 pages, respectively.

that man can employ power without forfeiting his humanity. For he will have only two choices: to match the greatness of his power with the strength of his humanity, or to surrender his humanity to power and perish."

Man has now perfected mightily his God-given task to control nature. In the new epoch, man's will to rule, shared by the Creator, must be expressed by the control of power itself through the agents of power which man has himself created: business corporations, workers' unions, legislative bodies and governmental bureaus, universities, professional associations, research teams and civic groups. Through these human relationships, many times multiplied into interlocking social systems, man exercises his dominion over nature, drawing forth from nature, and from man himself, the necessities of life and all that makes for "the fullness of a more excellent life."

Guardini is a thinker; he offers no program of action. While admitting that, on the whole, "an autonomous technical-economic-political system holds all life in thrall," he avoids determinism. He insists that man is still in the driver's seat, "that man himself is responsible for the turn history will take and for whatever becomes of the world and of human existence. . . . What we see is a world which does not run itself, which must be led. . . . What this world demands . . . is the genuine ruler."

The genuine ruler must receive a new kind of political education, rooted in ethical and spiritual convictions. "He will assimilate technology into the sense of life itself; he will be able to live with constant danger, will know how to command as well as to obey." But this new ruler is not some solitary statesman. He is manifold. "The new type of man is as apt to be a soldier as he is to be a priest, a businessman as a farmer, a doctor as an artist, a factory worker as a research scientist." These must all perfect and attune themselves for leadership, in their several areas of power and responsibility, by ascetics and contemplation, by freshly rediscovered human attainments adapted to the day's realities.

While Guardini does not elaborate, we can see these *several* new rulers as indicating the advantages of pluralism. Their *several* centers of power are mindful of the concepts of countervailing power, applied by John K. Galbraith to economic power concentrations, and the principle of subsidiary function and intermediate groups advanced by Catholic social teaching. Society must be so structured that the centers of power are spread among the many functional and creative poles which attract men into human associations.

But each of these polarities and groupings and power centers must understand its place in the larger social fabric. They must coordinate themselves accordingly. The will to power for its own sake—insubordinate power loosed upon the world by sin—can only be curbed and creatively directed by humility.

Humility, the virtue of the strong, is the principal Christian contribution to the dilemmas of modern power. Humility arises from the truth that, although man exercises God-given dominion over creatures, he is also a creature. While possessing so much, and charged by God to acquire more—more knowledge, more control over nature, more presence throughout space—still we are, in ourselves, nothing. We totter along the brink of annihilation. We dangle over the void of nonexistence.

Guardini sees that humility—rightly grasped, deepened, widespread within massed power—is hope. And hope is the decisive message of Christ. Humility will save mankind not only for heaven, but also here on earth. "All creaturely humility has its origin in the act by which the Son of God became man." In the words of St. Paul, Christ "humbled himself, becoming obedient unto death, even to the death of the cross." (Phil. 2:8.) God took on the form and weakness of a creature for no personal need whatsoever. He acted "out of pure freedom, because He, the Sovereign, willed it. The name of this 'because' is Love."

It seems foolish to some people to propose humility to the

proud world of multiplying power, childish to suggest love to conflicting nations, blocs and ideologies. But what seems foolish to human creatures could be so highly esteemed by the Creator that He makes it the secret of freedom and of peace, the soul of life and of all creation.

For what was the secret of Pope John, but his peasant simplicity, almost childlikeness, enlivened by his Christian concern for all his family? And since he so endeared himself to the whole world, we know that even socialization man is alive to love, and he can be awakened to love in return.

Chapter Thirteen

THE FORM AND SPIRIT
OF THE OTHER DIALOGUE

While the other dialogue has indeed begun, it has only proceeded far enough for us to begin discovering the dimension and depth of its promise. The experiences of this dialogue to date, although it is still in the young, probing stage, give us some indications of how it might progress satisfactorily in the future.

It must first be recognized that most issues of the other dialogue fall par excellence within the competence of the laity in the Church. All clerics, bishops and priests, brothers and sisters, must strive to grasp this role of lay men and women, that they are by their vocation, both natural and religious, called to be creators, ministers and stewards of the things of this-world. The main responsibility of the clergy, those by definition "set apart" from the world, is to teach, to inspire, to animate, to sanctify. And only in exceptional cases —if lay leaders adequate to the task are lacking, or if the issue is pressing and crucial—should they assume direct leaderhip in the temporal order.

For these reasons, the training of adult leaders must be given higher priority in the Church. It must not be assumed that a Catholic education, even through college, meets the rigorous requirements of intellectual and spiritual preparation adequate for dealing with the problems of socialization man. Formal educational systems have a distressing tendency to lag a few years—sometimes even generations—behind the times. Further, even granting that the curriculum, methods and faculty are keyed to the realities of the world (as is increasingly true in Catholic schools), by the time the graduate is out of school ten or twenty years, much that was contemporary in his student days has passed him by. New physical, political, economic and social realities become his Monday morning responsibility. Challenges, newer still, loom over tomorrow's horizon.

The physicist, doctor, businessman, legislator, lawyer, communications expert, or military man constantly updates himself in his professional specialty by training seminars, conferences and meetings, by intensive study of trade and professional publications, and by participation in his appropriate specialized society or association. He must increase his competence in all that touches his daily work; otherwise he makes no progress, receives no promotion. Unfortunately, the intellectual nourishment received by our Catholic adults *as Catholics* in no way compares to their marvelous and constant mental growth in the things of this-world. We have such confidence in our school system that we tend to consider the graduate a finished product—at least judging from the anemic content of our sermons and discussion clubs, the lack of social awareness in most missions and retreat conferences, and the failure to forge new educational instruments for our emerging laity.

The challenges and opportunities of today's other dialogue demand rethinking and a re-evaluation of our Catholic school system, so that the *continuing education of adults* becomes a major concern. Funds and teaching personnel should be re-allocated to provide a full-time staff at the parish and community level, and serious training institutes for weekend, week-long and month-long courses *in residence* at the diocesan and area levels. Their content must be in the context of today's society and its revolutions, current and future.

Many American Catholics are now becoming national and international leaders in business and labor, science and engineering, the professions, and political and cultural affairs. They wing their way around the world to confer with the policy- and decision-makers of our time. Most of them would welcome high-level seminars, among Christians and with other men of good will, on the principles and issues of the other dialogue. Often the religious understanding which they bring to their workaday problems is of a grade-school level compared with the moral demands made by the complexities and dilemmas of the power they must daily exercise.

We have not yet given serious attention to the need to update the religious knowledge and inspiration of our laity as they grow to national and world stature. A few books and a handful of Catholic publications do their praiseworthy part toward filling the gap. But the Church's educational system as a whole does not meet the need. Indeed, Catholics in positions of responsibility and leadership have probably learned more about Pope John's *aggiornamento* from secular news media and books than from sermons, societies and other traditional sources. In great part because we have become so engrossed in our school system, which did admirable and necessary work for the past century, we now depend heavily on secular weekly news magazines and the daily papers to bring Christ's message to our own Catholic lay leaders and to the modern world.

A man is between seventeen and twenty-five years old when he is graduated from high school, university, or training school in his vocational specialty. Another ten, twenty, thirty years may be required for him to acquire a full grasp of his work, to achieve status, and to qualify for civic and professional leadership. Assume that he did receive an adequate Christian orientation on the great social issues as a high school or college student—a whopping presumption, it must be admitted—still, the physical and moral dimensions of today's world problems quickly outgrow that preparation. How many students received factual—much less moral—orientation on the United Nations, on foreign aid and on trade twenty years ago? Or on interracial justice, other than exposure perhaps to *America* or *Commonweal,* a decade ago? Or on "the pill" and the fact of a world population problem as recently as five years ago?

All of these great issues have swooped down upon us since the Second World War. Laymen now in their forties and fifties must deal with them. Even the most enlightened educators could not have been expected to anticipate them. And once they clamor for attention from each morning's headlines and each evening's news report, where does the conscientious school administrator find the faculty, and how does he squeeze more time into the curriculum. It is illuminating to discover how often Catholic students begin their dialogue with the modern world, not through the regular school subjects, but through extracurricular activities such as debating teams and voluntary discussion groups on current affairs. This, alas, is especially true in seminaries and houses of study for religious.

Besides, less than half the Catholics in the United States graduate from Catholic secondary schools or colleges. The present writer once found through a parish survey, which included 30 percent of his parishioners in the sample, that 76 percent of the fathers of families had been to college an average of three and a half years. Of these, only 12 percent had gone through Catholic colleges. It must be noted that this is not typical of American Catholicism as a whole; this was a suburban parish located in the South, which is only about 7 percent Catholic. In this sampling, 52 percent of the couples interviewed were mixed marriages; that is, more than one half the spouses were not Catholic.

Still, this data should focus attention upon the very high number of college graduates now found in suburban congregations. These are the managers and technologists and professionals who deal daily with the great issues at local, state, national and world level. If they are to lead the other dialogue—and it will remain merely theoretical and largely sterile unless they do—they need a continuing intellectual growth in religious truth and social teaching, comparable to their constant advance in professional ability. Many of them now seek this deeper understanding. They seek too the inner formation and personal spirituality which must round out and enliven the newly grasped truths and principles of action.

Purported frustration among the emerging laymen of the Church is due in great part to the woeful lack of modernization in the Church's educational program for adults. The American parish and diocese, as a whole, is child-oriented to an appalling degree, for reasons historically understandable, but now gone with the winds of change. A cursory glance at parish budgets or the goals of a diocesan fund campaign reveals, in most instances, the predominant emphasis placed on elementary and secondary schools, seminaries, youth recreational centers and institutions for children. While millions are spent for these laudable purposes, problems concerning family life, urban renewal, racial tension, world peace and others which involve great issues must scrape and scrounge to limp along, usually outside the boundaries of official Church concern. It is as though the Piuses, John and Paul—and Christ—never said a word or gave a care about the human family in the arena of this-world realities.

Some first moves toward redress are now beginning to appear, giving body and hope to the other dialogue. Strong episcopal and chancery support for interracial justice has already been noted. Still, in but few places has this taken on significant meaning at the parish and neighborhood levels. The family movement and some professional societies are beginning to show greater promise. And the outburst of interest in Latin America and other overseas areas shows a sudden awakening to the new "we" of one world. Families, societies, parishes, dioceses and religious orders are now committing personnel and resources for work in Latin America, work that is often in the social field.

Centers for applied social research are also beginning to

appear in the United States under Catholic auspices. It is curious that in our country, which leads the world in sociological investigation and in the application of the behavioral sciences, the Church should have been so slow to understand the advantage, even the necessity, of social research. Precise statistics and empirical knowledge of values and motives, changing attitudes and trends are basic equipment for policy- and decision-making among leaders of the modern world. But we Catholics pretty much felt that the norms of ancient codes and the behavioral patterns of immigrant grandparents were sufficient for our needs as pastors of millions of families and as administrators of properties valued at hundreds of millions of dollars, in the most complex, fastest-changing society man has ever known.

Other hopeful signs are the increased attention being given to secular university faculties and to graduate students by the Newman movement. These campus apostolates are now going beyond the strictly pastoral and sacramental roles into the great issues of the other dialogue, with undergraduates as well as advanced students. Some Catholic universities have launched a more intense effort to update and refresh the accomplishments of their alumni. They are becoming centers for seminars and conferences of major consequence among policy- and decision-makers in secular society. One example of this departure is Georgetown University's series of workshops on economic development and foreign policy. Notre Dame University is building a special center for the continuing education of adults, which will draw together leaders of all persuasions for research and dialogue on the great issues.

On the parish and community levels, full-time adult educators are now being employed, at salaries sufficient to attract a gifted, apostolic man with a family to care for. Father Eugene Zimmers of the University of San Francisco is the principal pioneer of this movement, which is still modest but is likely to gain momentum. He accepts Catholic men, with five to twenty years of business or professional experience, as candidates for a year of full-time study and training in a special institute attached to the university. Parishes then contract for the services of these men to set up and direct adult education programs. Some fifty men, all with five to twenty successful years in the "downtown world," have completed their training and have taken up duties on this new career-vocation in the three years since Father Zimmers began his creative breakthrough. While these first full-time additions to parish staffs have understandably concentrated rather strictly on the religious education of adults, it becomes apparent that they will in due order evolve into first-line communicators in both dialogues in the parish and diocese, and thereafter at the area and national levels.

The role of lay Christians in the other dialogue will be carried on principally through their participation in the professional and trade associations of their respective specialties, and in political, cultural and civic affairs. Much of their formation will come from experience and action in real-life situations. But they must be offered systematic intellectual nourishment equal to their enormous tasks.

This writer is thoroughly delighted with the liturgical renewal now underway. The liturgical forms of the future will undoubtedly contribute much to the continuing education of the laity and the clergy, and to their joint spiritual deepening. But a strong demurral must be registered against those who promise too much from renewal of the liturgy alone. The public prayer of the Church cannot be thought of as an educational agent adequate to the tasks the layman must shoulder today. The *aggiornamento* must include other modernizations in Christian life for upgrading and updating adult understanding. These educational innovations must expressly include the issues of the other dialogue, and must be open to the participation of all men of good will.

If the laity need intellectual updating and upgrading, we clergy need these even more—because our task in forming and inspiring lay leaders is more demanding, and because, by our withdrawn seminary training and sheltered rectory and community life, we are so removed from the harsh realities of factory, market place, laboratory and public forum. The Vatican Council has brought, too, a host of theological perspectives and pastoral orientations which must be integrated into our whole apostolate, the directly supernatural as well as the social.

The bishops of the United States speak openly and gratefully of their own *aggiornamento* through the Council sessions. They spent themselves and their time with the admirable zest of first-year theologians on a daily round of lectures and panels on the problems of the Church, inside and outside, at home and in Europe, in the West and in the developing continents. With a dedication that should inspire clergy and laity back home, they studied books and ploughed through foot-high stacks of schemata, preliminary drafts, and historic documents. They gathered around committee tables in earnest attention and debate for many a weary day. Humbly they sat again at the feet of theologians, scripture scholars and other thinkers, with some of whom many felt marked disagreement, at least at first.

Certainly all clergy, religious and laity should be willing to do no less. They too must undertake the fresh search for understanding, stimulated by the new horizons the Council has opened upon the world. Pope John's *aggiornamento* cannot remain at the high level of the college of bishops if it is truly to renew the face of the earth. Its living waters must course down into chanceries and provincialates, monasteries and college faculties, parishes and homes. All believers in Christ, in keeping with the role and opportunity of each, must, with the successors of the apostles, drink deep the living waters of truth and grace, which our Lord offers anew at Jacob's well. And we must welcome all who would join us.

The introduction to this book indicated that the dialogue among Christians should, for the moment, be concerned, in great part, with the other dialogue—"beyond the frontiers of

Christianity," in the words of Paul. This writer shares the "chastened optimism" of Robert McAfee Brown, the prominent Protestant historian and delegate-observer to the Council. It does not appear realistic to expect that the theological and juridical differences which divide us will be resolved in the foreseeable future to the point of visible, organizational unity. Granting the power of God to heal and to move, it seems positively harmful to raise extravagant hopes which will, in all likelihood, be dashed by wounding disappointment, at least for the near future. But the very fact that we Christians are again talking to each other does make Christ's message more "hearable" to the rest of mankind. And more meaningful to us.

The dialogue among Christians can profit mightily by addressing itself deliberately to the great issues of the other dialogue: the need and poverty of so much of the human family, their hunger for justice, their thirst for peace and for knowledge, for dignity and equality—for "the fullness of a more excellent life." Since most of the complex problems of this world begin in the interior of man—in his mind and heart and soul—they can be ameliorated and solved only by changes within the human mind and heart and soul: a conversion and transformation which is pre-eminently within the power of religion.

It is heartening to know that when the civil rights bill passed the United States Senate in June 1964, several of the most prominent southern senators lamented that their defeat —and equal rights under the law for Negroes—had been brought about, to a large degree, by the churches and synagogues. Presidents Kennedy and Johnson showed keen insight into the heart of the matter and the soul of the nation by stressing that the Negro's right to equality has become a moral issue.

Senator Everett Dirksen, the Republican minority leader, whose strong and admirable leadership did so much to carry the day, explained in his speech, which concluded eighty-three days of debate, why he had become a crusader for Negro rights, especially in view of opposition within his own party. He based his stand, not ultimately on Jefferson or Lincoln, but on a Christian writer and minister, John Donne, Dean of St. Paul's in London in the early 1600s. Senator Dirksen concluded his speech, the debate and the issue by quoting the clergyman-poet's well-known line: "Any man's death diminishes me, because I am involved in mankind." The Senator continued, "Whatever the color of a man's skin, we are all mankind. So every denial of freedom, of equal opportunity for a livelihood, or for an education, diminishes me. There is the moral basis for this legislation. Mr. President, I am prepared to vote."

The power of ideas across the centuries has not been stifled among the power structures of socialization man. As in the racial question on the American scene, so in the great issues of the universal common good and world social justice, moral principles rooted in religious truths have the power to move men, to transform and to save. This will be increasingly true as the religious bitterness among Christians of the past four centuries is replaced by friendship and love and joint concern for one another, and for all the human family. Many people of other faiths, who do not share with us "one Lord, one faith, one baptism," are also ready to collaborate.

The ideas of Pierre Teilhard de Chardin have attracted deep interest within and without Christian circles in the past ten years. The French priest-paleontologist, who died in New York in 1955, has presented powerful seminal ideas which intellectually could nourish and sustain the realities of socialization, evolution and human progress.

During the twenty-five years prior to his death, Teilhard's superiors, both Jesuit and Roman, forbade publication in book form of his philosophical and religious thought. However, mimeograph copies of his raw manuscripts circulated around Europe since 1940. Since his death in 1955 Teilhard's

writings have appeared in print. The Roman Curia has is-
sued a warning, especially for seminarians, against untutored
and uncritical exposure to these volumes. Between 1959 and
1962 three of his books were published in English translation: *The Phenomenon of Man, The Divine Milieu,* and *Letters From a Traveller.* The first and last have introductions
by Sir Julian Huxley.

Scholarly and popular articles about Teilhard's work pro-
liferate, and commentary now evolves into books by the
dozen in several languages. Seminars and lectures on the
French priest's philosophic and religious thought are increasingly programmed on Catholic and secular campuses, where
his field findings on Peking man and Java man, and attendant
scientific theories on human development, have been frequent
fare for three decades in schools of geology and paleontology.
Faculty members of Ivy League divinity schools and Protestant seminarians are reading and discussing Teilhard, privately and publicly.

His influence is spreading notably in Latin America, where
the philosophies of the Enlightenment and of positivism have
enjoyed great vogue until our decade. Marxism has replaced
these schools of thought among many faculties of law, economics, humanities, education and philosophy, in some major universities of Mexico, Venezuela, Chile, Argentina, and
Brazil. Now Teilhard's "ultraphysics" (not metaphysics), applied to history, evolution, social progress, human perfection
and socialization, is receiving a serious hearing from Latin
American materialists and Christians alike. Intellectuals and
writers who espouse and elaborate the ideologies of drastic
reform and social revolution seek inspiration from his fertile
ideas.

The Jesuit priest's thought has not yet become a school
or system. It still lacks the wholeness and consistency of a
finished product. He has launched certain impulses and attractions which, in the minds of serious critics, may have

dangerous consequences to Thomist philosophy and Catholic theology as now conceived.

Does his evolutionary *élan vital* "force" God to create, and to keep on creating?

Does Teilhard play down sin and evil, overexalting nature's innate goodness, and underplaying the supernatural role of God's free grace and the power for both good and evil in man's free will?

Does he posit a substantial continuum in his progressive steps from inanimate elements and rocks to living plants and animals, and on to rational creatures—from lithosphere to biosphere to noosphere?

Is pantheism implicit in the forces he discovers bringing these successive spheres of increased complexity into being, leading to the eschatological Omega, which will divinize all creation? Does the human person retain his individual identity in the convergence of all into the absolute of Omega?

Is his "becoming" really different from being?

Some critics have stated or suggested that some of these tendencies appear to be implicit in some of Teilhard's propositions. He must be handled with care, in view of this, and of the sweeping power of his ideas.

Henri de Lubac, the French Jesuit, published in 1962 the first serious study by a major theologian on Teilhard's religious thought, drawn comprehensively from all his numerous books, notes and monographs. This significant book, *La Pensée Religieuse du Père Pierre Teilhard de Chardin* (Aubier, 1962), has not yet appeared in English at this writing. That a theologian of Father de Lubac's stature would take time out at this juncture in the *aggiornamento* to assimilate and evaluate Teilhard's voluminous writing, and to review and rebut the charges of his critics, offers authoritative testimony that Teilhard is a thinker of major import. De Lubac shows that his original visions and initiatives are now being hammered by debate into a consistent school of thought.

This Teilhardian school could have epochal significance in the other dialogue for our generation and beyond. Time and space do not permit even a brief review of de Lubac's appreciative essay on Teilhard's thought. His main rebuttal of critics is that they read him piecemeal and that they analyze portions of his writing outside the whole context of his life-long search "to see."

Further, de Lubac alleges that Teilhard's "pick-and-choose" critics fail to distinguish adequately the three different levels at which the priest-scholar expresses himself: as a scientific paleontologist, as a philosopher who generalizes theories by extrapolation from ultraphysical premises, and as a religious mystic who "touches" intuitively the divine. De Lubac shows that to an unusual degree Teilhard regularly tries to identify these three levels of thought, and to keep their respective premises and developments clearly separate. This, says de Lubac, makes the confusion, in the minds of Teilhard's critics (who include the eminent Charles Journet), all the more surprising.

Three "lines of force"—the adapted terminology of modern science is his trademark—are discernible in Teilhard's total statement. These are given here in a summary so audaciously brief as to be almost brazen, in view of the complexity and gradual evolution of his concepts. Nevertheless, in propositions drastically truncated, Teilhard's main religious theses are these three:

1. Everything in the world has *sacramental* character, tells of God, and is to be progressively divinized to higher degrees, giving pervasive meaning and value to all human endeavor and daily work.

2. The optimistic activism inherent above receives the constant counterpoint innate to all creaturehood: the passivities of *diminution*—deterioration, death, sin, suffering, the Cross —because as creatures we receive our existence from Another, from the Absolute, from God.

3. The universal experience of all creatures is essentially

eschatological, aimed at a final purpose, directed through twists and turns which tend toward ultimate goals of perfection. This upward spiral of the human and other creature phenomena leads progressively, via evolution, through ever greater complexity, converging more and more into socialization, into God-with-all, the Divine Milieu, the whole cosmic Christ, the Omega.

It is quite possible that the Teilhardian school of thought which is now taking shape will offer intellectual nourishment at the deepest levels, as well as the basis for an overarching unity for the other dialogue's many participating groups and ideologies, on a worldwide scale.

Some Christians fear that the Church is now exposed to the grave temptation of becoming overly involved in the things of this-world by action programs and by thinking and talking too much about social issues and mundane affairs. The Church, these critics point out, is a spiritual entity, with supernatural means and other-world ends provided her by revelation from on high, established and sustained by a Redeemer and Savior Who is not of this-world. The Church's role is oriented to the eternal, they insist, not to the here and now of passing human events. As the spotless Bride of Christ, they warn, the Church must avoid contamination from the snares and wickedness of this-world.

She must, therefore, beware of the great social issues which would enmesh her in politics, economics, technics and sociology. Too often in the past, history sadly relates, the Church meddled in mundane affairs. Her churchmen assumed major roles in national conflicts over property, power politics, cultural achievement. They became worldly and enamored of the things of Caesar; they failed to render to God the things of God.

Most of these warnings are true—to a degree sufficient to demand consideration. But they fail to set forth the whole truth of the "whoness" and "whatness" of the Church. While appropriately stressing the transcendence of the Church, they fail to recognize adequately her immanence, her presence in the world, because she is incarnate, like Christ, Whom the Church continues in time and place, is incarnate, God joined to human flesh and to the whole human family, indeed to all creation.

Cardinal Emmanuel Suhard of Paris explained the two-fold nature of the Church with depth and precision in his pastoral letters of the 1940s.[1] His treatment of the Church in "Growth or Decline?" is especially illuminating, and in many aspects foreshadows the pastoral approach of Pope John, who was papal nuncio while Suhard was Archbishop of Paris. Let it be made abundantly clear that the Church *is* transcendent. She is not the mere product of this-world, of economic forces, sociological pressures and man's cultural creations. As Suhard says, "the Church absolutely transcends all human societies." He quotes Pope Leo XIII:

God has made the Church by far the most excellent society of all. For the destiny which she claims for her members is as superior to that of other societies as divine grace is to nature, or things immortal to things which come to an end. And so in origin the Church is divine; her destiny and the means by which she achieves it are supernatural. [Encyclical, *Satis Cognitum,* Acts of the Holy See, 27, p. 274.]

Cardinal Suhard, noted for mounting the social apostolate which revived the Church in postwar France, keeps insisting on her nonworldly nature: "The Church is not an 'entity' comparable to any of our moral or juridical 'persons.' The unity which binds the faithful to God and each other in Christ and the Holy Spirit is an 'ontological' unity."

[1] English translations of Cardinal Suhard's seven principal pastorals are available in *The Church Today* (Fides, 1953), which is used here. Their appearance ten years ago in the United States probably did more than any other single publication to prepare the American Church for the *aggiornamento.* This is surely true of the present writer.

The Cardinal of Paris, who is famed for daring the ultra-modern experiment of the worker-priests, goes back to the fathers of the early Church to support this truth of the Church's uniqueness. He cites Clement of Alexandria, who says the Church "transcends everything in this world and encounters nothing equal to her." (Stromata 7, 17.) And St. John Chrysostom: "The power of the Church is as far above the civil power in value as heaven is above the earth, or rather it transcends it even more." (Migne, Greek Fathers 61, 507.)

But, Suhard warns, this sublime reality must not blind us to another, "namely that the Church is also in time, in history, among the affairs of this-world. For the Church is a body. . . . Because she is the body of Christ, His incarnation in the history and geography of the earth, the Church is first of all contingent. She belongs to a special time and place."

Further, the Cardinal explains, "Because she is also a body, the Church does not remain stationary; she develops, changes and grows." Her actualizations in time are influenced by social forms and passing civilizations, which cannot be foreseen or fully controlled. Still, in all these historical incarnations, the Church undergoes an organic development, moving in a given direction among the shifting sands of time and changing stages of society. She moves toward the ultimate goal of completing Christ, drawing all creation back under His headship; "And at the end she will be His 'pleroma'"—that is, the ultimate, full self-realization of Christ, Who attains this absolute plenitude when all creation is properly ordered and joined to Him, at the end of the world. The strong parallels between this clear official doctrine and the Teilhard projection of the cosmic Christ as Omega should be noted.

So the Church as the continuing incarnation of Christ, permanent to history, perpetuates the mystery of Christ: "In Him two natures were united: He was both God and Man. Similarly, two worlds are made one in the Church: the invisible reality, and the visible society or communion of the faithful. If one of these two is left out the Church is destroyed."

By this present union of the divine and the natural, the eternal and the temporal, the Church not only continues the incarnation of Christ but completes the incarnation of Christ. She must daily, so to speak, take on the flesh of this-world, in much the same way that Christ took His flesh from Mary, and thus became incarnate at the Annunciation, nine months before His Nativity. The incarnation of the whole Christ is not yet achieved. Rather, this proceeds day by day, and becomes indeed the principal theme of all human history.

Seen from that angle, Suhard shows that the total, long-range "world view" of Christians is frankly optimistic: "It shows that the world has a meaning, that it is not the plaything of a blind materialistic dialectical process, but is warp and woof of the eternal 'predestination' of all things in Jesus Christ. It shows that nothing can be outside His Redemption, that everything has been washed with His blood." Suhard quotes the breviary hymn for Passion Sunday: "'The land and ocean, the world and stars are all washed by the flood [of Christ's saving blood],' and therefore, from that moment, the world has been sealed with love."

These realities, literally world-shaking realities, provide the bases for the Church's concern for the things of this-world, and for the spirituality which should inspirit the other dialogue. Far from fleeing the world into the ghetto, the Christian has the vocation of completing and assuming the world —for and in and through Christ. Yes, even as Christ.

Instead of closing his eyes to progress, the Christian believes in it and works for it, so as to "complete creation" and bring forward the day of the "second coming," when the entire universe—the Mystical Body and the whole of creation—will show forth the triumph of Christ the King by realizing His plenitude and achieving the total Christ.

The world certainly presents temptations and dangers, just as the flesh brought with it temptations and dangers to the

Son of God. But it was the willingness of Christ to join Himself to matter which effectively demonstrated the power of the Spirit, and the true relationship of God to His creatures —a dominion of love. Christ showed that God could become united with the human flesh and psyche, with created matter and energy in the full range of its this-world expressions, and the two could live and be and act as one—through a union of love.

The Church must continue daily this demonstration, this showing forth, of the power of the Holy Spirit who ensouls her, by her action amidst the matter and energy of this-world —understanding, loving, uplifting the things of time so that they become configured to Christ the Eternal Lord, from whom we all come and to whom we would all return.

That is what the other dialogue is all about.

Date Due